634.8

P9-AFV-467

Practical Viticulture

. . . presents all aspects of grape-growing. Clarity, simplicity and a logical exposition of the subject have been the paramount objectives of the author throughout this work.

The specialized fields of the author — anatomy and morphology, selection of propagation material, pruning and ampelography — are discussed extensively. The discussion from chapter to chapter is co-ordinated in such a way that the reader will be able to relate the various topics and to integrate them into a whole. The criticisms and reservations which the author expresses are as outspoken as his enthusiasm and admiration for the great viticulturists of the continent of Europe.

A notable feature of this book is the inclusion throughout of carefully selected line-drawings instead of photographs. These illustrations are sometimes adopted from the classic works on viticulture, largely unknown in the English-speaking world because written in continental languages. Many of the illustrations are by the author.

A bibliography is appended of works in French, German, Hungarian, English, Afrikaans, Russian and Italian, which languages, with the exception of Italian, the author speaks and writes.

This book should become the indispensable companion for all those seriously interested in the science and practice of viticulture.

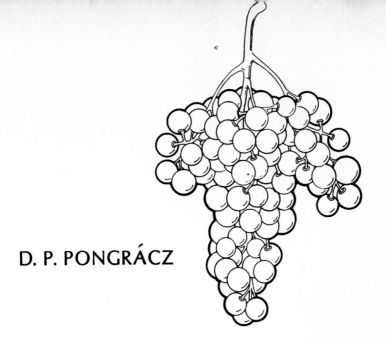

D. P. PONGRÁCZ

Practical Viticulture

GLEN ~~CANCELLED~~ PUBLIC LIBRARY

David Philip (dp) Publisher CAPE TOWN

First published in 1978 by David Philip, Publisher (Pty.) Ltd., 217 Werdmuller
Centre, Newry Street, Claremont, Cape Province, South Africa
ISBN 0 908396 01 5
© D. P. Pongrácz 1978

All rights reserved, no part of this publication may be reproduced, stored in a
retrieval system, or transmitted, in any form or by any means, electronic,
mechanical photocopying, recording, or otherwise, without the prior permission
of David Philip, Publisher (Pty.) Ltd.

Printed by Printpak (Cape) Ltd., Dacres Avenue, Epping, Cape, South Africa

Contents

TO THE MEMORY OF THE LATE PROFESSOR A.I. PEROLD,
THE GREAT PIONEER OF SOUTH AFRICAN VITICULTURE

Preface

This book has been specifically prepared as a practical guide for grape-growers, wine-makers, students of viticulture and wine-lovers in the English-speaking grape-growing countries. Grape-growing (viticulture) and wine-making (oenology) go hand in hand, because good wine is made in the vineyard, and not only in the cellar. A working knowledge of viticulture is part of a wine-maker's essential equipment.

While I know of several excellent books published in French, German, Hungarian, Italian and Russian dealing with the science and practice of viticulture, I am not aware of any similar work in English, with the single exception of the late Professor A.I. Perold's *A Treatise on Viticulture*, which was published in 1926, and has been out of print and unobtainable for many years.

The chapters dealing with the classification of *Vitis* species, anatomy and morphology of the vine, biology of the vine and ampelography may be of more interest to the student than to the practical grape-grower or wine-lover. These topics have, however, been extensively discussed since they are neglected in all recent textbooks in English.

Trade names are sometimes used to describe certain fungicides or herbicides, because this is how they are referred to in ordinary discussion in the vineyard. No endorsement of specific products is implied.

Because ampelography is such a vast subject, very careful thought went into the exclusions. Finally, only the distinguished *V. vinifera* wine-grape varieties from which the world's most famous wines are made, were included. To have exhaustively listed and described even a small percentage of all cultivated varieties would have unbalanced the content of the book and destroyed its purpose.

As far as rootstocks are concerned, only those preferred in the grape-growing countries around the coast of the Mediterranean, i.e. the oldest, one of the warmest, and definitely the driest and largest grape-growing region in the world, are described and discussed.

The South African reader, and especially the grower, will ask why, with the exception of Cabernet Sauvignon and Syrah/Shiraz, and the rootstock

99 Richter, he will not find the description of any of the varieties cultivated on a commercial scale in South Africa. The answer is simple: all
varieties known to the South African public are not cultivated at all outside South Africa (Pinotage, Tinta Barocca, Greengrape, Valse Riesling,
Raisin blanc, White Hermitage, etc.) or are considered to be suitable only
for the production of medium (Steen/Chenin blanc), and low-medium-
class table wines (Cinsaut, Colombard, Clairette, etc.) in some limited
regions of a few grape-growing countries, or are cultivated only for the
production of distilling wines.

Because of excellent cellar technology, South African medium and
low-medium-class table wines are incomparably good for their prices,
but, with the exception of Cabernets, there are no top-class quality wines.
The varieties from which the premium-quality wines of the world are
made are simply not available to local growers, although most of them
were imported 8 to 14 years ago.

As far as local rootstocks are concerned, Jacquez and 143 B were rejected in all grape-growing countries 90 years ago, and 101–14 Mgt has
long been replaced by better rootstock varieties. *V. champini* var. Salt
Creek is being tested and recommended only in California, Australia,
South Africa and Israel. Viala and Ravaz rejected *V. champini* as a rootstock in 1892. The vineyards of the whole Old World were reconstituted
according to the recommendations of Viala and Ravaz. This fact makes
any further discussion on the subject irrelevant.

For a fuller discussion and comment on the South African situation,
please see the Appendix.

The reader may find that I sometimes appear iconoclastic. It is certainly not my intention to stir up controversy. Rather, it is my sincere
conviction that truth needs no excuse. The opinions and conclusions
expressed in this book are my own, and I wish to retain full and undivided responsibility for them. My own philosophy is summarized by the
words of Martin Luther to the Imperial Diet at Worms on 18 April 1521:
'I cannot and I will not recant anything, for to go against conscience is
neither right nor safe. Here I stand, I cannot do otherwise!'

DESIDERIUS P. PONGRÁCZ

'Dackelheim'
Somerset West, Cape
May 1978

Acknowledgements

My warmest thanks go to the grape-growers of South Africa for their interest and confidence in my work from the first moment that I came into contact with them fifteen years ago.

My hearty thanks are also due to my friends, colleagues and tutors Messrs. J.J.A. (Koos) Meissenheimer and J.C. (Oom Jan) Ruppersberg. Their profound knowledge of every branch of practical viticulture — gained during lifelong hard work in the vineyards — and their love for the vine, inspired me with the love for my work.

I wish to acknowledge my indebtedness to Dr. J.A. (Pan) van Zyl, Assistant General Manager of the K.W.V., who was my Director at the O.V.R.I., for his understanding, confidence and support for my research projects, which greatly encouraged me in my opposition to the intervention of the 'virus-school' from outside the O.V.R.I.

To Dr. P.J. (Piet) Venter I would like to express my sincerest appreciation for appointing me, twice in my life — in 1963 in his capacity as Deputy Chief of the O.V.R.I., and in 1973 as Production Manager of Distillers Corporation — to posts which have given me the greatest pleasure and satisfaction.

I am grateful to Dr. Julius László, Manager, Wine Production of Distillers Corporation, my fellow Hungarian from Rumanian-occupied Transylvania, who also found refuge in South Africa, for his invaluable advice and criticism, which contributed in no small measure to the completion of this book.

My friend and former colleague, Dr. Hans Ambrosi, Managing Director of the wine-producing estates of the German Government in the Rhineland at Eltville, will be gratified to know that the grape-growers of the Cape, who were aware of the work we began all those years ago — and which was frustrated for so long — are finally about to achieve what we all aimed at in 1963. The recently started 'interim scheme' ('tussentyd se skema') of the Department of Agricultural and Technical Services is nothing but a copy of 'scheme Ambrosi', presented to nurserymen under a different label, nearly fifteen years later.

I must not conclude this preface without acknowledging my great debt to Mr. Murray Coombes of David Philip, Publisher (Pty.) Ltd., for giving his experienced care and attention to the very considerable amount of work that has been involved in re-reading and correcting the manuscript.

The work of Mr. P.H. Holtzhausen, F.F.T.R.I., in preparing the photomicrographs and some of the leaf-photos is gratefully acknowledged.

Coggaus. D.4.80 269910 #19-95-20%

CHAPTER 1

History and Geographical Distribution of Grape-growing

1. HISTORY

The grape has a far longer history than man. Fossilised leaves and seeds of the vine indicate that vines were growing in their natural habitat long before the appearance of man on earth. Prehistoric man probably ate the berries of the vines that climbed on the trees of the forest, as a primary food. Ancient man, having learned to gather and save food against the colder months, no doubt stored grapes as well. Fermentation was the unavoidable natural process resulting from the storage of the grapes. Sooner or later, the fermented juice was drunk, and man became a consumer of wine. No one knows exactly when men deliberately set out to make wine, but it was for many years regarded as a gift from the gods: the Egyptians attributed it to Osiris, the Greeks to Dionysos.

The earliest records of wine in Egypt are the sealing inscriptions found in pre-dynastic tombs. The wall-paintings and reliefs in the tombs of the Middle Kingdom and the New Empire show workers harvesting grapes with curved knives.

Fig. 1.1. Harvesting and wine-making in Ancient Egypt. From the tomb of Nakht, Thebes, XVIII dynasty 1420–1411 B.C. From Hegedüs et al. (4).

The Egyptians used fermenting-vats of acacia wood, in which the grapes were also trodden. The treading was almost ritualistic, with chants and hand-clapping. Egyptian wines were sealed in earthenware amphorae. On the feast of Bubatsis, a great quantity of wine was consumed in honour of Bast, the cat-headed goddess of pleasure and the dance.

The culture of grapes was extended from Egypt to Crete, and from there to Asia Minor and Greece, probably by the seafaring Phoenicians, before 600 B.C. Wine-making flourished also in ancient Cyprus, the island of Aphrodite.

The Greeks of Homer were wine-drinkers. They venerated Dionysos the god of wine, ecstasy and fertility. As they were also adventurous sailors, explorers and colonists, by the end of the seventh century B.C. there were Greek cities along the coast of Sicily as well as on the southern part of the Italian mainland. It is generally assumed that the Romans learned viticulture from these Greek settlers. The worship of Dionysos, latinized as Bacchus, found its way from Greece to Rome, where he enjoyed immense popularity as the Liberator, who had brought all the joys of the East to the West. The Romans became great wine-lovers. Virgil and Pliny wrote instructions for grape-growers. Columella described the method of pruning with such exactness that, to a great extent, we can follow it even today.

Wherever the Roman legions went, the culture of grapes went with them. Viticulture was established by the Roman conquest in Hispania (Spain), Gallia Transalpina (Southern France), Germania, Pannonia (Hungary), Dacia (Rumania), and in North Africa. Hispania and Gaul became the most Roman of the provinces outside what is now known

Fig. 1.2. Roman wine-merchants filling wine amphorae from the bulk transporters of their time. From Basserman-Jordan (1).

Fig. 1.3. The vineyards of France and Germany at the fall of the Roman Empire. The dates of their founding are mainly conjectural. Vineyards in the Languedoc and Marseilles (B.C. dates in italics) were founded by the Greeks. From *World Atlas of Wine* (5).

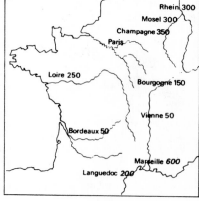

as Italy. Trade with Gaul became so extensive that one import — the famous wines of Southern Gaul — was restricted to protect Roman wine-makers. The technique of the aging of wines also progressed under Roman expertise. They were not limited to the earthenware amphorae of the Greeks. The Romans used barrels not unlike modern barrels, and bottles quite similar to modern ones (1, 5, 6).

Rome exacted tribute from the peoples of the Empire, but gave much in return: the rule of law within the imperial boundaries, and protection against the barbarian invasion from without. The Romans did not, as a matter of policy, destroy cultural traditions or attempt to suppress local languages and religions. In its heyday, Rome controlled one of the greatest empires in history, and the *Pax Romana* was considered by Gibbon (3) to have been the happiest in human history.

The fall of the Roman Empire is a classic example of cultural eclipse. In an incredibly short time all the wealth and splendour that was Rome was demolished. All the great material triumphs of the past were lost and destroyed. Roads, aqueducts, baths, amphitheatres — and vineyards — crumbled to ruins. 'Many cities were left vacant, and in several districts of Italy the harvest and the vintage withered on the ground'(3). In the fifth and sixth centuries Europe relapsed into barbarism.

Out of centuries of chaos, the Roman Church emerged as the strongest source of leadership on many levels, but particularly in matters of administration and organization. The political and economic structure of the Roman Empire was in ruins, and the Church under the firm leadership of the Papacy moved into the political vacuum. The Bishop of Rome had always been recognized as first among the patriarchs, and with the fall of the Western Empire he took over the ancient title of *Pontifex Maximus* which the Roman Emperors had held. The Church clung to the tradition of the Roman Empire and to the idea that it was the natural instrument of European unity.

Because they were the only real source of trained manpower, the Christian monastic orders that were now arising in the Western world made a very important contribution to the social recrystallization which started in the eighth and ninth centuries, after the breakdown in the sixth and seventh centuries (8, 9).

The spread of monasteries of the Benedictine type in the eighth and ninth centuries was very considerable. 'Everywhere we find them as centres of light, restoring, maintaining, and raising the standard of cultivation, preserving some sort of elementary education, spreading useful arts, multiplying and storing books, and keeping before the eyes of the world the spectacle of a social backbone. For eight centuries thenceforth the European monastic system remained a system of patches and fibres of enlightenment in what might otherwise have been a wholly chaotic world' (9).

And it was these monasteries that played a very important and beneficial role in establishing viticulture in the former Roman provinces. For centuries the Church owned most of the famous vineyards of Europe. Cistercian monks founded Clos de Vougeot in about A.D. 1100. This abbey played a leading part in the development of Burgundian viticulture (5).

Emperor Otto the Great ordered the replanting of the vineyards in the Ostmark in A.D. 995. Here, as elsewhere, the vines were to be tended principally by monks of the monasteries of southern Germany. In Germany, wine became the concern of the Church. Although Napoleon secularized the German vineyards along the Rhine and the Moselle and in the Palatinate in 1806, and only a few of the great holdings survived, the estates retained the boundaries inherited from the monasteries (1, 5, 6).

In about A.D. 1000, at the request of the kings of Hungary, German monks established monasteries and planted the first vines in the western part of Hungary after the departure of the Romans.

'By the time of Herodotus (460 B.C.) the wines of Armenia had won great renown. The Georgians learned early to cultivate their vines. Archaeologists have discovered painted wine jars and large amphorae dating from, at least, the second millennium B.C. Xenophon related that the inhabitants of the Black Sea shores made robust wines, pleasant and aromatic when mixed with water.' (6)

Table-grape culture was introduced into conquered Spain and Portugal by the conquering Arabs of North Africa.

The first vines in the New World were planted in Peru by the Spaniards in the first half of the sixteenth century. From Peru the culture of grapes was carried to Chile, where the first wine was made in 1556. Don Pedro del Castillo founded Mendoza in 1561, bringing *Vitis vinifera* grape varieties to Argentina from Chile (5, 6).

A Jesuit priest, Father Juan Ugarte, planted what were probably the first wine-grapes to be grown on the west coast of North America in about 1697 at the Mission San Francisco Xavier in what is now Lower California. This was a European variety and was named, appropriately enough, 'Mission'. (6)

The real advance towards a commercial industry in California was made only in the second half of the nineteenth century. This expansion was made possible by the coming to California of many experienced European viticulturists, most of them South Germans, Italians and Hungarians who had fled from political repression in their native countries after the failure of the revolutions of 1848–9 (6, 10).

According to Lichine (6), 'the most extraordinary newcomer on the scene was Colonel Agoston Haraszthy, a Hungarian nobleman, who has since been recognised as the father of Californian viticulture'. Haraszthy was convinced that the finest European varieties could grow in California and he advocated planting only the best varieties and concentrating the first vineyards in areas of the most favourable environment.

'In 1861 he was assigned by Governor John G. Downey to a viticultural expedition to gather varieties that might prove satisfactory. He selected some 100 000 cuttings from 300 varieties, and all were shipped to California in the course of one year. The great plunge into the wine industry attracted inexperienced farmers and seekers after immediate profits, indifferent as to the choice of varieties, soil, or location. The realization of Haraszthy's dream was postponed and even today it has not been fully achieved.' (6)

It was at the end of the year 1654 that the first cuttings from Holland arrived at the Cape. They were probably varieties from the Rhineland. In February 1659 wine was made for the first time at the Cape (6).

The culture of grapes in Australia is as old as the settlement itself. Captain Arthur Philipp landed in Sydney on 26 January 1788, and planted the first vines on the site where the Botanical Gardens now stand (6).

Nature has sometimes produced good wines, but it was not until the end of the seventeenth century that *grands crus* emerged. The interest in classical mythology and the desire for the resurrection of the ideas of the Graeco-Roman civilization have been recurring phenomena of our Western civilization ever since the Italian Renaissance. Of the deities of the Hellenic world, the cult of Dionysos attracted more attention than any other, and inspired the works of such great thinkers as Hölderlin, Nietzsche and Gerhard Hauptmann.

'The laws of conservation of energy demand eternal recurrence. Dionysos, cut to pieces, is a promise of life, and it will eternally be reborn again from destruction.' — Nietzsche.

From data presented in Table 1.2 (p. 6), it is evident that the populations of five Mediterranean countries — of countries settled with people of the Mediterranean races — and largely Roman Catholic or Orthodox in religion — are by far the biggest wine-consumers in the world.

2. GEOGRAPHICAL DISTRIBUTION

TABLE 1.1
The fifteen biggest wine-producing countries of the world in 1973 (2)

Country	Areas planted with vines in hectares	Production of wine in hectolitres
Italy	1 185 276	64 271 000
France	1 322 166	61 330 782
Russia	1 104 200	28 723 000
Spain	1 584 950	23 675 000
Argentina	299 600	22 052 950
U.S.A.	235 000	11 909 870
Portugal	350 101	8 977 700
Algeria	290 000	8 250 000
Rumania	351 279	7 700 000
West Germany	92 064	6 027 000
Yugoslavia	251 619	5 545 549
South Africa	101 330	5 532 900
Greece	211 974	4 771 200
Hungary	222 000	4 459 000
Chile	127 180	4 000 000

TABLE 1.2
The ten biggest wine-consuming countries in the world in 1973 (2)

Country	Population in millions	Consumption per capita in litres per annum
Italy	54,6	111
France	51,0	107
Portugal	9,5	91,3
Argentina	24,0	85,3
Spain	33,0	60
Chile	10,0	43,9
Switzerland	6,2	40,7
Greece	8,8	40,0
Austria	7,3	39,8
Hungary	10,3	32,0

It is interesting to note that in rich industrial countries the consumption of wine per capita is low: in Western Germany it is only 18,3 litres per annum; in South Africa 11,2 litres; in Australia 8,7 litres; in Sweden 6,4 litres; in Holland 5,7 litres; in the U.S.A. 4,95 litres; in England 3,7 litres; and in Canada 3,0 litres.

For a more comprehensive study of all countries that produce significant quantities of wines, *Encyclopaedia of Wines and Spirits* by Alexis
Lichine (6) can be recommended. No other book in any language can
approach this one in its range and its wealth of up-to-date statistics.

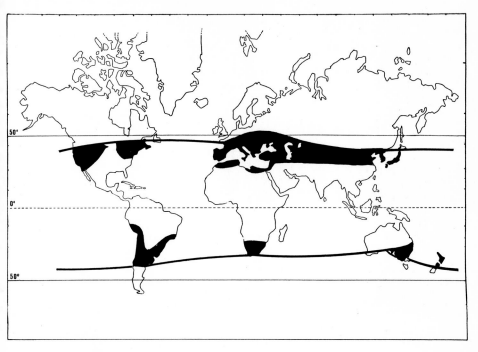

Fig, 1.4. Climatic limitations of grape-growing. From Simon et al. (7).

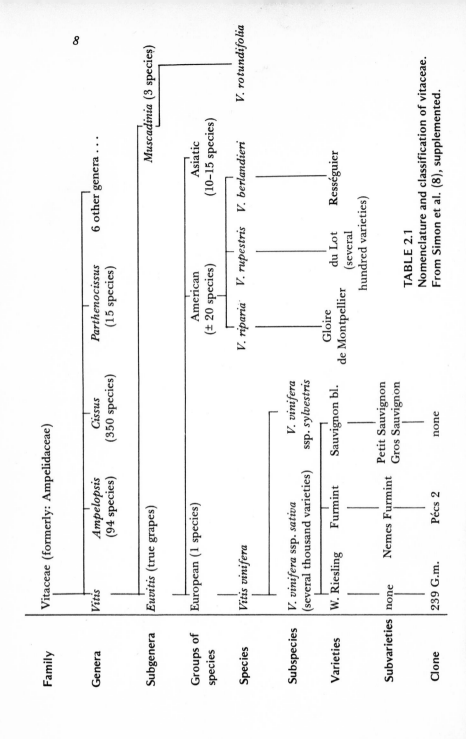

TABLE 2.1
Nomenclature and classification of vitaceae.
From Simon et al. (8), supplemented.

CHAPTER 2

Classification of the Genus Vitis

Grape-vines belong to the botanical family Vitaceae, formerly known as Ampelidaceae. Of the ten genera of the family (7), only one — the genus *Vitis* — is important to the grape-grower. The classification of the species of *Vitis* is based on the work of Planchon (7).

The word *vitis* was used by the Romans. It describes the tendrils and shoots of the vine. According to Wittstein (1835), quoted by Hegedüs et al. (4), the word *vitis* may be derived from the Latin verb *vincire*, which means to bind, to tie, indicating probably the ability of the vine to attach its long and tender shoots to trees with the help of its tendrils. Today *vitis* is generally regarded as being derived from the Latin *viere*, to twist. In all Indo-European languages viticultural terms are mostly derived from the Latin words *vinum* (wine), *vita* (life), *vinitor* (grape-grower), *mustum* (must), *uva* (berry) etc.

The botanical genus *Vitis* includes two subgenera: *Euvitis* Planchon and *Muscadinia* Planchon (7).

Euvitis

Euvitis — the true grape — has forked tendrils, shedding bark, and a diaphragm at the nodes. The number of chromosomes is 19 (3, 9).

(1) The single species of *Euvitis* that is indigenous to Europe, to Asia Minor, and to the Caucasus Mountains, is *Vitis vinifera* Linnaeus. Some classification divides *V. vinifera* L., into two subspecies, *V. vinifera* ssp. *sativa,* and *V. vinifera* ssp. *silvestris* C. Gmel. Most botanists agree that *V. vinifera* L., the species from which all cultivated varieties were derived before the discovery of North America, originated from the region between and south of the Black and Caspian seas (3, 4, 10).

The word *vinifera* is of Latin origin: *vinum,* wine, and *ferens,* bearing. The L. behind *Vitis vinifera* indicates the name of the great botanist Carl von Linnée or Linnaeus (1707–78), who first classified it as a plant species, in his famous work *Species Plantarum* (1753). The classification of the several thousands of varieties of *V. vinifera* is a matter of great difficulty and, thus far, there is no perfect classification in existence. The most logical and generally accepted is Negrul's classification (5). It is based on morphological and biological characteristics obtained spontaneously through geographical and ecological influences. Negrul (5) divides the varieties of *V. vinifera* into three main groups:

(a) *Vitis vinifera proles pontica.*
(b) *Vitis vinifera proles occidentalis.*
(c) *Vitis vinifera proles orientalis.*

Proles pontica is subdivided into subproles *georgica* (moderately pubescent leaves), and *balcanica* (strongly pubescent leaves). The subproles *balcanica* is divided into *macrocarpa* (very large berries) and *corinthiaca* (seedless berries) types. The *proles occidentalis* is not subdivided by Negrul. The *proles orientalis* is subdivided into subproles *caspica* (round, medium-sized berries) and *antiasiatica* (large, fleshy berries). The subproles *caspica* is further divided by Negrul into three different groups: *conculta apiana* (Muscadel group), *aminea* (Chasselas group) and *apirinea* (seedless group).

Negrul's system of classification was supplemented and completed by Németh (6). He subdivided *proles occidentalis* into subproles *gallica* with five subprovarieties, *microcarpa* (small berries and one subprovariety), *mesocarpa* (medium-sized berries), and into subproles *iberica* with one subprovariety *microcarpa* and one *mesocarpa*.

(2) The American species of *Euvitis.*

Early settlers in eastern America found wild grapes growing in the warm soils of New England, in the woods of the Mississippi Valley, on the Great Plains, in the limestone hills of the Allegheny Mountains, in the Rocky Mountains and on the Pacific coast. Morphologically, American species of *Euvitis* are as different as the environments in which they grow.

After a due amount of study and experiment, it was found that in America, instead of a single species as in the Old World, about twenty distinct species could be identified. There are numerous natural hybrids of these species, for example *solonis* (riparia X candicans), which is often referred to as *V. solonis* Hort. Berol.

Hedrick (1907), quoted by Winkler (10), lists some 1 400 varieties of American grapes. Analysis of the genetic origin of these varieties shows that 27,4 per cent are pure species, 53 per cent are hybrids of known parentage, and the remaining 19,6 per cent are of unknown origin.

In American *Vitis* species the skin slips easily from the pulp, and the berries have a characteristic foxy flavour. Some of them produce fruit that may be regarded as palatable.

The classification of the American species of *Euvitis* is still based on the work of Planchon (7), who divided them into seven major groups. Behind the names of the species, the names of the authors who first described them are indicated.

Subgenera *Euvitis* Planchon:
  1st group: *Labruscae*
          V. labrusca Linnaeus
  2nd group: *Labruscoideae*
          V. californica Bentham
          V. caribaea de Candolle
          V. coriacea Shuttleworth
          V. candicans Engelmann
  3rd group: *Aestivales*
          V. lincecumii Buckley
          V. bicolor le Conte
          V. aestivalis Michaux
  4th group: *Cinerascentes*
          V. berlandieri Planchon
          V. cordifolia Michaux
          V. cinerea Engelmann
  5th group: *Rupestres*
          V. rupestris Scheele
          V. monticola Buckley
          V. arizonica Engelmann
  6th group: *Riparia*
          V. riparia Michaux (*V. vulpina* Linnaeus)
          V. rubra Michaux
  7th group: *Arachnoideae*
          V. champini Planchon (natural hybrid of rupestris ✕ candicans)

According to Winkler (10), descriptions and further information on these and other American species may be found in Bailey (1), and in Munson (1909). Neither these, nor any other classifications, are completely satisfactory.

There are 10–15 species of *Euvitis* native to Asia: *V. amurensis* Rupr., *V. coignetiae* Pull., *V. thunbergii* Sieb. et Jucc. etc. These species contributed little to grape-growing (2, 10).

Muscadinia

The subgenera *Muscadinia* Planchon can easily be identified by a tight bark that does not shed, simple tendrils that do not fork, nodes without a diaphragm, and small clusters with berries that detach as they mature. The number of chromosomes is 20 (3, 9, 10). There are three species of *Muscadinia: V. rotundifolia* Michaux, *V. munsoniana* Simpson, and *V. popenoei* Fen (2).

The term 'cultivar'

While the term cultivar is gaining currency in popular language to indicate a cultivated variety, it is avoided in this book for the following reasons:

(a) Botanists are interested in variations which can be found in a particular species. Whether such a variation is cultivated or not is for botanists unimportant.

(b) In the case of some American *Vitis* species such as *V. riparia, V. rupestris* and *V. berlandieri* there are numerous varieties which are not cultivated at all, but which have been used widely for hybridization and have become the parents of our most widely cultivated rootstock varieties. To call varieties such as Rupestris Martin, Berlandieri Rességuier, Berlandieri Las Sorres, etc., 'cultivars' is thus not only inaccurate, but misleading.

(c) The French never adopted the word cultivar. As Professor J. Branas of Montpellier put it in 1974, 'the words "cépage" and "variété" are expressions which have existed for centuries in everyday language, so the word "cultivar" is superfluous' (2). The same applies to German, Slav and other languages.

(d) Recent textbooks on viticulture published in English do not use the term cultivar.

CHAPTER 3

Morphology and Anatomy

The vine lives partly in the air and partly in the soil. There is a close relation between the biological functions of the parts of the vine above the ground and those in the ground. In order to understand the annual life-cycle of the vine we must have a basic knowledge of the relation of the cells, tissues and organs of the vine to the performance of the plant as a whole (16, 20).

In this chapter we shall first discuss the external morphology, and then the internal structure, i.e. anatomy, of the various parts of the vine.

The word *morphology* is derived from the Greek words *morphé,* form, and *logos,* science, and means the science concerned with the outer form and inner structure and development of the different parts of the plant (21). If we take very thin sections of any part of the plant and examine these under the microscope, we notice that all the parts of the plant are built up out of a large number of very small units, each called a CELL. Cells of similar structure, which together perform a particular function, constitute a TISSUE. A distinct and visibly differentiated part of a plant is called an ORGAN. The science which deals with the study of the internal structure of the plant is called *anatomy,* derived from the Greek word *anatome,* dissection (8, 16, 20).

The grapevine consists of the following organs: the roots, the root-stump, the undivided main permanent stem or trunk, the arms of the trunk, and the growing stem in its first year, i.e. the shoot system, bearing the leaf, the flower and the fruit (10, 16, 20, 29, 30).

THE ROOT

According to their origin, we distinguish between GERMINATION ROOTS and ADVENTITIOUS ROOTS. The former are produced when grape seed germinates, whereas the latter arise out of the stem (16, 20, 27). Commercially cultivated varieties of the grapevine are, however, always propagated vegetatively from cuttings of one-year-old canes. Consequently the detailed knowledge of germination roots is of no practical importance to the grape-grower.

Morphology

Kroemer (16) distinguishes the following four zones in the young root: the root tip, the zone of elongation, the zone of absorption and the zone of conduction. Unlike the shoots, roots are not divided into nodes and internodes.

The ROOT TIP is 2–4 mm long. Its exclusive function is the formation of new cell tissues. The external layers of its tissues are called the ROOT-CAP (8, 16, 20, 25, 27).

Immediately after the root tip comes the ZONE OF ELONGATION which is several millimetres in length (16, 25, 27).

The ZONE OF ABSORPTION of water and salts from the soil is longer (about 10 cm). It can be recognized by its yellowish colour and the presence of fine ROOT-HAIRS (16, 25).

The ZONE OF CONDUCTION extends over the rest of the root, and can easily be recognized by its brown colour. Where the zone of absorption meets the zone of conduction, lateral (secondary or branch) roots develop. The finest of these are called ROOTLETS. Thousands of rootlets are produced by the vine during active growth (16, 25). On a one-year-old Riesling vine, Kroemer (16) observed forty adventitious roots. Their length varied between 15 and 45 cm. On these roots he counted 1 112 lateral roots of the first order, 2 772 of the second, and 960 of the third order. The annual increase in the absorption surface of the root system is thus enormous.

Distribution and depth of the root system

The growth of the roots depends mainly on the physical nature and depth of the soil, and a favourable water supply. Stagnant water in the root zone will cause the deep roots to die off. Hence the phenomenon that vines which are subject to 'wet feet' in winter are the first to suffer from drought during the summer months (6).

According to the observations of Branas and Vergnes (5) more than 50 per cent of the roots of all the investigated varieties could be found at a depth of 24–45 cm. Kasimatis, quoted by Weaver (29), reported that, in coarse sands or gravelly soils, roots of the vine can penetrate 7,5 m (25 ft) or deeper but their penetration is usually less as the soil texture becomes finer.

Considerable effort has been devoted to studying the influence of air temperature on the growth and composition of grapevines and their fruits. Information is scarce, however, on the influence of root temperature on fruit and shoot development. An exception is the work of Woodham and Alexander (31), who investigated the effect of root temperatures from 11 °C to 30 °C on the development of Sultana vines. The optimal temperature for root growth was found to be about 25 °C; root growth diminishes below 11 °C and above 30 °C.

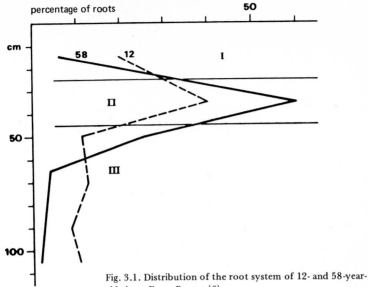

Fig. 3.1. Distribution of the root system of 12- and 58-year-old vines. From Branas (6).

The weight of the root system increases with the age of the vine. It varies from 4,5 to 7 kg per vine, or 20 to 31 tonnes per hectare, for *V. rupestris* aged 12 and 58 years respectively. It can increase up to 50–60 tonnes per hectare with the hybrids of *V. berlandieri* (9). The amount of water absorbed by the roots of the vine is about 15 to 40 cubic metres per hectare, depending mainly on the amount of water transpired through the leaves. During the summer, a vine can absorb 0,2 to 1,5 litres of water in a 24-hour period (6, 13).

The different species of *Vitis* differ considerably in the development of their root systems. Investigations (22) carried out on a large number of one-year-old root systems of 23 rootstocks, grown under identical conditions showed that:

(a) *V. riparia* and those of its hybrids with *V. riparia* characteristics predominating, all have a shallow-growing root system which consists of a large number of well-ramified thin roots with a smooth surface;

(b) *V. rupestris,* and those of its hybrids with *V. rupestris* characteristics predominating, all have deep-growing root systems which consist of a large number of medium-sized, well-ramified roots arising from all the nodes of the root-stump;

(c) *V. berlandieri,* and those of its hybrids with *V. berlandieri* characteristics predominating, have deep-growing root systems consisting of fairly thick, poorly ramified roots arising mainly from the base of the root-stump.

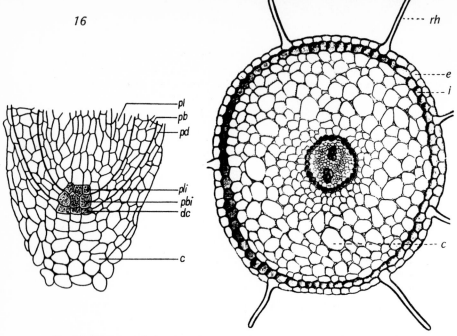

Fig. 3.2. Diagrammatic longitudinal section of the root tip of the vine, indicating distribution of meristematic activity. (*Meristem:* tissue in which cell division predominates. Pratt 1974.) After Baranov from Ampelografia SSSR (3).

Abbreviations: *pl* — plerome, meristem forming the core of the axis composed of the primary vascular tissues and associated ground tissue; *pb* — periblem, meristem forming the cortex; *pd* — protoderm, meristematic tissue giving rise to the epidermis; *pli* — plerome-initials; *pbi* — periblem-initials; *dc* — dermo-calyptrogen, meristem giving rise to the root-cap; and *c* — calyptra.

Fig. 3.3. Primary structure of the root. Diagrammatic transverse section of the root of the vine in the absorption zone. From Kroemer (16).

Abbreviations: *e* — epidermis; many epidermal cells have elongated perpendicularly to the surface to form root-hairs, *rh*; the root-hairs soon die, and the root is then covered by intercutis, *i*; *c* — cortex, which is distinguished by its well-developed intercellular spaces. In the centre is the vascular bundle with two strands of xylem and phloem respectively, enclosed by the endodermis. The number of vascular bundles varies from 2 to 8, depending on species and root size (13, 16, 17, 20, 25).

Anatomy

When cuttings of dormant one-year-old canes are planted during spring in moist soil, they readily form adventitious roots. Callus originates from the cambial region at the base of the cuttings. Roots originate adventitiously near the interfascicular cambium mainly at the nodes. There are no pre-formed initials nor do roots develop directly from callus (25).

Secondary structure of the root

Where the zone of absorption changes into the zone of conduction, the secondary structure of the root commences. VASCULAR CAMBIUM arises inside the primary phloem bundles, crosses the multiseriate medullary rays, and develops in the pericycle outside the primary xylem. The FASCICULAR CAMBIUM forms xylem cells on its inside, and phloem cells on its outside by periclinal division ('*Periclinal*: tangential or parallel to the surface of the plant organ, commonly used to describe a plane of cell division in meristematic tissue.' Pratt 1974.) Simultaneously with the formation of the cambium ring, the cell walls of the endodermis are suberized, thus cutting off all nutrition of the cortex from the tissues of the central cylinder. The cortex therefore dies. Before the cortex is completely lost, new tangential cell divisions take place in the cells that lie immediately inside the endodermis. A PHELLOGEN, or CORK CAMBIUM, develops in the pericycle, producing several layers of suberized PHELLEM (cork) towards the outside, and a lesser amount of PHELLODERM towards the inside. The secondary protective tissue that is derived from the phellogen is termed PERIDERM (8, 13, 17, 25).

During the root's progressive growth in thickness, new layers of periderm are continually formed deeper in the phloem, each of which in turn cuts off the outer parts from all nutrition. They therefore die and remain as loose bits of dead bark, termed RHYTIDOME, on the surface of the root. The deep-seated origin of the periderm was found to be characteristic of 31 *Vitis* species. Only in *V. rotundifolia* does the periderm arise superficially (16, 20, 25, 27).

The principal food-conducting tissue of the vascular plant is the SECONDARY PHLOEM. The axial system of the secondary phloem of *Vitis* roots and stems consists of tangential bands of FIBRES, alternating with bands containing SIEVE TUBES, COMPANION CELLS and PHLOEM PARENCHYMA. In the roots and stems of *V. rotundifolia* the phloem fibres do not form tangential bands and are scattered (7, 9, 16, 25, 27).

The SECONDARY XYLEM is the principal water-conducting tissue in vascular plants. The xylem of *Vitis* roots consists of radially alternating blocks of axial (xylem strands) and radial (ray) systems. The MEDULLARY RAYS transverse both the phloem and xylem, flaring out in the phloem. They consist of quadrangular parenchyma cells without intercellular spaces. There are two kinds of medullary rays: (a) those that originate between the primary vascular bundles and penetrate to the primary xylem strands are called medullary rays of the first order; and (b) those that are initiated in the interfascicular cambium are called medullary rays of the second and third order (7, 25).

Two kinds of trachery cells can be found in the secondary xylem of

Vitis roots: the TRACHEIDS and the VESSEL MEMBERS (8, 13, 16, 17, 25). Like the phloem, the xylem is continuous from the top to the bottom of the vascular plant.

The PITH of *Vitis* roots is very small.

Fig. 3.4. Transverse section of one-year-old *V. vinifera* var. White French (A), and of one-year-old 420 A (riparia x berlandieri) root (B), indicating remarkable anatomical differences. From the M.Sc. thesis of the author, University of Stellenbosch.

A

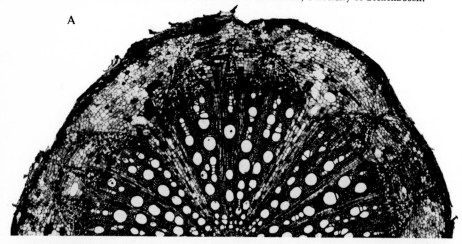

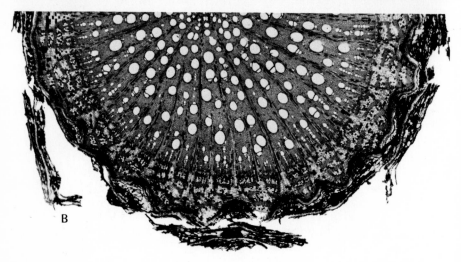

B

Comparative anatomy of Vitis roots

As indicated in Fig. 3.4, A and B, the different species of *Vitis* differ considerably in the internal structure of their roots. According to available literature:

(a) very wide medullary rays are a typical anatomical characteristic of *V. vinifera* roots (10, 13, 16, 17, 23, 27);

(b) a strong tendency to develop numerous, sequent periderms is characteristic of the phylloxera-resistant American *Vitis* species (17, 23); even at the end of the second growing-season, Kroemer (16), found no evidence of the forming of a second periderm in *V. vinifera* roots;

(c) the one-year-old roots of *V. vinifera* possess a markedly larger pith tissue; in the roots of American *Vitis* species the poorly thickened cell walls of the pith are compressed by the strong development of xylem strands (17, 23);

(d) the one-year-old roots of *V. vinifera* represent a strikingly broad phloem section, i.e. 43,95 per cent of the radius of the xylem (23);

(e) one-year-old roots of the vine show more significant anatomical differences than three-year-old roots; consequently the former are more suitable for identification purposes (23).

THE TRUNK AND ITS ARMS

The undivided main stem or TRUNK of the vine may be considered as the body of the plant. It grows in diameter each year and may attain enormous size. The trunk forms a connecting link between the roots and the above-ground parts of the vine. The underground portion of the trunk always gets thicker than the root-stump. However, when varieties of *V. vinifera* are grafted onto American rootstocks, the thickening of the trunk just above the graft union can be very considerable. The French call this thickening of the trunk 'bourrelet'. The trunk divides into ARMS, on which BEARING UNITS, i.e. one-year-old canes, pruned back from 2 to 12 eyes, are situated.

Fig. 3.5. Old grafted-vine showing the various organs of the plant. From Hayne (11). Abbreviations: *c* — one-year-old cane pruned back to two eyes to serve as a short bearing unit; *a* — arm: *tr* — trunk; *b* — bourrelet; *j* — joint or graft-union; *rst* — root-stump.

THE GROWING STEM IN ITS FIRST YEAR: THE SHOOT SYSTEM

The close association of the stem with the tendrils, flower clusters and leaves makes this part of the vine more complex than that of the root.

Shoots, leaves, flower clusters (or inflorescences) and tendrils, all make their appearance in a short active growing-season from buds situated on the nodes of a one-year-old cane (13, 16, 20, 27, 30).

The shoot (when mature, the cane)

Morphology

The shoots of the grapevine are divided into NODES and INTERNODES. The thickened parts are called nodes, and here the leaves, and opposite the leaves the inflorescences, or tendrils, are born. Starting from the base of the shoot, we find the inflorescences, usually opposite the third and fourth leaves. The next node bears only a leaf followed by two tendril-

Fig. 3.6. Diagrammatic representation of the morphology of the cane. From Branas (6).
Abbreviations: d — dorsal side; v — ventral side; p — flat side; c — grooved (caniculated) side.

Fig. 3.7. Development of summer lateral. The compound bud or winter eye (e) is on the dorsal side, while the smaller bud, out of which summer lateral (l) arises, is on the dorsal side of the shoot. After Goethe, from Kroemer (16).

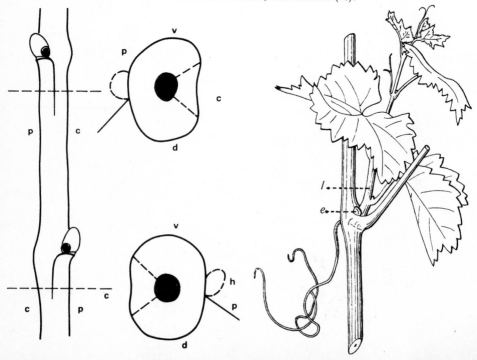

bearing nodes, followed by a tendril-less node. The part of the shoot
between two nodes is called the internode (4, 6, 9, 10, 16, 20, 27, 30).

In all *Vitis* species, except *V. rotundifolia* and *monsonia,* the pith is
interrupted at the node by a hard, woody tissue called DIAPHRAGM.
The thickness and shape of the diaphragm varies with different species.
It is narrow in the canes of *V. riparia,* wide in *V. vinifera, V. berlandieri*
and *V. champini* (16, 22, 27).

DORSIVENTRAL structure (having two distinct nonsymmetrical surfaces or planes) is characteristic of *Vitis* shoots. ('*Dorsal:* in general botanical use is equivalent to *abaxial.*' Pratt 1974.) In dorsiventral shoots
of *Vitis* the side of the shoot to which tendrils and buds (out of which
summer laterals arise) are attached is where the vascular tissues are thinner
(19, 25). ('*Ventral:* in general botanical usage *adaxial.*' Pratt 1974.) In
dorsiventral shoots of *Vitis,* the side of the shoot to which the leaves are
attached is where the vascular tissues are the thickest (25). If the shoot
is pinched early in the growing-season, the axillary bud develops a
SUMMER LATERAL. According to Pratt (25) 'this shoot develops
soon after leaf expansion, from the bud axillary to a foliage leaf on the
current year's shoot. It shows a dorsiventral structure in the insertion of
the prophyll on the dorsal side of the shoot. The plane of leaves is
roughly at right angles to that of the main shoot.'

Anatomy

The precursors of the primary tissues of the shoot are produced by a
group of meristematic cells at the tip of the shoot, called APICAL MERI-
STEM, or SHOOT TIP (8, 12).

The leaf primordium is initiated on the flank of the apical meristem by
periclinal divisions on the second layer. The tendril is initiated by periclinal divisions in the third layer of the apical meristem (16, 25).

Hegedüs (12) described the ontogeny ('*Ontogeny:* the life history, or
development of an individual organism.' Esau 1964) of the elongating
shoot of *V. vinifera.* He reports that a new leaf primordium is produced
every 2–3 days when the shoot is growing 3–4 cm per day.

Primary structure

The young shoot, like the root, consists of three tissue systems, the
dermal (epidermis), the fundamental or ground (cortex etc.), and the
vascular (8).

The epidermis bears stomata, contains chloroplasts, and is photosynthetic (15). The cortex is relatively less developed than in the young
root. The vascular bundles are grouped around the edge of the central
cylinder in such a way that the phloem is next to the cortex, and the
xylem opposite the phloem. Here, therefore, we have the OPEN or

COLLATERAL GROUPING of the vascular cylinder (12, 16, 20, 25). Elongated series of parenchyma cells develop into separate fibres which form a 'cap' outside each primary phloem bundle (12, 25). The pith is very large. It consists of short parenchymatous cells with thin walls and complete protoplasts (16, 25).

Secondary structure of one-year-old canes (see figs 3.8 and 3.9)

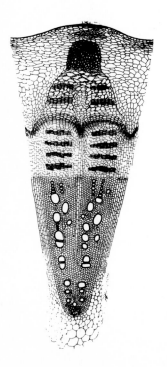 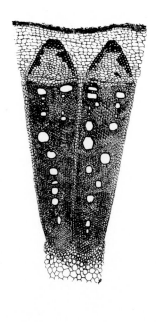

Fig. 3.8. Transverse section of a one-year-old cane of *V. vinifera* showing deepseated periderm, tangentially arranged phloem fibres, phloem, xylem, residues of the primary xylem, very narrow medullary rays and pith.

On the periphery of the vascular cylinder septate fibres occur in *Vitis* stems which form a 'cap' outside each primary phloem bundle. These fibres do not originate as part of the phloem, but outside of it (8, 13, 16). According to the terminology used by Esau (8), these fibres are referred to in this book as perivascular fibres. From Viala and Péchoutre (27).

Fig. 3.9. Transverse section of one-year-old *V. rotundifolia* showing superficial periderm, retention of the cortex, and all the phloem distribution of the secondary phloem fibres on margin of the phloem, xylem and pith. From Viala and Péchoutre (27).

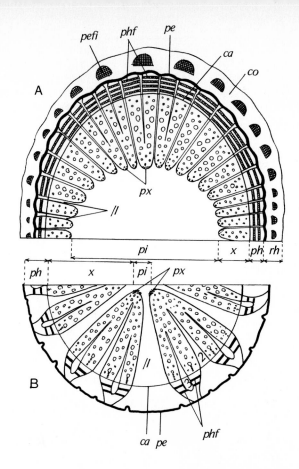

Fig. 3.10. Comparative anatomy of one-year-old *V. vinifera* cane (A) and root (B): transverse sections.

Although the internal structure of the secondary vascular cylinder (phloem, xylem and pith) is similar in *Vitis* stems and roots, the relations of the various tissues in the vascular cylinder differ considerably. Consequently, the anatomy of one-year-old cane (A) can easily be distinguished from that of the one-year-old root (B) by:

(a) its strikingly larger pith;
(b) its very numerous and much narrower medullary rays;
(c) its narrower phloem section;
(d) the presence of perivascular fibres outside each phloem bundle;
(e) the presence of a thick dead bark, and
(f) its dorsiventral structure.

Abbreviations: *rh* — rhytidoma (dead bark); *co* — dead cortex; *ca* — cambium; *pe* — periderm; *phf* — phloem fibres; *pefi* — perivascular fibres; *ph* — phloem; *x* — xylem; */1* — medullary ray of the first order; */2* — medullary ray of the second order; */3* — medullary ray of the third order; *px* — residues of the primary xylem; and *pi* — pith.

The compound bud or eye

As already stated, the shoot is only the product of the development of a bud. What appears to be a single bud visible on the cane is found to be a well-developed central bud with two buds on either side (Figs 3.11 and 3.12). According to Pratt (25), 'The primary, secondary and tertiary buds, enclosed in the prophyll of the summer lateral and the two basal bracts of the primary bud, constitute the *compound bud,* viticulturally termed *'eye',* of the dormant cane.' ('A *bract* is a small scalelike leaf; if borne at the first one or more nodes of a stem, it is called a *prophyll.'* Pratt 1974.)

If the primary or main bud is destroyed, one of the secondary buds will take its place to make certain that grapes will be borne. Tertiary buds usually bear no flower clusters (6, 16, 25). Speaking superficially, we may say that in every leaf-axil a new bud is formed on young shoots. Hence they are called AXILLARY BUDS. On closer examination it soon becomes apparent that as a rule two buds are formed in every leaf-axil. The larger bud consists in reality of three buds, as seen in Fig. 3.11 and 3.12; hence such a bud is called a COMPOUND BUD or EYE to distinguish it from a smaller single bud, which develops in every leaf-axil during the growing-season in which it is formed (16, 20, 25). It may

Fig. 3.11. Diagrammatic transverse section through a compound bud (eye) of *V. labruscana* (Concord) showing relative position of leaf scar (LS), lateral shoot (LAT), and three dormant buds (1, 2, 3). Primary bud (1) in axil of prophyll (solid black) of lateral shoot. From Pratt (25).

Fig. 3.12. Compound bud and part of the cane in longitudinal section. From Kroemer (16).
Abbreviations: a — apical meristem of the shoot arising from the primary bud; b — rudimentary leaf; c — rudimentary inflorescences; d — rudimentary tendril; ph — phloem; x — xylem; pi — pith; d — diaphragm.

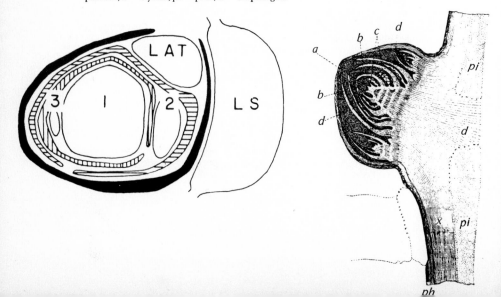

remain undeveloped for a season or it may become active and produce
a lateral shoot if, for example, the main shoot is pinched or topped. On
varieties that have fruitful eyes at the base of the canes, summer laterals
will bear fruit in the same season that they are formed. Such grapes are
known as SECOND CROP (20, 30).

If a vine has been overseverely pruned, eyes that previously were invisible may develop out of the old wood. They are called ADVENTITIOUS
EYES. An ADVENTITIOUS BUD is thus a bud that develops anywhere
except in the leaf-axil. The shoots developing out of adventitious eyes
are called WATER SPROUTS (16, 20, 29). Unlike trees, the shoots of
the vine never form terminal buds. Eyes may be either WOOD-EYES or
FRUIT-EYES. It is impossible to distinguish fruit-eyes from wood-eyes
by their outer appearance. We usually find the fruit-eyes at some distance
from the base of the cane. Grape varieties show considerable differences
in this respect, and this must be borne in mind when pruning (1, 2, 14,
16, 20, 27).

Fig. 3.13. Discontinuous tendrils (a), characteristic of all *Vitis* species, with the
exception of *V. labrusca,* which has continuous tendrils (b) opposite the leaves at
nearly every upper node. From Viala and Péchoutre (27).

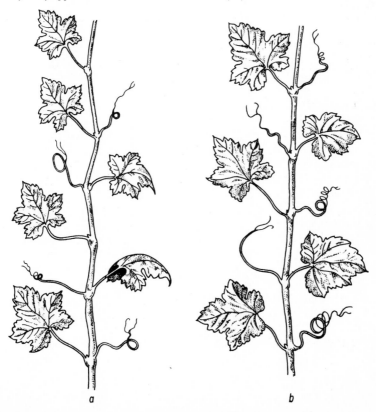

a   b

The tendril

Tendrils and flower clusters, or inflorescences, occupy the same position on the shoot, and intermediate forms between tendril and inflorescence are frequently observed (4, 6, 9, 16, 20, 27). According to Pratt (25), 'The grapevine tendril is usually considered homologous to an inflorescence, but it is really similar to that only in its origin on the apex and its development as far as the first bract and initiation of arms.'

Like the lateral bud, the tendril occurs on the dorsal side of the shoot. Strassburger (26) considered the tendril of the grapevine to be a metamorphosed shoot.

The function of the tendril is to serve as a means of attachment to whatever supports the vine. With the help of the tendrils the vine can tie its fragile shoots to stakes, trees, wires, etc. Its tips circumnutate away from the light until they meet a support. Then stronger growth on the opposite side causes them to coil around the support. The location and nature of the pressure-sensitive cells have not been satisfactorily defined. (25).

The flower

Morphology

The flowers of the grapevine are always small, varying in size from 2 mm for the smallest (*V. berlandieri*) to 6–7 mm for the largest (*V. labrusca*). The majority of *V. vinifera* grape varieties have flowers from 4 to 5 mm (9).

The individual flowers are grouped together in a FLOWER CLUSTER, or INFLORESCENCE. The grape inflorescence is neither terminal nor axillary to a foliage leaf, as are inflorescences of most plants. The cluster occurs opposite a foliage leaf in the same position as a tendril. The inflorescence and the tendril are commonly regarded as closely related (homologous) organs (4, 16, 24, 27).

About two and a half months after the inflorescences emerge with the leaves from the compound bud (fruit-eye), the flowers start blooming. The flower is attached to a short stalk, the PEDICEL, which is thickened at the top and forms a low rim around the base of the flower. The CALYX encloses the other flower parts during their earliest development. It is usually made up of five SEPALS which stop growth and dry up soon after the clusters appear. The COROLLA (cap or calyptra) usually consists of five greenish PETALS which are firmly united at the top; for this reason, the corolla always becomes detached at the base and is shed as a little cap at the time of blooming (6, 16, 20, 24, 27, 30).

Fig. 3.14. Hermaphroditic flowers of the grapevine showing various stages of their development. From Viala and Péchoutre (27).

The opened flower shows the male and female genital organs. The former are called STAMENS, the pollen-bearing organs of the flower. Each stamen is made up of a STALK or FILAMENT, with the ANTHER at the tip. The stamens surround the female part of the flower, called the PISTIL, which looks like a champagne bottle (6, 16, 20, 24, 27, 29).

Flower types

'The types of flowers may be divided into three main groups: (1) hermaphroditic or perfect flowers (both the stamens and pistils functional); (2) pistillate (female) flowers with a well developed functional pistil, but with stamens more or less reflexed and pollen sterile; (3) staminate (male) flowers with erect functional stamens and a more or less aborted pistil. There are also several types of abnormal flowers.' Quoted from Pratt (24).

Most varieties of *V. vinifera* have hermaphroditic flowers but as a result of interspecific hybridization, some are female or male (16, 27).

Anatomy

The primordium of the inflorescence is present in the compound bud in a fruit-eye. It is initiated in the year prior to flowering (1, 2, 6, 14, 16, 24). According to Pratt (24), 'as it grows, the primordium produces a bract with two arms in its axil. The outer (abaxial) arm develops into the lowest branch of the inflorescence, and the inner (adaxial) arm into the main body of the cluster.'

The anther of the grape comprises four sacs. The POLLEN SAC pro-

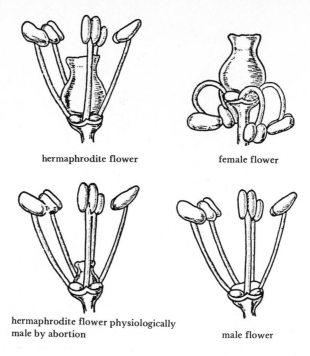

hermaphrodite flower   female flower

hermaphrodite flower physiologically
male by abortion   male flower

Fig. 3.15. From Vogt (28).

duces POLLEN GRAINS. The basal portion of the pistil (female part of
the flower), the OVARY, is enlarged. In each half of the ovary there are
two OVULES. Each ovule has an EMBRYO SAC, containing an egg,
which after fertilization may develop into a seed. Fruits of stenospermocarpic seedless grapes contain aborted and sterile ovules. Surrounding
the ovary is the PERICARP, a fleshy layer. The elongated tissue extending upward from the ovary is called the STYLEwhich connects the
STIGMA with the interior of the ovary. The style is a hollow cylinder.
It is through this style canal that the pollen tube passes on its way to the
ovary. The stigma holds the pollen grains that fall onto it with the help
of a sweet and sticky solution that it secretes (6, 16, 27, 30).

THE LEAF
The leaf is 'a flattened lateral appendage produced by the apical meristem at each node of the stem' (25). As the seat of the process of photosynthesis, the leaf is one of the most important organs of the grapevine.

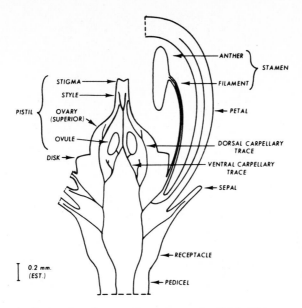

Fig. 3.16. Longitudinal section of a grape flower (hermaphroditic) of 'Muscat Hamburg' grape, showing vascularization. From Pratt (24).

Morphology

'The foliage leaf of *Vitis* consists of two *stipules* (short-lived scales which surround the node), the *petiole* (stalk) and *blade,* containing photosynthetic tissue.' (25).

The LEAF-BLADE (lamina) is transversed by five main NERVES or VEINS which arise together out of the petiole where it is attached to the blade. Lateral veins spring from all main nerves. The veins serve to transport the aqueous solution of plant food in the leaf and to keep it spread out for proper exposure to the sunlight (9, 14, 16, 18, 20). Few *V. vinifera* grape varieties possess 'entire' leaves. Usually they are lobed. The bay between two lobes is called a SINUS. The sinus at the attachment of the petiole to the leaf is known as the PETIOLAR SINUS (4, 9, 16, 20, 27). The vine leaf is asymmetric, i.e. the two halves of a leaf are not precisely alike (16).

Anatomy

The initiation and vascular connections of a leaf to a shoot are intrinsically part of the development of the shoot. 'At each node, five traces to a leaf leave the ring of stem vascular bundles through separate gaps. The

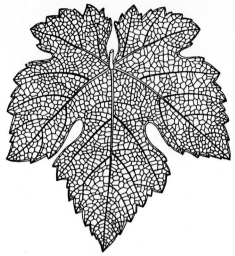

Fig. 3.17. Five-lobed vineleaf showing the largest veins and the highly complex branched network of smaller lateral veins. Each of these veins is connected to still smaller veins. From Kroemer (16).

traces divide and anastomose to form the complicated network of palmate venation in the leaf' (25). According to Esau (8) the LEAF TRACE can be defined as a 'vascular bundle in the stem extending between its connection with a leaf and that with another vascular unit in the stem'.

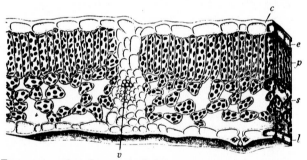

Fig. 3.18. Transverse section of mature leaf of *V. vinifera*. From Kroemer (16). Abbreviations: *c* — cuticle; *e* — upper epidermis of the mature leaf which contains almost no stomata. The palissade (*p*) comprises slightly more than half of the leaf. It consists of one layer of cells which are abundantly supplied with chloroplasts. The spongy mesophyll (*s*) consists of more or less lobed cells containing abundant chloroplasts and surrounded by extensive air spaces. The lower epidermis (*l*) has many stomata. The vascular bundles in the leaf are commonly called veins (*v*). The leaves of the grapevine have the largest veins along the longitudinal axis of the leaf (8, 16, 18, 25).

Abscission: At leaf fall, epidermal and cortical cells separate and vascular connections are broken. Periderm formed below the abscission layer covers the leaf scar (13, 25).

THE FRUIT

Morphology

Fruit set generally results from pollination that achieves fertilization and seed development (29). The ovules become the grape seeds, and the whole inflorescence becomes the GRAPE BUNCH or CLUSTER, which consists of STALK, PEDICELS, and BERRIES (20). The bunches of nearly all varieties are more or less conical, tapering from the stalk to the tip. Some have one, others two shoulders. Within any one variety the shape of the bunches may vary considerably (16, 20).

The stalk branches repeatedly until its terminal branches, to which a variable number of pedicels are attached, each pedicel bearing a berry. The end of the pedicel projecting into the berry is called the BRUSH (16, 20).

The stalks and the pedicels constitute 2–6 per cent of the total weight at maturity (9).

After fertilization the ovary develops into a fleshy fruit called a berry. The grape berry consists of SKIN, FLESH or PULP, and SEEDS.

The flesh of all European grapes is tender and juicy, and separates readily from the seeds but not from the skin. The flesh of American *Vitis* species is a rather tough, pulpy mass, sometimes stringy, which separates not easily from the seeds but fairly easily from the skin (slip-skin). The skins of some varieties are thick and do not burst easily, clinging to their pedicels until full maturity. Others have skins so thin that they burst before fully ripe. The most apparent characteristic of grape-skins is their colour, which varies from greenish-yellow to dark red or bluish-black (16, 20, 27).

The different varieties of grapes have their typical colours. However, owing to spontaneous mutations, sometimes white and red bunches occur on the same shoot; sometimes even white and red berries occur in the same bunch.

The skin owes its colour to grains of pigments deposited in the outer layers of cells. These pigments are insoluble in water but are readily soluble in alcohol. For this reason the separation of the skins from the juice of the grapes does not take place during the vinification of red wines until fermentation is over and much of the colour is extracted from the skins by the alcohol derived from fermentation.

The skin of the berries accounts for 5–12 per cent of the total weight at maturity (9).

The inner cells of the skin which come into contact with the pulp contain the AROMATIC SUBSTANCES which give the wine its characteristic flavour (6, 9, 16, 20, 27, 29). It is especially during the last days of ripening that grapes develop their full characteristic taste and flavour.

At maturity the skins of all grapes have to a greater or lesser degree a delicate, powdery, waxy coating, called BLOOM.

Anatomy

The internal structure of the pedicel is similar to the stem, consisting of epidermis with few stomata, cortex, and vascular bundles with cambium and pith (24).

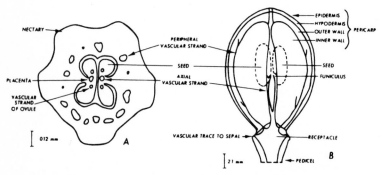

Fig. 3.19. 'Concord' grape berries. A: transverse section through the base of the locule at bloom. B: longitudinal section of a mature berry. From Pratt (24).

The berry develops only from cells that were formed in the ovary. Thus no new cells are formed during its development; the existing cells merely enlarge. Cell enlargement is continuous during the development of the berry, except during the period of maturation (6, 16, 20, 24). By the time the berry is ripe, the epidermal cells are tabular, wider tangentially than radially. The flesh consists of large parenchymatous cells with big vacuoles. The vascular system of the berry is derived from the ovary. There appears to be no information how the vascular system grows into the berry (24).

THE GRAPE SEED

The seeds are 0–4 in number, usually 2–3. They constitute up to 10 per cent of the weight of the berry (9).

The seed is the entire product developed out of the ovule. It possesses a fairly complicated structure and consists of the SEED-COAT, ENDO-SPERM and EMBRYO (6, 9, 13, 16, 20, 24, 27).

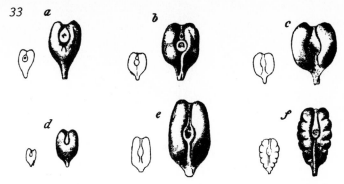

Fig. 3.20. The shape, size and colour of the seed varies considerably, depending on the species.

a–b, *V. vinifera*; c, *V. labrusca*; d, *V. riparia*; e, *V. monticola*; and f, *V. rotundifolia*.

From Kroemer (16).

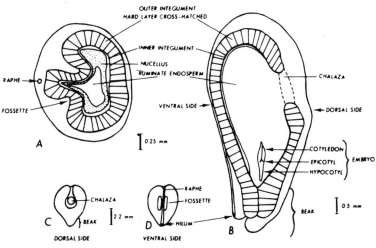

Fig. 3.21. Grape seeds. A: transverse section of a seed above the level of the embryo about four weeks after pollination. B: longitudinal section of a mature 'Concord' seed. C, D: surface view of mature 'Concord' seeds. From Pratt (24).

34

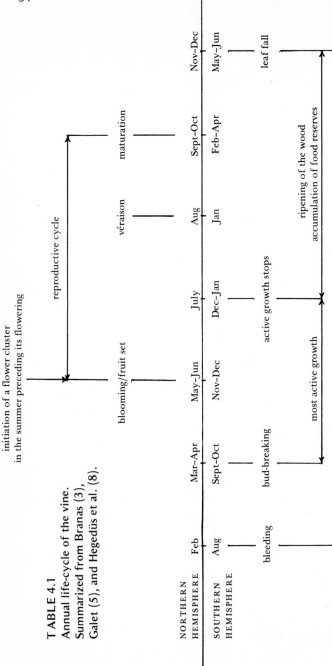

TABLE 4.1
Annual life-cycle of the vine.
Summarized from Branas (3),
Galet (5), and Hegedüs et al. (8).

initiation of a flower cluster
in the summer preceding its flowering

reproductive cycle

	blooming/fruit set		véraison	maturation	
NORTHERN HEMISPHERE	Feb	Mar–Apr	May–Jun	July	Aug	Sept–Oct	Nov–Dec
SOUTHERN HEMISPHERE	Aug	Sept–Oct	Nov–Dec	Dec–Jan	Jan	Feb–Apr	May–Jun
	bleeding	bud-breaking		active growth stops			leaf fall
			most active growth		ripening of the wood accumulation of food reserves		rest
dormancy							

vegetative cycle

CHAPTER 4

Biology of the Vine

The word *biology,* derived from the Greek words *bios* (life) and *logos* (science), is the science dealing with the study of the vital activities of the plant.

In this chapter we discuss the different stages in the annual life-cycle of the vine in the order in which they occur. Because of the correlation between vegetative development and reproduction, Hegedüs et al. (8), Galet (5) and Branas (3) considered it necessary to distinguish between VEGETATIVE and REPRODUCTIVE phases (Table 4.1).

VEGETATIVE CYCLE

1. The bleeding of the vine

The bleeding of the vine is the first external manifestation of the awakening of its life after its winter rest, or DORMANCY. If the vine is pruned towards the end of the winter, a watery liquid is discharged from the wound. A closer look at the bleeding surface of the pruned cane reveals that the liquid flows out of the tracheae and tracheides of the wood (xylem). The bleeding of the vine is ascribed to the absorption of water by the newly formed rootlets (6, 12, 17).

Houdaille and Guillon, quoted by Perold (17), found that the vines start bleeding when the temperature of the soil at a depth of 25 cm reaches 10,2 °C. This bleeding occurs suddenly, rapidly increases in intensity, and then decreases gradually. The quantity of sap lost during the bleeding varies from 0,5 to 5,5 litres per vine. Although the plant is not injured by this loss of liquid, the vines should be pruned at a time when they do not bleed very much (6, 12, 17).

2. Bud-breaking, or budding

In the spring, when the daily temperature reaches about 10 °C, the buds on the canes begin to swell. According to Guillon (6), it takes twenty to thirty days from the time the vine starts bleeding until the buds begin to open. Many factors, such as the grape variety, the date of

GLEN INNES PUBLIC LIBRARY

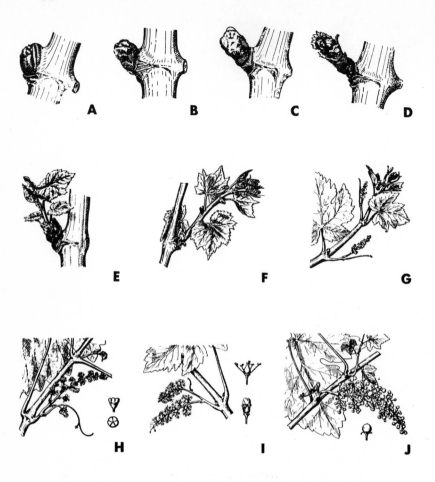

Fig. 4.1. Successive stages of the early development of the vine from the swelling of the compound bud (A) until the berries have set (J). From Baggiolini (1).

winter pruning, the method of pruning, vigour of the vine, the nature of the soil, the temperature of the soil, etc., can influence the date of bud-breaking (3, 6, 12, 17).

The fact that unrooted cuttings that have been planted out begin budding before they have developed roots, proves that the opening of the dormant bud is not dependent upon the formation of roots (12, 17).

From the dates of the bud-breaking of 25 varieties in South Africa during 1914–17, given by Perold (17), the following facts emerged:

(a) that the same variety did not bud on the same date in different years;

(b) that the earliest bud-break in any year took place on 5 August (Madeleine Angevine in 1917), and the latest on 20 September (Red Hanepoot in 1914);

(c) that climate influenced the date of bud-break. In normal seasons, at the Cape, when the rains and cold weather are over, the vines bud from about 20 August until about 15 September.

3. Growth of the vine

'Every cell is formed by cell division out of an already present cell. Wherever there is vine growth, there are young cells dividing themselves into two daughter cells. During this cell division the nucleus first divides mitotically into two identical daughter nuclei, between which there is then formed a new cell wall in the middle of the mother or dividing cell and at right angles to its cell walls. This new cell wall at the same time divides the rest of the protoplast (chromatophores and cytoplasm) equally between the two daughter cells. These latter grow until they have reached the size of the original mother cell, and then in their turn proceed to divide each into two equal halves. Through the continuation of this process a group of similar cells is formed which constitute a *cell tissue.*' From Kroemer, quoted by Perold (17).

Growth does not occur in all parts of a plant, but is initiated only in certain tissues of restricted distribution called MERISTEMS. The most important meristems in the body of vascular plants are the APICAL-ROOT and APICAL-SHOOT MERISTEMS, and the VASCULAR CAMBIUM (4, 7, 8, 12, 17, 20).

To the grapegrower, growth usually means elongation of the shoot. A shoot, as the name implies, shoots out from a bursting bud and grows rapidly in length. The growth of the young shoot is irregular during its active growing period. After bud-break, growth is slow at first, and then, as the daily temperature rises, the young shoots rapidly become longer. About the time the berries start enlarging, shoot elongation slows down. At first the decrease in the rate of growth is quite rapid, then for a while constant, gradually slowing until it ceases (1, 2, 3, 5, 6, 7, 12, 17, 25).

Growth of the shoot in diameter, as a result of cell division in the cambium, follows a similar pattern, but begins several weeks later (12, 20, 25).

Apical dominance

A lateral bud is always present in the axil of every leaf of the vine. If the apical meristem of the growing shoot is destroyed or artificially removed (topping), development of the lateral buds usually starts at once. This inhibiting effect of an apical meristem upon lateral bud development is called APICAL DOMINANCE and it is very pronounced in *Vitis* species (8, 12, 14, 24).

Although there is no doubt that auxins play a key role in the phenomenon of apical dominance, the exact mechanism of their controlling effect is not known with certainty (14).

4. The ripening of the wood and the dropping of the leaves

Some time after the shoots have acquired their full length and thickness, a reddish-brown or light to dark brown coloration of the surface begins from the internodes at the base of the shoot. This gradually proceeds towards the tip of the shoot. As previously mentioned, the dead epidermis, cortex and periderm form the brown covering of the mature shoot, which is now called a CANE. Kövessi (11) appears to be the first to have made an in-depth study of the ripening of the wood. He mentions the following external characteristics of a WELL-MATURED CANE: the wood (xylem) is stringily developed, well-lignified and differs clearly from the brown pith. A large quantity of reserve food, consisting mainly of starch grains, is accumulated in the parenchymatous tissue of the vascular cylinder. The cane is hard, and breaks when bent; the dead bark can easily be torn off. The leaves shed early.

A BADLY-MATURED CANE is soft and does not break when it is bent. Such canes are green towards their tips and shed their leaves very late. The presence of a large quantity of water in the tissues of badly ripened canes is the reason why they cannot stand the cold of winter (17).

Accumulation of food reserves

After berry growth slows down and the rate of shoot growth almost stops, the rate of accumulation of carbohydrates increases.

Starch and sugars are the main food reserves. In the dormant season, available carbohydrate is stored mainly as sugar. The roots represent the main food storage organ of the vine, but carbohydrate is also found in the trunk and canes (24).

The reserve food, mainly carbohydrates, accumulated in all parts of the vine during summer and autumn, remains stored until the following spring, when it is utilized in the starting of new growth (12, 24, 25). The basic reason why there is no appreciable transfer of plant nutrients from the canes to the roots after leaf-fall was clarified by Esau (4), who found that — at Davis, California — the phloem of the vine is inactive from late November until mid-March.

It is of utmost importance to remember that the leaves are needed to ripen not merely the grapes, but also the canes. Therefore the leaves should remain on the vines as long as possible (11, 17).

In autumn the leaves gradually assume their autumnal colours. They have now completed their task, and therefore drop off after a while. The dropping of the leaves closes the annual life-cycle of the vine, which now enters its winter rest.

REPRODUCTIVE CYCLE

1. Initiation of an inflorescence

The first stage in the reproduction of the grape is the initiation of an inflorescence or flower cluster in the summer preceding its flowering and fruiting (3, 5, 7, 19). According to Winkler et al. (25) differentiation that results in the formation of fruit-eyes begins in early June at Davis, involving the compound buds on the lower part of the shoot. Differentiation is somewhat retarded in the buds at the base of the shoot. They mature early, but the accumulation of carbohydrates starts later than in the buds borne between nodes four to eight. Once begun, differentiation proceeds rapidly.

Perold (17) reported that differentiation occurs at about the same time in South Africa as in Australia — mid-November to early December. In Central Europe differentiation begins about mid-June and is complete by mid-August (9).

Circumstances that upset the normal cycle of seasonal development retard the initiation of fruit-eyes, and also reduce the number and size of flower clusters per shoot. For example, overcropping, severe drought, epidemic outbreak of downy mildew, etc., during the previous season will inevitably have a deleterious effect on the growth of the vines during the following spring, and thus on the initiation of flower clusters in the developing compound buds (2, 9, 24, 25). In very hot regions fruitfulness of the buds is also reduced. This is thought to result from a more active and continued growth of the vines (25).

The rudimentary flower clusters formed at the time of differentiation continue to develop until late in the summer, when they enter into winter rest that extends into early spring. Rudimentary flower clusters in the buds on the upper part of the shoot do not advance so far in their development before the rest period begins. This is the reason why bunches on shoots arising from these buds are usually small and not typical in shape for the variety (25).

2. Blooming

Blooming, or FLORAISON, is the period when the caps, or calyptras, fall from the flowers. The time between bud-breaking and flowering is usually about eight weeks. The number of days during which the vines are in bloom depends on the weather, on the variety and on the year. Eight to ten days may be taken as normal when conditions for flowering are favourable (6, 7, 12, 17, 24). Blooming is a critical period in the annual cycle of the vine. During this time the weather is of the utmost importance, for on it depends the success of the grape-grower's crop.

POLLINATION AND FERTILIZATION is a complicated process, summed up by Weaver (24) as follows: 'When the calyptras fall from the flower a cloud of pollen is released from the anthers of the stamens which move away from the pistil. Pollen grains fall on the stigma and germinate if conditions are favourable. A pollen tube grows down the style to the embryo sac and serves as a pathway by which two sperm reach the embryo sac. One sperm then unites with the egg cell to form the zygote from which the embryo plant develops.' ANTHESIS, or bud-opening, occurs between 6 a.m. and 9 a.m. with rising temperatures, and sometimes also from 2 p.m. to 4 p.m. (19). Female flowers ordinarily cannot form fruit without cross-pollination, as their pollen is sterile (17).

Flowers that fail to develop into berries drop from the flower cluster. The heaviest drop of flowers occurs during the first twelve days after blooming (2, 5). Huglin (9) furnishes the following data:

TABLE 4.2
Percentages of flowers that develop into normal berries in the varieties cultivated in Alsace

Variety	Average number of flowers per flower-cluster	Average number of berries per cluster	Percentage of berry-set %
Gewürztraminer	100,8	39,6	39,2
Riesling	188,8	60,8	32,2
Pinot gris	149,2	41,3	27,7
Auxerrois	186,4	69,1	37,1
Sylvaner	95,2	50,3	52,9
Chasselas	163,6	48,3	29,6

3. Setting of the berries

Pollination and fertilization are critical processes in berry development. The term FRUIT-SET designates the early stages of fruit development immediately after fertilization, during which time rapid growth of the ovary wall prevents an abscission layer from being formed in the pedicels of those berries which 'set'. The length of the fruit-set period in grape-vines varies greatly from region to region and is strongly influenced by temperature. The end of the period is marked by berry shatter, in which all berries not set fall off (10).

Stout's (22) six types of ovules in grapes are summarized by Pratt (19) as follows: (a) those which will develop into viable, hard seeds; (b) those which can develop into viable seed without fertilization; (c) those which are fertilized but will soon cease development, i.e. aborted or stenospermic and empty seeds; and (d) those which are not fertilizable (sterile).

Millerandage

Müller-Thurgau (16) appears to have been the first to recognize that some so-called seedless varieties are characterized by berries containing small, soft seeds without embryo or endosperm, as distinguished from completely seedless varieties in which the ovules do not enlarge at all. Since there has been pollination and fertilization followed by embryo abortion, the fruit-set in these varieties is by STENOSPERMOCARPY (3, 19, 24, 25).

Such berries are always round, even when the normal berries are elongated, and ripen earlier than normal berries. The bunches thus consist of grapes of varying sizes. The French call this MILLERANDAGE (3, 17). Sultanina is the most prominent representative of the varieties which have stenospermocarpic berries.

Some varieties set fruit without fertilization, a process known as PARTHENOCARPY, which means 'virgin fruit formation' (3, 17, 25). Black Corinth usually requires only the stimulus of pollination. Artificially parthenocarpic berries can be induced in normally seeded varieties by giberrelin or kinin treatment at bloom (25). The complete seedlessness and small size of Black Corinth berries are characteristics that have made it one of the world's important varieties.

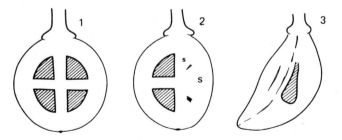

Fig. 4.2. The shape of the mature berry is related to the number of partially developed seeds. 1: Normal berry with four seeds. 2: Berry with two stenospermic seeds (s). 3: Arched berry whose concave surface corresponds to a stenospermic seed. From Branas (3).

Fig. 4.3 Millerandage. Cluster of Muscat d'Alexandrie, showing small, round, seed-less, and fully developed seeded oval berries.

Fig. 4.4. Coulure. Cluster of Muscat d'Alexandrie.

Coulure or shelling

A heavier than normal drop of flowers, creating straggly clusters, is called COULURE or SHELLING(25).

The symptoms of millerandage and coulure are often confused with each other. They are, however, *not* related phenomena. In the case of coulure, the pedicels and pistils drop after flowering, so that nothing of the flower remains behind (3, 16, 17). Coulure is thought to be caused by poor pollination, incomplete fertilization, defective flower parts, poor carbohydrate nutrition of the flowers before anthesis, or virus diseases (3, 25).

Development of the grape berries

After fertilization the ovary and its seeds develop into the fleshy fruit called a berry. In its development from ovary into mature fruit the grape berry follows a pattern common to berries: a short period of cell division after anthesis, passing gradually into a longer period of cell enlargement.

Cell enlargement is continuous during the development of the berry, except during the period of maturation (7, 19).

Botanists divide the development of the grape berry into three stages: (a) the green or growing stage; (b) the ripening stage; and (c) the overripe stage (3, 5, 8, 12, 17).

(a) THE GREEN OR GROWING STAGE lasts from the setting of the berries until the VÉRAISON, when they change colour. During this stage berries and stalks are green. The chemical composition of the berry does not alter appreciably during this period, and differs little from that of the other parts of the vine (5, 6, 8, 12, 17, 25). During the first period of rapid growth of the berries, the percentage of sugars is very low, and it changes little until near the end of the green stage. During this stage the sugars produced in the leaves are being used to help the growth of the shoots, leaves and roots, and to increase the berry size (8, 23, 25). Total acidity increases until the end of the green stage, after which it decreases continuously.

(b) THE RIPENING STAGE of the grape commences with the *vérai-son,* when the berries are almost full grown. By the time the berry has

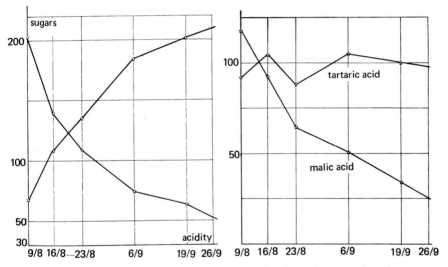

Fig. 4,5. Evolution of the formation of sugars and acidity during the maturation of Cabernet Sauvignon (Saint-Emilion, 1966). The sugars are expressed in grams per litre; acidity in grams of sulphuric acid. From Peynaud (18).

Fig. 4,6. Evolution of the formation of the principal acids during the maturation of Cabernet Sauvignon (Margeaux, 1966). Content in milli-equivalents for 1 000 berries. The graphic clearly indicates that malic acid is mainly present in unripe grapes, while the predominant acid of ripe grapes is always tartaric acid. From Peynaud (18).

reached about three-quarters of its full size, the growth of the vine almost stops, and the leaves lose turgor pressure. The leaves, nevertheless, continue to function normally, and carbohydrates produced in the leaves are translocated to the berries. Such movement results in the very rapid accumulation of sugars in the berries at the beginning of ripening (6, 8, 12, 18, 25).

The SUGARS of the grape are primarily glucose and fructose. According to Winkler (25), on the basis of available data, it may be assumed that (a) glucose predominates during the growth of the berries, (b) at maturity the proportion of glucose to fructose is about equal, and (c) in overripe grapes fructose is the major sugar.

The PRINCIPAL ACIDS of the grape are tartaric, malic, citric, ascorbic and phosphoric acids. The tartaric and malic acids constitute well over 90 per cent of the total acidity (8, 18, 25). The acids are metabolized in respiration at high temperatures, whereas low temperatures at night stimulate the formation of acids (3).

TABLE 4.3
Evolution in the composition of the berry during its ripening. Variety: Cabernet Sauvignon Pauillac (Médoc) in 1967. From Peynaud (18)

| Date | Weight of 100 berries in grams | Contents in grams per litre | | |
		reducing sugars	total acidity	tartaric acid	malic acid
16 Aug.	83	96	17,9	12,5	14,5
21 Aug.	95	124	11,2	8,6	9,8
28 Aug.	103	156	8,4	8,1	6,4
11 Sept.	117	184	6,8	7,4	4,3
18 Sept.	120	192	5,3	6,9	6,2
26 Sept.	184	226	5,2	6,7	2,7
2 Oct.	179	228	4,0	5,9	2,0

The berries constitute about 92 to 98 per cent of the bunches. The pulp generally constitutes 65 to 91 per cent, the skins 6,5 to 20 per cent, and the grape seed 2 to 6 per cent of the weight of the berries (5). Although the size of the berry is mainly a varietal characteristic, seasonal conditions, particularly the amount of rain during summer, markedly influence the weight of the berries of the same variety (18).

The relative proportions of weight of stalk, skins, pulp, and grape seed and the chemical composition of the must vary with the different varieties, and are also influenced by the soil, climate, cultivation, manuring, size of the crop, rootstock, and the degree of ripeness at which the grapes are examined (3, 5, 8, 17, 25).

TABLE 4.4
Evolution in the weight of 100 berries, given in grams, during maturation.
From Galet (5)

	after Peynaud			after Moreau and Vinet	
Date	Sémillon	Cabernet	Malbec	Date	Gamay
9 Aug.	94	64	105	18 Aug.	172
19 Aug.	126	75	135	25 Aug.	185
29 Aug.	155	89	168	1 Sept.	212
8 Sept.	177	100	183	8 Sept.	215
19 Sept.	185	115	198	15 Sept.	220
29 Sept.	200	121	216	22 Sept.	243

COLOURING SUBSTANCES of the ripe berries occur almost exclusively in the cells of the skin. Armand Gautier, quoted by Perold (17), has shown that pigments of red grapes are formed in a colourless state in the leaves, from where they are conducted to the berries as soon as they begin to colour. Here they change into the coloured form (pigment) by oxidation. Riberau-Gayon (21) found that the grapes of red varieties of *V. vinifera* contain monoglucosides, whereas the red colour of varieties of American *Vitis* species contain cyanidin and paeonidin, which are diglucosides.

During the ripening stage the grape develops various AROMATIC SUBSTANCES that give each variety its special aroma. The aromatic substances are largely, but not entirely, confined to the skin of the berries. According to Winkler (25), although the precursor materials of aromatic substances are produced in the leaves, the aroma is synthesised in the berries.

The flavour of the grape variety often carries over into wines. Frequently, wine flavours which are varietal, i.e. which differ with the specific variety used, are additionally different as a result of flavour modifications during fermentation and wine processing. Certain varieties, especially noble white varieties such as W. Riesling, Pinot gris, etc., and certain reds, notably Cabernet franc and Pinot noir, become much less distinctive when grown in warm areas under irrigation.

All parts of the vine and its fruit contain TANNINS, which play an active role in the respiratory process. During ripening the tannins are hydrolized (25).

During the ripening period of the fruit a WAXY BLOOM forms on the skin. The function of the bloom is not merely to improve the outward appearance of the grapes; it assists in the formation and preservation of the aromatic substances, and protects the berries against sunburning.

(c) THE OVERRIPE STAGE begins after the grape has passed the peak quality for its intended use. Overripe grapes are easily attacked by fungi and insects. Berries shrivel and in some varieties the shatter of berries increases (24).

VITAL BIOLOGICAL ACTIVITIES OF THE VINE

The grapevine, like any other green plant with a root system, consists of an underground and an above-ground portion. From the soil the roots absorb water, a variety of minerals and food ingredients in a very aqueous solution. From the air certain carbohydrates are synthesised from carbon dioxide (CO_2) and water by chlorophyllous cells mainly in the leaves, in the presence of light; oxygen being the by-product. This process is generally called CARBON ASSIMILATION or PHOTOSYNTHESIS (3, 5, 8, 12, 14, 17, 24, 25).

1. Transpiration

The loss of water in vapour form from living plants is called TRANSPIRATION (14, 24, 25).

All forms of life in the first instance depend upon a sufficient supply of water. An overwhelmingly large proportion of water absorbed from the soil by the roots is lost by the plant into the atmosphere by transpiration. Generally speaking the leaves are the principal organs of transpiration. Although most vapour diffuses through the stomata, some may be lost through the leaf cuticle (14, 24, 25). A rise in air temperature is invariably accompanied by an increase in water loss through transpiration. According to Winkler (25), this greater loss results from an increase in the steepness of the diffusion gradient between the water vapour of the outside air and that within the leaf.

Water moves upward from the roots through the xylem to the leaves, from which vapour escapes to the atmosphere. According to Weaver (24), a plausible theory about the process involved in the ascent of water is known as the TRANSPIRATION PULL AND WATER COHESION THEORY. The column of water in the xylem is pulled up from the roots through the stem by the force of water evaporation from the leaf cells and the imbibitional forces that develop there.

2. Absorption of water by the roots

The large amount of water lost from the plant by transpiration must be replaced by water absorption through the roots. Water enters the roots principally through the walls of root-hairs and epidermal cells of the root tips (3, 8, 12, 14, 17, 25).

The mechanism of the absorption of water by the roots is summed up by Meyer et al. (14) as follows:

'The development of a diffusion-pressure deficit in the mesophyll cells of leaves causes the water in the xylem vessels or tracheids to pass into a state of tension which results in an increase in the diffusion-pressure deficit of the water in the xylem ducts. As soon as the diffusion-pressure deficit of the water in the xylem ducts in the absorbing region of the root exceeds that in contiguous cells, a gradient of diffusion-pressure deficits is established across the root, increasing consistently from cell to cell its epidermal layer to the xylem conduits. Whenever the diffusion-pressure deficit of the water in the peripheral walls of the young root cells exceeds that of the water in the soil, water will move from the soil into the root.'

3. Absorption of mineral nutrients

All substances that enter the roots from the soil must be in a solution of water. Solutes enter the peripheral cells of young roots from the soil by DIFFUSION, which is 'the net movement of molecules from a region of their greater diffusion pressure to the region of their lesser diffusion pressure' (14). The process can continue only as long as differences of concentration are maintained. This movement of nutrients from a region of low concentration to one of high concentration is termed ACTIVE SOLUTE ABSORPTION or ACCUMULATION (24).

Chemical elements essential for plant growth

The ten classical nutrient elements considered to be essential for the normal growth of green plants, and in brackets, the form in which they are absorbed, are as follows: carbon (as carbon dioxide), hydrogen and oxygen (as water), phosphorus (as phosphates), potassium (as potash salts), calcium (as calcium salts), magnesium (as magnesium salts), sulphur (as sulphates), and iron (as iron salts, ferrous or ferric). The elements boron, manganese, copper, zinc and molybdenum may be added to the group recognized as essential in the metabolism of green plants. Since they are required only in minute quantities, they are called TRACE ELEMENTS (14).

Biological function of the elements

CARBON is by far the most important plant nutrient. About 50 per cent of the total dry matter of plants consists of carbon. Carbon, hydrogen and oxygen are essential parts of the protoplasm and cell walls, and they compose the principal energy materials: carbohydrates, fats and oils (25).

HYDROGEN and OXYGEN constitute water. Water fulfils different functions in plant growth: it serves as a pathway for solutes to enter the roots and move through the tissues; it is a raw material for photosynthesis; and it is essential for the maintenance of cell turgidity, without which cells cannot function properly (24).

NITROGEN is used in relatively large quantities by the vine. Of the major elements needed by the vine, nitrogen is the most likely to be deficient. It is a component of proteins, a constituent of the amino-acids, and a part of the chlorophyll molecule (14, 24, 25).

PHOSPHORUS: Its most important function in the plant is in the building of nucleoproteins. Phosphorus is necessary not only for photosynthesis, but it is also indispensable in respiration (25).

POTASSIUM fulfils its most important biological function in the leaves and is absolutely essential for plant growth. Young and actively growing parts of the vine are always rich in potassium. The vine places a heavy demand on the potassium supply of the soil, a demand comparable to, and for the shoots even greater than, the demand for nitrogen (13, 14, 25).

CALCIUM is necessary for the continued growth of apical meristems and is also known to have a role in the nitrogen metabolism of plants (13, 14).

MAGNESIUM forms part of the chlorophyll molecule.

IRON is indispensable in the synthesis of chlorophyll. Plants that do not absorb sufficient iron salts suffer from chlorosis (13, 25).

4. Translocation

Movement of organic or inorganic solutes from one part of the plant to another is called TRANSLOCATION, TRANSPORT or CONDUCTION of solutes. Of the various tissues of the stem and root, only the xylem and phloem possess structures suggesting that a relatively rapid longitudinal movement of solutes can occur through them (14).

Movement of most mineral nutrients occurs in the vessels of the xylem and it is usually upward. Downward translocation of organic compounds occurs through the phloem tissue. The movement of assimilates (carbohydrates) is usually from the region of production (leaves) to that of utilization (meristematic tissues, young berries, etc) (24).

The rates at which solutes are translocated upward through the xylem of a stem correspond to the rates of translocation of water.

5. Carbon assimilation or photosynthesis

Photosynthesis is without question the most important biological process of green plants. As already stated, it is the process in which certain carbohydrates are synthesised from carbon dioxide (CO_2) and water by chlorophyllous cells in the presence of light, oxygen being the by-product. All the organic matter in the vine is ultimately provided by photosynthesis. The summary equation representing the process of photosynthesis is conventionally written as follows (14):

$$6\,CO_2 + 6\,H_2O \xrightarrow[\text{chlorophyllous cells}]{\substack{673\ kg\text{-}cal \\ \text{radiant energy}}} C_6H_{12}O_6 + 6\,O_2$$

In vascular plants photosynthesis occurs chiefly in the leaves. Carbon dioxide (CO_2) is obtained from the air. It enters the leaves through the stomata by diffusion. The stomata open in the morning when light strikes the leaves. The carbon dioxide goes into solution when it makes contact with the walls of the mesophyll cells of the leaf; it then moves into the cells and reaches the chloroplasts, where it is used (14).

Fig. 4.5. Diagram of a growing shoot at six different development stages showing main direction of movement of photosynthate. After W. Koblet, from Vogt/Götz (23).

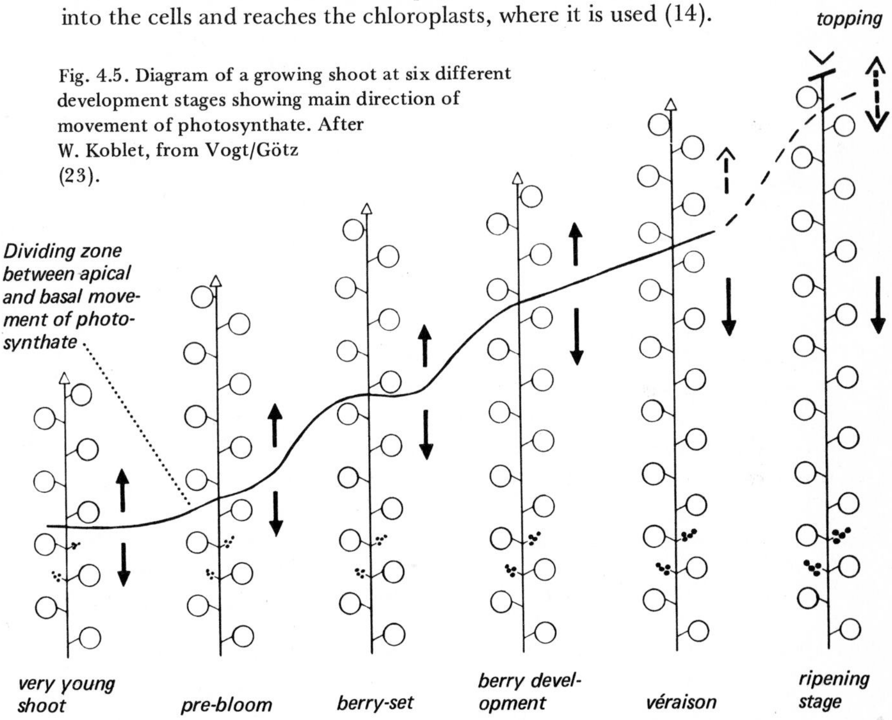

In a very young shoot up to the pre-bloom stage the movement of photosynthate is evenly bi-directional. After berry-set there is apical movement of photosynthate from 4–5 leaves below the shoot tip. Below this region the movement is basal. Predominating basal movement of photosynthate from the leaves increases steadily during the development of the berries until the véraison, i.e. the beginning of the ripening stage. During the ripening period there is practically no apical movement of photosynthate. This biological phenomenon enables the vine to concentrate all its energy into the ripening of its fruit.

According to Meyer et al. (14), 'The chloroplast is regarded as a complete photosynthetic unit containing a multi-enzyme system divided into three main groups, each controlling an increasingly complex phase of photosynthesis: photolysis of water, photosynthetic phosphorylation, and CO_2 fixation.'

Vines that wilt close their stomata: as a result CO_2 intake is reduced, causing a reduction on photosynthesis (24).

Motorina (15) found that the temperature for maximum photosynthetic activity of the vine ranges from 22 to 30 °C, at 60–70 per cent relative humidity. High temperatures inhibit photosynthesis. Above 30 °C the rate decreases and practically ceases at 45 °C (25). According to Kriedemann et al. (1970) quoted by Winkler et al. (25), the rate of photosynthesis increases greatly during the period of active growth, reaching its maximum activity when the leaf attains full size, about 30 to 40 days after unfolding. Thereafter photosynthetic activity declines gradually until the leaf becomes senescent.

6. Respiration

The grapevine, like any other living organism, has to breathe. For the purposes of respiration the vine takes oxygen from the air and oxidizes part of its organic food to carbon dioxide and water. On the assumption that hexose is the substrate, the summary chemical equation for aerobic respiration is:

$$C_6H_{12}O_6 + 6O_2 \longrightarrow 6CO_2 + 6H_2O + 673 \text{ kg-cal}$$

This respiration is an oxidation process, in which, for the oxidation of one molecule of a hexose, six molecules of oxygen are required (8, 14, 24, 25).

As a general rule, respiration rates are found to be greatest in meristematic tissues, such as root or shoot tips. The water produced in respiration is often termed METABOLIC WATER (14, 24).

Respiration of the roots

The above-ground parts of the plant absorb oxygen from the air through the stomata, and they never experience a lack of oxygen. The root system, however, also respires constantly and it obtains oxygen from the soil water in which the oxygen is dissolved. If too much water is present in the soil, the air is forced out of it and plant roots may be deprived of oxygen. That is why plants die in waterlogged soils. It is, therefore, essential that the grapegrower should drain soils containing excessive moisture. Flooding the vines during the dormant season does not appear to be harmful (13, 24).

The formation of root-hairs is said to be largely dependent on the presence of sufficient oxygen. Salt absorption by plants is not possible without root respiration (13).

Metabolism

The carbohydrates manufactured during photosynthesis provide growing plants with the matter and energy whereby they are able to develop and maintain themselves. The activity of living protoplasm, however, resides *not* in carbohydrates, but in nitrogen-containing compounds. It is for this reason that nitrogen metabolism is a subject of vital importance to the understanding of the physiology of living plants. METABOLISM refers to the synthesis and degradation of the organic materials in living organisms (24).

For most higher plants the immediate source of nitrogen is the inorganic nitrate ion (NO_3) that enters the plant by way of the roots from the soil. Since the nitrogen in nitrates is in a highly oxidized state, while in amino-acids it is usually in a highly reduced state, it is evident that reduction of nitrogen is one of the steps in the synthesis of amino-acids and other organic compounds whenever nitrates are the source of nitrogen. It seems probable that nitrate is reduced in the leaves to some transitory compound which combines with an intermediate product of photosynthesis, resulting in the formation of amino-acids. Glutamic acid is an amino-acid which appears to play a key role in the nitrogen metabolism of both plants and animals. It is probably synthesised in plant cells by a reaction between ammonia, often originating from the reduction of nitrates, and alpha-ketoglutaric acid, originating in the Krebs cycle (14).

A close relationship exists between photosynthesis and amino-acid synthesis as it occurs in chlorophyllous organs (14). 'On the average about 85 per cent of the weight of amino-acid molecules represents non-nitrogenous components, chiefly carbon, hydrogen, and oxygen. It is evident, therefore, that amino-acid synthesis cannot occur without an adequate supply of carbon compounds' (14).

CHAPTER **5**

Soils and Climate

SOILS FOR GRAPES

'Soils consist of more or less weathered particles that, together with organic matter, water, and air, provide a medium in which plants can grow.' (4)

Vines are able to adapt themselves to a very wide range of soil types. In fact, if the climate is suited to viticulture, soils which will not support vines will prove unsuitable for most other agricultural crops. Grapevines generally produce their finest fruit in calcareous, or slate soils, and where soil composition is large, grained, and consequently well drained. The fact that in various parts of the world grapes are grown commercially in almost all types of soils emphasizes the wide adaptability of *Vitis* for soils. However, heavy clays, very shallow, poorly drained soils, and soils containing relatively high concentrations of alkali salts, boron or other toxic substances, should be avoided (1, 2, 3, 5, 7, 8).

An experienced grape-grower can tell with little difficulty where the vine will grow well; however, to tell where and which variety will produce a wine of superior quality, is a matter of time, field trial, and a large measure of luck. The novice in grape-growing usually rushes to the nearest experimental station with a sample of soil to be analysed. The

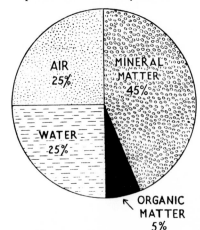

Fig. 5.1. Diagram showing the composition of a moist soil, consisting of mineral matter, organic matter, water and air. From Malherbe (4).

results are often disappointing. The soil chemist can tell him what is in the soil, but not which grapevines to choose. Without doubt, the physical texture of a soil usually is more important than its chemical constituency.

Influence of soil types on wine quality

Viticulturists and oenologists maintain that four factors determine the quality of any wine: variety, climate, soil, and man. As Winkler (8) aptly summed up, 'The combination of specific environmental conditions with the qualities of a given variety has made possible the Rieslings of Germany, the Clarets and Burgundies of France, the Chiantis of Italy, the Constantias of South Africa, and other renowned wines.'

The influence of specific soil types on the quality of the wine is disputed. French viticulturists attribute great importance to the lime content of their soil. Italian viticulturists, in contrast, attach no special value to lime content. In Germany much beneficial influence is attributed to the slate-stone and shale soils. It is a fact, though, that a number of noble-grape varieties of the highest quality produce excellent wines grown on a number of quite different soil types in the famous wine-producing regions of the world. 'Thus, the differences in the character of wines can hardly be attributed mainly to specific soil types. If the soil were so important a factor as is often claimed, there should be some uniformity in one or more characteristics between the soils of the various good districts.' (3, 8).

Soil depth

The depth of viticultural soils varies widely, but it is usual to differentiate between the TOPSOIL and the SUBSOIL.

The subsoil, which is usually lighter in colour, becomes mostly more stony or gravelly as it is penetrated, until the parent rock on which the soil rests is reached (4).

It is very important that the grape-grower should be well acquainted with the nature of the subsoils of his vineyards, because to a large extent, the productivity and water-holding capacity of his vineyard-soil and the adaptation of a specific rootstock variety etc. depend on it. If the subsoil is more clayey at a certain depth than the topsoil, very dense, unfractured layers, called HARDPAN, sometimes develop. Such hardpans are impervious to both water and roots. Soils with such impervious layers within 0,5 to 1,5 m of the surface have shallow water-tables (Fig. 5.2). During the winter, or if irrigation is applied injudiciously, water will accumulate above the hardpan, with consequent damage to the roots (6, 7).

The importance of soil texture

Malherbe (4) emphasizes that 'a knowledge of the exact texture or

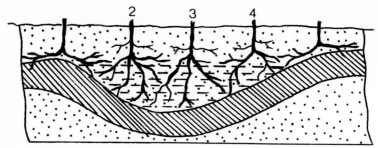

Fig. 5.2. Vertical section of a soil layer indicating how a basin-shaped impervious layer causes the accumulation of excessive water, drowning the roots of vines 2, 3 and 4.

mechanical composition of soils enables us to classify them and to gather valuable information in connection with their agricultural possibilities and weaknesses.'

SANDY SOILS are well aerated, easy to cultivate, and well drained; they are warm soils, but they have a low water-holding capacity. Generally speaking, the sand portions contain very little plant food such as potash, phosphate, magnesia, lime, etc. The incorporation of organic matter into sandy soils gives them body, and so increases their capacity for retaining water (4).

If the fine-sand content predominates, cultivated soil has a tendency to form a hard surface crust on drying after rain or irrigation. Because soil texture cannot be altered, surface crusting cannot be permanently eliminated (6).

Many soils, especially in the coastal regions of the Cape, contain a high percentage of gravel. So there are gravelly sands, gravelly loams, gravelly silt loams and also true gravel, or stony, soils with over 70–80 per cent gravel (4). The main disadvantage of the coarse sandy soils in South Africa is their poor water-retaining capacity. Excess water application leads to rapid leaching of plant nutrients.

CLAY SOILS retain water and plant nutrients well. On the other hand clay soils usually drain slowly with the result that they are apt to become waterlogged. They should only be cultivated when they have the correct moisture content. If cultivated too wet, they puddle and afterwards form hard clods and big cracks. If cultivated when too dry they break up into large clods. Under the same rainfall conditions, clayey soils are not as acid as sandy soils, and yet, under intensive cultivation they require more lime than sandy soils, because lime renders the clay more friable (4).

Table 5.1 clearly shows:

(a) that results of mechanical soil analyses enable us to gather valuable information about the physical properties of soils;

(b) why a soil consisting mainly of one or two closely related types

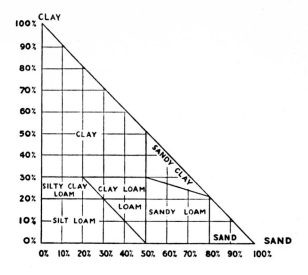

Fig. 5.3. Diagram from which the texture of soils can be deduced. From Malherbe (4).

would be less suitable for plant growth than a soil that contains moderate quantities of all different types (4).

TABLE 5.1
Soil texture and physical properties. From Malherbe (4)

| Physical property | Degree in which the soil content concerned exhibits the property | | | |
	Coarse sand	Fine sand	Silt	Clay
Water capacity	Very low	Medium	High	Very high
Capillarity	Very low	Good	Great	Very great
Rate of water movement	Very fast down	Fast down and up	Slowly down and up	Very slowly down and up
Absorption capacity (for gases, water, and plant nutrients)	Very slight	Slight	Good	Very high
Cohesion and plasticity	None	Slight	High	Very high
Relative temperature	Warm	Fairly warm	Cold	Very cold
Aeration	Very good	Fairly good	Poor	Very poor

The structure of the soil

'*Soil texture* refers to the size of the soil particles, but *soil structure* refers to the arrangement of the particles, especially of finer soil particles. There are two extremes in soil structure with intermediate conditions between them. The one extreme is a so-called *single-grain structure* of which the best example is, perhaps, a pure sand containing very little clay and humus. The other extreme in the arrangement of soil particles is a *crumb structure.* In this case groups of the soil colloids are united with other finer soil particles into small granules, aggregates, or crumbs. This is the ideal condition for an arable soil' (4).

Microbial life, which is so important in soil fertility, flourishes under the above-mentioned conditions and roots expend the least amount of energy in penetrating the soil.

The question presents itself to the grape-grower: given a certain soil and climate, what can be done to bring about favourable crumb structure in the soil?

According to Malherbe (4) there are at least four measures:

(a) the application of organic matter;

(b) the application of lime or lime-containing fertilizers;

(c) tillage, provided the soil has a favourable moisture content; better aeration and an increased microbial activity will be among the beneficial results;

(d) turning arable soils into perennial pastures for some years.

Formation and decomposition of humus in soils

In virgin soils the organic content is derived from animal and plant life in and on the soil. The root systems of plants are naturally in the soil and after the plant dies the organic matter of the roots becomes part of the soil. Usually animal excrement is nothing but digested and undigested plant material.

In cultivated soils organic matter is added to the soil. When fresh plant material or animal products are incorporated with moist soils, a rapid decomposition of most of their constituents is brought about by living microbes. 'After a relatively rapid decomposition of the above-mentioned substances a small, variable residue that is very fine and mainly dark in colour is left in the soil. This residue is called *humus.*' (4) Humus can be considered as a comparatively permanent constituent of every agricultural soil, but it also undergoes a further slow decomposition by new generations of soil microbes.

The COMPOSITION OF HUMUS varies in different soils and under different climatic conditions, but in round figures humus contains more or less the following (4):

57

carbon	50 per cent
oxygen	35
hydrogen	5
nitrogen	5
mineral constituents	5

Soil acidity

'Soil colloids, consisting mainly of clay and humus, usually have five different *cations,* i.e. ions with positive electric charges, absorbed on their surface: hydrogen, calcium, magnesium, potassium and sodium. An acid soil is characterized by the fact that hydrogen predominates among the absorbed cations. If the ions of calcium (and magnesium) predominate, the soil will be slightly acid, neutral or slightly alkali. If ions of sodium (and potassium) predominate, we usually have a very alkaline soil' (4).

Where are acid soils found?

Soil particles (colloids) are deprived of their substances under high rainfall conditions, and these bases are replaced by hydrogen. Consequently, the likelihood of soil becoming acid increases as the annual rainfall increases.

Under the same precipitation sandy soils will be subject to greater leaching than loams and clay soils which have a higher water-holding capacity. The result is that sandy soils are usually more acid than the heavier soil types under the same rainfall conditions (4).

The degree of acidity of the soil solution is today commonly expressed in terms of pH. A neutral solution is a solution containing equal quantities of hydrogen ions (H^+) and hydroxyl (OH^-) ions, and its pH is 7. The more acid, the lower the figure (4).

Properties of alkali soils (brak, or brackish)

A saline soil is caused by the presence of too much soluble salt. 'The characteristic property of nearly all alkali (*brak*) soils is that their clay portion is largely saturated with sodium ions. A second characteristic is that they usually contain considerable quantities of water-soluble sodium salts such as sodium chloride (common salt), sodium sulphate (Glauber's salt), and sometimes also sodium carbonate (washing soda). The harmful effects of these salts on plant growth are due to the fact that the soil solution may become too concentrated as a result of their presence, and agricultural crops are not adapted to such high concentrations. The protoplasm of the plant cells shrinks (*plasmolysis*) if the salt concentration of the plant food solution is too high, with the result that the plant dies.' (4)

The pH of such soils is usually higher than 8,5.

Brak soils may be divided into two classes:

(1) SALINE *BRAK*. This type of soil contains an excess of sodium chloride or sodium sulphate or both. The soil has a good structure and the high salt concentration is the most important impediment to plant growth.

(2) ALKALINE *BRAK* ('Black Brak', 'Black Alkali' soils). The clay portion of such soils consists of deflocculated sodium clay, which is responsible for the undesirable properties. An alkaline *brak* soil is totally unsuitable for plant growth. Such soils are structureless, very compact, do not absorb water easily, drain badly and hence are also badly aerated (4, 7).

According to Neja et al. (1974) quoted by Weaver (7), the following factors accentuate salt accumulation:

(1) irrigation water of poor quality (high salinity);

(2) poor water management that allows too much salt to accumulate in the root area;

(3) high original salt content of the soil;

(4) poor drainage characteristics;

(5) semi-arid climate with low rainfall and high temperatures (low rainfall causes an insufficient winter leaching, and large amounts of water applied may then add more salts);

(6) heavy application of fertilizers;

(7) heavy, infrequent water applications during the growing-season to soils with shallow claypans;

(8) uneven topography and variable depth of soils over impervious soil layers.

Effect of saline soils on vines

According to Winkler (8) salinity injury 'first appears as a marginal burn, which is followed by progressive necrosis of the leaf blade toward the petiole until only the main veins remain green. The line of demarcation between the green and brown tissue is sharp.'

The remedy for salinity injury is to reduce the salt content of the soil. Usually drainage and leaching are required, and in the case of alkali the treatment includes certain soil amendments; for example, the application of gypsum (potassium sulphate) improves the structure of a *brak* soil. This physical effect on the soil is coupled with its antagonistic effect towards sodium ions, largely preventing the sodium uptake by plants (4).

Soil erosion

The water that reaches the surface of the earth in the form of rain may run off to lower-lying land and rivers. Run-off of rainwater and the transportation of soil constituents appear in an aggravated form as SOIL EROSION.

According to Malherbe (4) soil erosion is affected by, or is a function of, the following five factors: topography (slope); soil type; climate; vegetation; and human activity.

Vegetation is by far the most important single factor influencing soil erosion. It binds the soil, protects the surface layer against the harmful effects of rain on its structure, increases the humus content of the soil, and thus increases the penetrability of the surface soil for water.

The question of soil conservation is very comprehensive. Bennett, quoted by Malherbe (4), describes it as follows: 'Soil conservation calls for the techniques of the crop specialist, the livestock specialist, engineers, foresters, soil scientists and other specialists, all working together as a single co-ordinated whole. That is soil conservation. Soil conservation calls for using the land properly and protecting it for permanent productivity.'

CLIMATE

Climate is one of the most important factors influencing the production of grapes and the quality of their wines. We cannot change an unfavourable climate.

For best development, *V. vinifera* grape varieties require mild, dry weather in spring when the new period of growth commences. Rains early in the growing-season make the control of fungoid diseases difficult. Rains and especially cold weather during the flowering period may result in poor set of the berries. Once the berries have set, vinifera grapes require long, warm-to-hot and dry summers. They are not adapted to humid summers owing to their susceptibility to certain fungus diseases and insect pests that are practically uncontrollable under continuous humid and warm climatic conditions. It is of the greatest importance that little rain should fall from the time the grapes change colour (véraison). Wines of the best quality are usually produced in the hot years of the coolest viticultural regions of the world, whereas in the warm regions the cool years produce the higher quality wines (3).

Vinifera grapes require a winter rest period of about two months, with an average daily temperature below 10 °C, but no temperatures below minus 12 °C. Abundant rain is desirable during the winter. As the equator is approached, the altitude at which grapes can be grown increases. Generally speaking, the upper limit for grape-growing lies 2 000–2 500 metres below the snowline (5).

It is generally known that seas, large lakes, and large rivers exert a moderating influence upon the climate in their adjacent areas. Water acts as a 'regulating reservoir of heat' far more than soil or air does. The

Cape Peninsula illustrates these influences very well (5). Winkler (8) emphasizes that 'centuries of experience and research of European growers and oenologists have definitely established the effect of climate on wine grapes. Climate influences the rates of change in the constituents of the fruit during development and the composition at maturity. Moderately cold weather, under which ripening proceeds slowly, is favourable for the production of dry table wines of quality. In warm climates the aromatic qualities of the grapes lose delicacy and richness, and the other constituents of the fruit are less well balanced. This fact is pointed up in particular by the marked differences in the quality of wine of the same variety or varieties grown on similar soil types and texture, but under different conditions of heat summation.'

The influences of climate and soil-type on wine quality are overemphasized in South Africa, while the influences of the size of the crop and injudicious irrigation are overlooked. Consequently, no restrictions on irrigation or on the size of the crop are enforced in this country, to the great detriment of the quality of local table wines.

On the basis of a false assumption concerning the predominating influence of a cool climate on wine quality, some warm grapegrowing areas in South Africa, such as the Robertson–Ashton–Bonnievale regions, have been unjustly 'condemned' in the past as suitable only for the production of distilling wines. On the other hand, growers near the coast have been misled into believing that they can produce high-quality wines as long as their vines 'can see or smell the sea' and have enough water to irrigate them and enough nitrogen-containing fertilizers to push their growth.

CHAPTER 6

Means of Improving Propagation Material

THE SELECTION OF V. VINIFERA GRAPE VARIETIES

Heterogeneity of the grapevine

Before the laws of heredity became known during the second half of the previous century (Father G.J. Mendel 1822–84), vines were propagated by means of seedlings. The most promising seedlings were chosen for multiplication and were propagated further by seedlings again. Most *V. vinifera* grape varieties have HERMAPHRODITE FLOWERS, i.e. each flower has both male and female reproductive organs. Consequently, fecundation occurred. The flowers of a grapevine are also subject to wind- or insect-borne cross-pollination from flowers of neighbouring vines. Developed through centuries of evolution and improved by men who always selected the most vigorous and fertile seedlings for propagation, our cultivated varieties are products of a series of cross-pollinations. They are genetically not *homogeneous,* but *heterogeneous.* (The word heterogeneous is derived from the Greek words *heteros,* other, and *genos,* race.) No one knows, for example, when and by whom the first grapes of Cabernet Sauvignon, Riesling, Pinot noir, etc., were picked.

Because of the heterogeneity of the grapevine, the seedlings originating from the seed of the same vine resemble neither each other nor the mother-plant. For example the crossing of Riparia tomenteuse with Rupestris Martin by Couderc in 1881 produced 18 seeds forming the well-known 3300 series of rootstock varieties, out of which only the 3306 and 3309 are commercially cultivated. The descendants of all these 18 seedlings have the same GENOTYPE, but they can be distinguished from each other by means of small morphological characteristics due to their different PHENOTYPES. The various external characteristics (shape of the leaves, bunches, berries, etc.) by which we can recognize a particular variety, constitute its phenotype. It expresses the visible reaction of its genotype to environmental conditions (7, 11, 15).

Nothing in organic life is permanent. The evolution and constant alteration of grape varieties never stop. Organic evolution is a process that either preserves or rejects different genotypes. Consequently, our cultivated varieties, especially the older ones, are subject to MUTATIONS that give rise to a hereditary alteration in the genotype. Mutations are easily confused with VARIATIONS, which arise from different environmental conditions.

Mutations are divided into two major classes: those involving a change in a single gene and those involving a change in the structure or number of chromosomes. '*Gene mutations* implies that the genetic material can undergo some sort of change so that its action results in the production of an altered phenotype' (11).

Most new mutations are deleterious, owing to the long history of evolution that has preserved the favourable alleles and rejected those that are less favourable. 'As a consequence, a newly arisen mutation has only a small probability of producing a favourable phenotype under normal environmental conditions' (11). Consequently, a slow but constant degeneration of our cultivated grape varieties is an unavoidable biological process. The only way to counteract this process is to propagate only the most robust, most fertile and in external appearance the most constant individuals of a specific variety. *Man must be quicker with his selection than Nature with its degeneration.* Consequently, selection is a continual battle against the hereditary instability of the vine. It is a never-ending process, probably the most important duty research-workers and grapegrowers have to fulfil. *The basic principle of selection is based on the oldest and most uncompromising law of Nature: the survival of the fittest and the right of the strongest to propagate itself. The weak, on the other hand, must be prevented from propagating itself. It must perish. This is the apparently immutable law of Nature for the preservation of the species* (17, 18).

If possible, one must select material for propagation in very old vineyards, and where the vines have grown under difficult climatic and soil conditions. In such vineyards Nature itself has already made a selection by eliminating all vines which could not maintain the fight for survival (7, 10, 17, 20, 26, 30).

It must be emphasized, however, that we cannot change a basic characteristic of a particular variety by selection. We can only to some extent improve it. It would for example be wasted effort to try to 'select' a Palomino or Müller–Thurgau clone with high acidity, or a Colombard clone with low acidity. The limits of selection must be acknowledged (18, 30).

Methods of selection

(1) Mass-selection

The first phase in any attempt to improve propagation material is

POSITIVE MASS-SELECTION. It is the quickest and cheapest method of eliminating all inferior types of a variety-population from further propagation, as long as it is carried out with a profound knowledge of the varieties concerned (2, 10, 14, 17, 18, 20, 22, 26, 29).

The problems that arise and the questions that have to be solved are as follows:

(a) Are there individual vines in a particular vineyard which constantly perform better than the other vines of the same variety?

(b) Is the above-average performance of such vines due to hereditary factors or only to favourable environmental conditions, different methods of pruning, different rootstocks, etc.?

(c) Individual vines which have performed better than the average during at least three consecutive years: can we recognize them by their external appearance, such as for example leaf-, bunch-, berry-types, growth-habits, etc.? (25, 26, 29, 37).

It is well known that, for example, deeper lateral sinuses, extremely sharp-pointed dentition, looser bunches and larger berries than considered typical for the variety concerned, as well as susceptibility to *millerandage* and to *coulure,* are indications of the degeneration of a variety (25, 27, 37).

To establish the most valuable types of a specific variety by means of comparative evaluation is the aim of individual or clonal selection (2, 10, 14, 16, 25, 28, 29, 34, 37).

(2) Clonal selection

Clonal selection is a kind of continuation and perfection of mass- and type-selection. It is a comparative evaluation of the vegetative descendants of numerous mother-vines of the same *V. vinifera* grape variety. Such promising mother-vines are usually detected during mass-selection. Because the yield per vine is mainly dependent on the number of fruit-eyes retained during winter pruning, which cannot be controlled during a large-scale selection in summer when the vines are in foliage, attempts to improve the productivity of vines based exclusively on yield observations of the mother-vines could be misleading (3). Who could claim, for example, that he can find the most valuable five vines in a block of vineyard consisting of 5 000 vines? For this reason, mother-vines for clonal selection are approved on the basis of genetically anchored characteristics, such as shape of the leaves, size, shape and compactness of the bunches, size and shape of the berries, number of bunches per shoot, etc. The ultimate aim of clonal selection is to find the most valuable biotypes of premium-quality *V. vinifera* grape varieties, which have been cultivated for a very long time and have consequently degenerated. The various clones of, for example, Riesling, Pinot noir, Ruländer, Furmint, Chardonnay, Kadarka, etc., can be distinguished from each other either by their differing phenotypes or by the quality of their wines. To create numerous 'clones' from genetically homogeneous newly bred hybrids is not only a waste of time and money but, according to Professor J. Branas (6), 'scientifically speaking an absurdity'.

The performance of a clone usually corresponds closely to the performance of its mother-vine. If this is not the case, we have to do with clones whose performance is influenced by environmental conditions, the so-called *gebietsgebundene Klonen,* i.e. clones whose performance is bound to a specific region (16, 28).

Fig. 6.l. Successive phases of clonal selection adopted in Europe (10, 14, 16, 21, 25, 26, 29, 37). From Vogt/Götz (34).

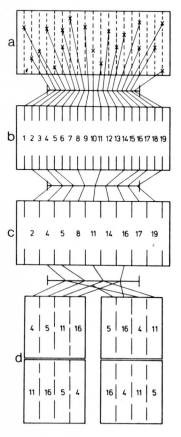

(a) *Selection of mother-vines* in commercial vineyards all over a country. Time required for approval: three consecutive years.

(b) *Preliminary phase:* comparative evaluation of the first clonal descendants of the most promising 19 mother-vines in a clonal garden. Number of vines per clone: 10.

(c) *Intermediate phase:* comparative evaluation of the second clonal descendants of the 9 most promising clones of the previous phase in the clonal garden. Number of vines per clone: 4 x 20 = 80.

(d) *Main* or *ecological phase,* in which we try to ascertain how well the four best clones of the previous phase have adapted themselves to different environmental conditions. For this purpose the material (about 200 vines per clone) must be planted and evaluated in four different viticultural regions of the country concerned.

If we compare Figs 6.1 and 6.2, we discover such fundamental differences that we might assume that research workers in Europe and in California work with plants belonging to two different botanical families and with two different aims.

The essence of the schema followed in the European grapegrowing countries is continual and never-ending selection. The essence of the method followed in Davis is the continuous indexing, heat treatment (thermotherapy) and re-indexing of propagation material. 'Because it was not possible to find most varieties in a clean state in commercial vineyards', in 1960 Dr. A.C. Goheen erected heat chambers 'in order to

Fig. 6.2. Successive phases of the 'virological approach' of improving propagation material, followed in Davis, California. From Alley (1).

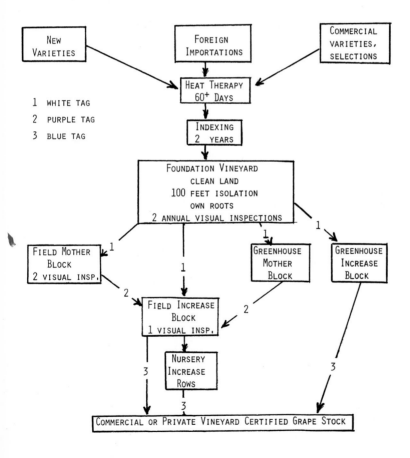

develop clean stocks from diseased vines' (1). No data are provided indicating the performance of the 'cleaned' material. The presumption that genetically inferior material can be improved by 'cleaning' it of viruses makes a mockery of the laws of heredity. Dr. J.V. Poshingham (1972), quoted by Myburgh (13), indicates, however, that even in the English-speaking grapegrowing countries serious doubt arose concerning the infallibility of the virologists:

'It is not certain that all viruses are harmful as some particularly high-yielding clones have identifiable virus infections. Horticulturists believe there is a risk in leaving this most important phase of vine improvement to virologists as there have been some embarassing cases of the most excellent virus-free vines turning out to be the wrong variety. Example: some heat-treated Gamay Beaujolais vines recently imported into Australia turned out to be Pinot noir.'

Similar experience occurred in South Africa with material imported from the Foundation block in Davis. 'Gamay Beaujolais', 'Petite Syrah' and certified '99 Richter' not only turned out to be completely different varieties but performed poorly when planted into the vineyards.

No references can be found in the literature that mass- or clonal selection, based on yield-records, wine-quality, etc., has ever been attempted in Davis. Starting the improvement of grapevine propagation material by heat treatment without prior genetical selection is like putting a roof on a house that has been built on sand without a proper foundation. On the other side of the Atlantic, thanks to the efforts of practically minded viticulturists and grapegrowers, clonal material thoroughly tested viticulturally could be cultivated on a large scale long before it became known that the vine could be affected by something like symptomless viruses (2, 28).

The urgent and necessary improvement of propagation material can be achieved only through systematic and continuous selection by viticulturists in the vineyard and *not* by continuous indexing and heat treatment in laboratories and heat chambers.

The grapegrower expects propagation material to graft easily, to produce grafted vines which grow vigorously, look healthy, bear regularly and well, and to produce grapes of the highest quality possible from the variety concerned. Symptomless viruses which do not deleteriously affect the performance of the material have no practical significance whatsoever for the grower, who must plant vines for a life of at least 25 years. To quote Vuittinez, the well-known French plant-pathologist, 'it would be absurd to destroy plant material which performs well, because it is infected with a virus which does it no harm' (35).

It must be emphasized that:

(a) By 'harmful' viruses viticulturists and growers in Europe understand a virus which deleteriously affects the performance of the grapevine.

(b) The method of clonal selection as practised in Europe for nearly 50 years, indicated in Fig. 6.1, is considered to be completely adequate for excluding all harmful viruses from further propagation (10, 14, 16, 25, 28, 29, 34, 37).

(c) No one in Europe would dream of suggesting that (viticulturally) thoroughly tested clonal material which looks healthy and performs splendidly in the vineyards should be 'cleaned' from symptomless viruses by thermotherapy before it can be put at the disposal of the growers.

The shortcomings of the virological approach are:

(1) Not all virus races have yet been identified, and new virus races are being 'discovered' continually by virologists, while other diseases, which had for years been assumed to be caused by viruses now appear to have other origins. For example, Pierce's disease is now shown, by recent research, to be associated with a Rickettsia-like organism (36).

The causal organism of corky-bark, reported as a virus disease only from California, South Africa and Italy according to Branas (1974), is still disputed. French and German viticulturists and plant-pathologists presume that its symptoms are being confused with those of flavescence dorée (Vergilbungskrankheit), which, according to our present knowledge, is *not* a virus disease.

(2) It has not yet been proved that material which has been found, by means of indexing, 'free' from the known viruses of the vine, performs better in the vineyard than viticulturally tested clonal material, approved visually for propagation after many years of evaluation (2, 6, 25). On the contrary, South African plant-pathologists, using only the Californian method of indexing, 'detected' symptomless viruses in internationally famous clones such as W. Riesling 239 G.m., Ruländer H 1., Pinot noir 2/10, Nemes Furmint Pécs 1, etc. The material, imported to South Africa during the 1960s, performs excellently in the field and shows no symptoms of viruses whatsoever.

(3) The results of indexing of the same material can vary from one year to another, because the distribution of the virus might be uneven in the various arms of the vine and even in various parts of the same cane (8).

(4) The sensitivity of court-noué (fanleaf) virus to heat treatment, termed 'thermosensibility' by Ravaz, has been known since 1921 (5). However, the whole question of heat treatment is, according to Galet (7), still in an experimental stage: (a) we do not yet know which virus races might resist the thermotherapy; (b) we do not yet know the effect of the combination of two or more viruses on the performance of the vine; and (c) even if virologists succeed in providing material free from all harmful viruses of the vine, without knowing the possible host-plants

and vectors there is no effective means of preventing a reinfection of the material. There are strong indications, based on practical experience, that a reinfection could be fatal to the plant.

Indexing results indicate that *fanleaf* virus is comparatively easily eliminated with heat treatment from shoot tips after 30 days treatment. *Leafroll,* however, requires longer heat periods, three months and beyond, and is less consistently eliminated; and grapevine *yellow speckle* could not be eliminated even after heat treatment periods up to 11 months!

(5) Heat-treated rootstocks grow very vigorously in the field, but the problem to be answered still remains: how will an excessive vigour and the inevitably lower fertility affect the quality of a *V. vinifera* grape variety? It has been experienced in France that a clone of Gewürztraminer, which was well known for the high quality of its wines, grew more vigorously after heat treatment, but the quality of its wines deteriorated.

(6) Although there has been more than 25 years of intensive and expensive virus-research, the author is not aware of a single block of vineyard in the world in which material 'cleaned' from viruses performs better than internationally known clones of the same variety, selected and approved for their practical performance according to the method of clonal selection followed in Europe.

The biological problem of improving propagation material has not, and it appears, will not be solved by a dogmatic approach.

I would like to give grapegrowers in the English-speaking countries the following advice: Attend your vines properly; select the best of them for propagation systematically, as our predecessors in Europe did for centuries, and don't trouble your head with virology.

It is a curious fact that whenever man attempts his self-appointed task of improving Nature by unnatural means, as in this case replacing selection with heat-treatment, disaster is the inevitable price of his folly.

'If we first know *where* we are, and *whither* we are tending, we could better judge *what* to do and *how* to do it' — Abraham Lincoln.

THE SELECTION, BREEDING AND EVALUATION OF ROOTSTOCKS

Historical

The destruction of the European vineyards by the phylloxera, during the last decades of the previous century, represented the greatest crisis in the history of European viticulture.

The insect, a root louse, was named *Phylloxera vastatrix* by Professor Planchon of Montpellier, who discovered it on roots of infected vines in 1868. Laliman, an ampelographer from Bordeaux, observed in 1872 that roots of *V. aestivalis* were not destroyed by the insects, and argued very correctly that, as the phylloxera has existed from all time on wild American vines, there must be some quality in these vines that enabled them to resist the attacks of the insects. Laliman was the first to propose the grafting of the very susceptible *V. vinifera* grape varieties onto *Vitis* species indigenous to North America. The first consignment of cuttings arrived in France from America in 1873, and with the first grafting experiments a new era opened in viticulture (4, 5, 9, 23, 24, 32). Thousands of hectares were planted with American vines, but the results were at first disappointing. Many were found to perish even before grafting, while some thrived at first after grafting, and then perished. But some of them flourished exceptionally well and after grafting yielded heavier crops than had ever been obtained with *V. vinifera* grape varieties on the same soil.

This caused close attention to be paid to the different species and varieties of the American vines. It was found that in North America, instead of a single species as in Europe, eighteen distinct species were identified and grouped in two sections and six series. Each species embraces many different varieties, these varieties differing from one another as much as for example *V. vinifera* var. Cabernet Sauvignon from the seedless *V. vinifera* var. Sultanina. The confusion of species with varieties has proved the greatest difficulty in solving the question of the adaptation of American vines. The inability to recognize at once the fact that there are hundreds of varieties of *V. riparia, V. rupestris,* etc., and that some are valuable and the others are useless, has cost European viticulture vast sums of money (9, 12, 24, 31, 32, 33).

The most striking mistakes were made in attempting to reproduce the resistant stocks from seeds. This proved a dismal failure everywhere, for almost every seedling developed into a new variety, more or less worthless, since a grape seedling is seldom as good as the mother-vine (5, 9, 12, 24, 31, 32, 33).

The burden fell heaviest on the French, from whom the best viticulturists of the time were commissioned for the selection, breeding and evaluation of phylloxera-resistant rootstocks. This monumental task fully occupied for about 40 years (1870–1910) scientists like Millardet, Couderc, Foex, Ravaz, Viala, Teleki, etc., who, between them, represent the greatest names in viticulture.

As the *V. vinifera* grape varieties are grafted on American rootstocks to prevent them from being destroyed by the phylloxera, the resistance of a rootstock variety to the insect is by far the most important factor in deciding on its suitability as a rootstock (9, 12, 23, 24, 31, 32, 33).

In order to be able to indicate with some degree of certainty the resistance to the phylloxera — not the cultural value of the rootstock — an arbitrary scale has been adopted by scientists. On this scale, the maximum of resistance is indicated as 20, and the minimum as 0.

After about 25 years, the tremendous work of evaluating many hundreds of varieties of American *Vitis* species, as well as their hybrids, was completed. In 1892 Professors P. Viala and L. Ravaz published their recommendations for the reconstruction of the vineyards on phylloxera-resistant rootstocks in a book published in French and English, *American Vines: Adaptation, Culture, Grafting and Propagation*. This book is rightly considered one of the most important ever written on viticulture. The vineyards of the entire viticultural world have been grafted according to the suggestions of Viala and Ravaz (24, 32, 33).

The authors summarized their recommendations as follows: '*The numbers 16 to 20 correspond to a sufficient resistance for all soils; the numbers 15 and 14 express a resistance sufficient for sandy and deep soils, where the phylloxera does little harm; the numbers 13 and under, should be totally discarded for vineyards.*'

The arbitrary resistance scale, worked out by Professor Viala in grouping the best-known varieties, produces the following:

20: absolute immunity (?).

19: *V. rotundifolia*.

18: *V. riparia, V. rupestris,* Rupestris Ganzin, Rupestris Martin, *V. cordifolia,* riparia X rupestris, cordifolia X riparia, cordifolia X rupestris.

17: *V. berlandieri,* riparia X berlandieri, rupestris X berlandieri.

16: Rupestris du Lot, Rupestris Metallica, candicans X riparia.

15: *V. cinerea, V. aestivalis, V. candicans*.

14: Solonis, Viala, Novo-Mexicana, *V. champini* glabrous.

13: Taylor, Michigan.

12: Jacquez=Lenoir, Herbemont, *V. champini* tomenteuse.

Below 10: Clinton, Concord, Labrusca, Othello, Catawba, etc. The hybrids of vinifera X rupestris (1202 C and Aramon X RG) vary between 7 and 15.

The hybrids of vinifera X berlandieri (41B and 333 E.M.) possess a high resistance to chlorosis; Millardet considered them sufficiently resistant to phylloxera in deep, fertile, sandy soils in cold countries.

As indicated above, the vineyards of the entire viticultural world have been reconstituted according to the recommendations of Viala and Ravaz. The success which has been achieved, makes any dispute or discussion concerning the correctness of these recommendations irrelevant. Where the instructions of Viala and Ravaz were disregarded, as in South Africa[1] with 1202 C and Aramon X RG in the 'thirties, with 143 B in the 'fifties, and with Jacquez, vines grafted on to these rootstocks deteriorated or

[1] Unfortunately for South African viticulture, the late Professor A.I. Perold in 1926 considered Professor P. Viala's arbitrary scale to be of 'not much practical value to us', because 'there is no such thing as a fixed resistance of a stock to phylloxera'.

withered as the result of attacks of phylloxera. Future experience will show what will happen to *V. champini* var. Salt Creek. *V. champini* was rejected as a rootstock by Viala and Ravaz 80 years ago. Instead of profiting from the costly experiments of others, some research workers seem still to be inclined to start experimenting with rootstocks which were discredited 80 years ago by the French. The wheel was discovered long ago; it is unnecessary, and expensive, to try to rediscover it.

The general tendency was to reconstitute the devastated vineyards of Europe on Riparia gloire and on riparia X rupestris hybrids in those grapegrowing areas with moderate climate and sufficient rainfall. For countries with a warm, dry climate Rupestris du Lot and 41 B were preferred.

After the First World War, hybrids of berlandieri X riparia, mostly those selected by Teleki from 1896, began to replace the riparia X rupestris hybrids in Central Europe, North Italy, and in the German-speaking countries. But it was only after the Second World War that the berlandieri X rupestris hybrids of Richter, Paulsen and Ruggeri began to replace Rupestris du Lot and 41 B in arid areas with warm climates (5, 7). The only exceptions are: California, where Rupestris du Lot (called Rupestris Saint George), 1202 C, and Aramon X RG No. 1 are still the main rootstock varieties (1); and South Africa, where Jacquez=Lenoir and 101-14 Mgt are the two most widely used rootstocks (19).

But it must be remembered that mere resistance to phylloxera is *not* the only consideration in determining the value of a rootstock. There must be a natural adaptability to soil and climate, and to the scion variety. By a system of experimental selection, scientists found that varieties of *V. riparia, V. rupestris* and *V. berlandieri* as groups adapt themselves more readily to changed conditions, and especially to the European varieties grafted on them, than any other American *Vitis* species. With very few exceptions, most rootstocks used today are hybrids of these three American species. The other American species were found to be of little or no value as rootstocks.

IMPORTATIONS

The importation of a few cuttings of heat-treated material from the Foundation block of Davis will never solve the problem of improving the propagation material in viticulture. This extremely urgent problem can only be solved by the large-scale importation and quick propagation of viticulturally thoroughly tested clones of the most noble European grape varieties and rootstock selections. As has already been pointed out, it took the European viticulturists and grapegrowers decades to select and evaluate such clones. It would be possible in new areas to ascertain their adaptation within three to five years. It is by no means taken for granted that a grape variety which produces wine of superior quality in Europe will produce wines of the same quality in, for example, South Africa. But *it is absolutely certain, that only a variety which produces wines of high quality in Europe has a chance of producing wines of similar quality in, e.g. South Africa or Australia, where climatic conditions for the production of delicate wines are less favourable.*

Through the ages certain grape varieties have proved their superior value in the old wine-producing countries, and have become world-famous. There are no more than about seven to eight whites, W. Riesling, Chardonnay, Sauvignon blanc, Furmint, Ruländer, etc., and only four reds, Cabernet Sauvignon, Cabernet franc, Merlot and Pinot noir. This being so, it would seem to be common sense that, if certain facts have been established in many countries beyond the possibility of doubt, it is foolish and irresponsible to disregard them. 'Fools say that they learn by experience. I prefer to learn by other people's experience,' said Bismarck.

From 1963 until 1970 the author was able to import, among others, the best available clones of Weisser Riesling, Welsch-or-Italian Riesling, Furmint, Hárslevelü, Pinot noir, Pinot gris/Ruländer, Pinot blanc, Sylvaner, Kadarka, and the rootstocks 140 Ru, 1103 and 1447 P, 44-53 M, and Prosperi Super 99 R.

CHAPTER 7

Propagation

Vines may be propagated from seeds, layers, cuttings, or grafts.

1. GROWING GRAPES FROM SEED

It is as easy to grow grapes from seeds as it is any other fruit. The seeds, after having been taken from over-ripe berries must have a resting period of a few months. Keep them in moist, sandy soil and store in a cool place. Before planting out, the seeds must be soaked in water for three to four days. Then they are sown in well-manured garden-soil 3–4 cm apart and in rows 10–20 cm apart. In due course the young seedlings are transferred to a nursery.

Unfortunately, vines grown from seeds differ markedly not only from the parent vines but also from each other. Since most seedlings are inferior to the parent vines, the breeder must be prepared to discard 99,9 per cent of his seedlings as not worth further trial. To quote the late Professor B. Husfeld's remark, 'To find one superior hybrid in 10 000 seedlings requires more luck than knowledge.'

The inheritance of characteristics

The characteristics of grapes are inherited in accordance with Mendel's laws. The breeder should use as parents all varieties that promise to transmit characteristics that he wants in his new hybrid. But:

(a) Intraspecific hybridization does not produce totally new varieties in grapevines. A new variety originating from hybridization is but a re-combination of characteristics of the immediate and distant parents.

(b) It must not be taken for granted that varieties of high cultural value are likely to make the best parents on hybridization. Riesling, Cabernet Sauvignon, Merlot, Pinot noir, etc., have produced a very small percentage of good offspring in grapevine breeding. In support of this it may be noted that, in spite of millions of seedlings, and many thousands of evaluated hybrids during the last 80–100 years, not one vinifera × vinifera wine-grape hybrid is cultivated on a significant scale in the traditional wine-producing countries. A cross between a thorough-bred mare and a donkey can only be a mule.

2. PROPAGATION BY LAYERS

Layering is the most convenient way of filling occasional gaps in an established vineyard in countries or areas where the *V. vinifera* grape varieties are still cultivated on their own roots. A newly planted one-year-old rooted vine has little chance of surviving the competition of the roots of fully grown neighbours, but a layered plant from a nearby parent-vine readily establishes itself.

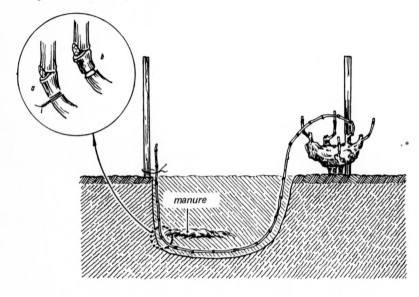

Fig. 7.1. Propagation by layer: A long, vigorous cane from a vine adjacent to a missing vine should be used as *layer*. Such a cane is bent down into a trench about 30–35 cm deep while still part of the parent vine. The tip of the layer should be exactly in position to replace the missing vine. A layer will strike roots at each node but, in order to promote root-formation at the base of the future plant, the layer should be girdled at the place where it is bent suddenly upwards from the trench. After about two years the layers can be severed from the mother vine. From Kozma (8).

3. PROPAGATION BY MEANS OF CUTTINGS

For commercial purposes all varieties, whether for the production of rootstocks or grapes, are propagated by cuttings. Segments of one-year-old canes (called cuttings) are always used. The sooner the cuttings are made after the vines become completely dormant, the better. Only well-matured material should be prepared for cuttings. The wood must be firm, the phloem should appear green, the pith must be of moderate size and of light-brownish colour (1, 9, 18, 21).

Length and thickness of the cuttings

The best cuttings are those of medium thickness (9-11 mm), with medium-long internodes. Cuttings that are too thick strike roots with great difficulty. If grafted, they often produce imperfect graft unions.

Rootstock cuttings, designed for grafting, should be cut just below the bottom node, and at the upper end at least 3-4 cm of wood must be left above the topmost bud. They are usually cut in lengths of 25-32 cm.

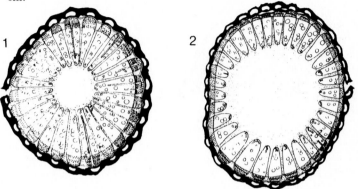

Fig. 7.2 (a) Transverse sections of well-matured (1) and badly matured (2) canes. Note the strikingly large pith and the very unfavourable wood : pith ratio in badly matured canes. Consequently, such material is not suitable for grafting purposes. From Vogt/Götz (18).

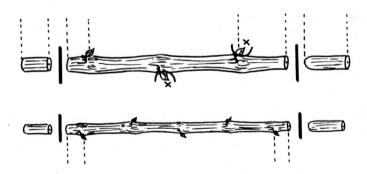

Fig. 7.2 (b) Preparation of rootstock cuttings: Cut to the desired length of about 25 cm in South Africa; in Europe they are cut considerably longer. The cuttings are then disbudded: all buds, save the basal bud, have to be removed with a knife to prevent the growth of rootstock suckers; cuttings designed for grafting (above), and cutting designed for planting out (below).

Cuttings for planting out (rootstock, direct producers, etc.) are cut just below the bottom node and just above the top node, as such cuttings must be terminated at each end by a node (1, 9).

Storing of cuttings

The finished cuttings are tied with two wires in bundles of 100 or 200 each, lying uniformly from the basal end. Where cuttings of various varieties are stored in the same place, a durable label should be tied to each bundle indicating the name and origin of the material.

At the Cape with its cool and rainy winters, rootstock cuttings are usually stored in the open. Care must be taken that they retain their original moisture content as far as possible. They are laid flat in trenches and in layers that are not too thick, with some soil between the bundles. Canes lying flat will not commence budding as readily as those standing more or less straight up (9).

In modern nursery technique, propagation material is stored in cold-storage rooms at more than 1 °C. In early winter, scion and rootstock material is first soaked in a solution of 0,3–0,5 per cent Chinosol for 15 hours and then packed in plastic bags. The bags are stored in cold-storage rooms. The air of such rooms must have a very high per cent relative humidity (2).

Planting out cuttings

The disbudding of ungrafted cuttings is not necessary. Such cuttings are planted in nursery rows about 75–90 cm apart and are set 4–5 cm in the row. The earliest possible planting is advisable. The cuttings must be set in trenches and only the top buds (eyes) of the cuttings should be above the soil level. Before covering the trenches the soil must be tamped down around the base of the cuttings (9).

4. PROPAGATION BY GRAFTS

Until phylloxera came to Europe from North America (between 1854 and 1860), the *V. vinifera* grape varieties, i.e. varieties that produce fruit of desirable character, were grown on their own roots. Cuttings taken from such vines were rooted and then planted out into the vineyards. During the last four decades of the previous century the phylloxera — a small root louse — devastated the vineyards of Europe because the roots of the varieties of *V. vinifera* are very susceptible to the attacks of the insects. (See more about phylloxera in chapter 12.) The only practical means of growing such susceptible varieties in soils badly infested with phylloxera is to graft them onto rootstocks of American origin whose roots are resistant to the insects.

There are many regions of South Africa where irrigation is extensively practised on very fertile, deep sandy soil which as yet is not infected with phylloxera. The grapegrowers of these regions refuse to believe that they have anything to fear. They may rest assured that they have no grounds for any hope of permanent immunity. With strict quarantine regulations they can delay the advent of phylloxera but cannot hope to be free from it forever.

Any *grafted vine* consists of two essential parts: the ROOTSTOCK, and grafted onto it the SCION, i.e. the desired fruiting variety of *V. vinifera*. The two are joined by a GRAFT UNION, or joint.

Establishment of a graft union between scion and rootstock

When cuttings having secondary growth are grafted, the establishment of graft union involves phenomena similar to those associated with wound healing. A meristematic tissue, composed of parenchymatous cells rich in protoplasm is formed by the cambium layers of the scion and, somewhat later, of the rootstock. On an obliquely cut scion (short- or long-whip grafting), callus tissue is formed in greater abundance below the eye than near the middle of the internode (Fig. 7.3). This CALLUS- or WOUND-TISSUE fills the space between scion and rootstock forming a preliminary union between them. Its purpose is to cover the wound, and to shelter it from exterior influences. The cells which are derived from the activity of generating layers (cambia) of scion and rootstock become joined. Therefore, the closest possible proximity of the cambia when scion and rootstock are put together facilitates the establishment of cambial connections. Soon the exterior cells become suberized, and in one or two layers they form a protective brownish cork-tissue. Inside the jelly-like mass of callus tissue a differentiation of tissues gradually takes place, until newly formed vascular strands (phloem and xylem) bridge the gap between scion and rootstock, uniting the corresponding tissues. From this moment the grafted vine performs its functions as though no wound had been made (3, 4, 7, 9, 13, 14).

For successful grafting the development of the rootstock must be in advance of that of the scion. Otherwise the buds of the scion will leaf out before the joint has been callused and the rootstock has formed proper roots for feeding the young shoots. Such grafts will perish for lack of water and nourishment (9).

The establishment of a graft union involves many problems, and causes of failure of grafts are incompletely known. The largest problem, however, is not the establishment of the union, but incompatibility between scion and rootstock (4).

Fig. 7.3. Callus development on an obliquely cut scion. From Hayne (6).

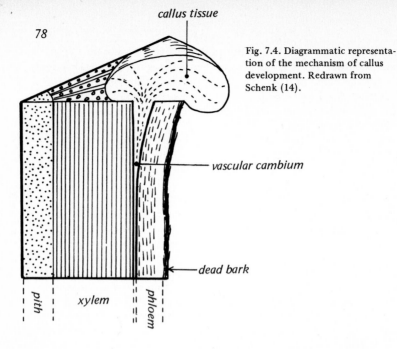

callus tissue

vascular cambium

dead bark

pith   xylem   phloem

Fig. 7.4. Diagrammatic representation of the mechanism of callus development. Redrawn from Schenk (14).

Factors influencing the successful union between scion and rootstock

(a) The intensity of callus development depends on the correlative influence of DORSIVENTRALITY and POLARITY. In the ventral sides of the cut surfaces of the canes callus development begins sooner and with more intensity than on the flat-and-groove sides, as indicated in Fig. 7.5.

The cut scion and rootstock also have a shoot-pole and a root-pole. Polarity always stimulates callus development on the root-pole, i.e. on the deepest point of the cutting (15). Knowledge of the influence of dorsiventrality and polarity on callus development is applied in practice by nurserymen in the execution of short-whip grafting. When scion and rootstock are placed together with the tongues interlocking, the short-whip graft transverses the deepest point of the cut surface to the groove-side, where dorsiventrality always retards callus development. By doing so its lack of callusing potency can be compensated by the stimulating effect of polarity on callus development (15).

(b) Affinity (compatibility) between scion and rootstock: 'Affinity is simply the behaviour of the European vine towards the American root-stock in the grafted stage. By a *bad affinity* or *lack of affinity* of a European variety for an American rootstock I mean that the one does not, in the long run, grow well or at all on the other' (9).

According to Teleki, quoted by Perold (9), it was Couderc who, at the

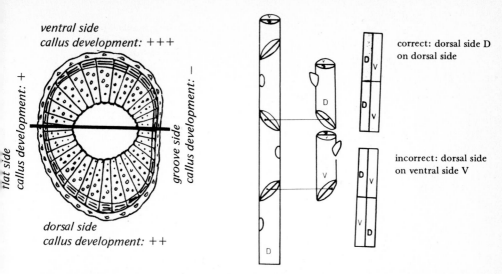

Fig. 7.5. Diagrammatic transverse section through a one-year-old cane, showing its dorsiventral structure, as well as the effect of dorsiventrality on the intensity of callus development.

Fig. 7.6. Arrangement of grafting partners (scion and rootstock) taking the influence of dorsiventrality on callus development into consideration. From Schenk (15).

Viticultural Congress in Mâcon in 1887 brought up the question of affinity.

In grafting *V. vinifera* grape varieties on phylloxera-resistant American rootstocks, we always have to do with an unequal relation between the functional capacities of scion and rootstock (1, 3, 7, 9, 21).

The physiological functions of *V. riparia* especially are different from those of *V. vinifera*. They are less marked in cases of other American *Vitis* species (*V. rupestris, V. berlandieri,* etc.), which approach more closely the viniferas (3).

When a *V. vinifera* grape variety is grafted onto *V. rotundifolia,* it may grow for a time, but the scion is so badly nourished that it soon perishes. The same is true in the case of grafts on the Ampelopsis, Cissus, etc. (3).

Lack of affinity of numerous varieties of *V. vinifera* such as Chardonnay, Ugni blanc, Colombard, Syrah, Bukettraube, Folle blanche, etc., has been observed in South Africa with 101-14 Mgt, and 143 B. (10, 11).

Malbec and the Pinots are more sensitive to chlorosis after grafting. Ungrafted Ugni blanc is vigorous on non-calcareous soils, while it is exceedingly liable to chlorosis when grafted, as also is Folle blanche (5, 7).

Vegetative incompatibility. Where two different *Vitis* species are

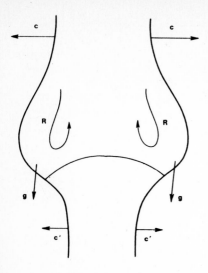

Fig. 7.7. Anatomical obstruction (*bourrelet*) formed above the graft union as seen in diagrammatic longitudinal section. From Branas (3).

Abbreviations: c — diametrical growth of the scion; c' — diametrical growth of the rootstock; R — reflux of assimilates; g — effect of gravity on the auxins.

grafted onto each other, the functional capacities of scion and rootstock are unequal. Hence the life of the grafted vine is continually in an unstable equilibrium (9). In addition to this we may have anatomical obstructions caused by the graft union. It is often observed that the stems of *V. riparia* and of its hybrids (101-14 Mgt, 3306 and 3309 C, 5 BB, SO 4, etc.) do not increase in diameter at the same rate as those of the *V. vinifera* grape varieties grafted onto them. Consequently, the stem of such grafted vines dilates strikingly above the graft union, forming what the French call a *bourrelet*. According to Branas (3), this anatomical obstruction causes the reflux of organic substances, synthesised in the leaves and carried downwards through the phloem of the scion to the roots. The scion then dies after a short period of common life with the rootstock.

SYSTEMS OF GRAFTING

1. Bench grafting

Bench grafting is the most common method of producing grafted vines. The work is carried out during mid- and late-winter, indoors or at least in a shed. Dormant single- or two-eyed scions are grafted onto rootstock cuttings. The newly made grafts are callused and stored until early spring when they are planted out in the nursery. Bench grafting may be carried out by hand (Fig. 7.8), but today machines are more often used.

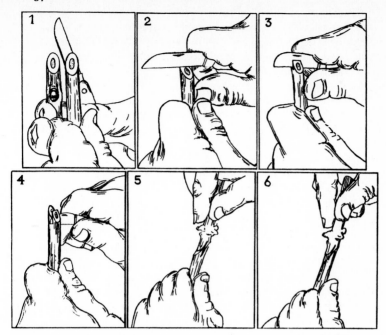

Fig. 7.8. Steps in short-whip (short-tongue) grafting by hand. From Vogt (17).

If everything is done properly, no cut surface will be visible. If the points overlap, the overlapping part should be cut off.

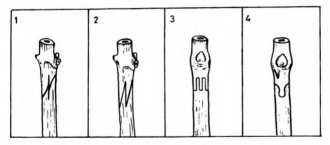

Fig. 7.9. Methods of grafting: (1) Short-whip; (2) Jupiter; (3) Saw-type (Hengl); (4) Omega. From Vogt/Götz (18).

Callusing of grafts

Long-whip, short-whip and machine grafts are usually callused. With this procedure it is not necessary to tie the joints of the grafts. Under favourable conditions, i.e. in the presence of enough heat and moist air, callus tissue is formed first at the bottom, i.e. the root-pole, of scion and rootstock.

In HOT-ROOM CALLUSING grafts are packed into boxes. Aeration assists greatly in the formation of callus. Growing cells respire more, hence they require a medium that is especially well supplied with oxygen. The degree of humidity also exerts a very great influence on the successful joining of scion and rootstock. For this reason, moist, coarse sawdust is mostly used as a packing medium. The callusing room is kept at a temperature of 26–28 °C. It is essential that the temperature should be sufficiently high, and always *regular*. After being in the callusing room for about 14–18 days, the joint between scion and rootstock will be covered by a whitish callus tissue (1, 5, 9, 19, 20).

When callusing is complete all around the joints, the boxes are transferred to a room where the temperature is fairly constant and preferably about 15 °C below that of the callusing room. In modern nursery practice, callused grafts are transferred again to the cold-storage room until they are planted out.

Waxing. In modern nursery technique the scion and the joint are dipped into melted paraffin to prevent moisture loss while the joint knits. For this purpose specially made grafting-wax is available with a very high melting-point (71 °C). The melted paraffin must be kept at 78–85 °C during the process. If the wax is too hot it may injure the tissues and eyes (18, 19).

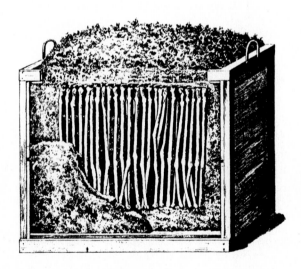

Fig. 7.10. Callusing box filled with about 800 grafts packed in sawdust and ready to go into the callusing room. From Bábó & Mach (1).

Planting

The best time for planting is determined by the ruling climatic conditions. The nursery should be on a well-drained, fertile, sufficiently moist and warm soil. In preparation for planting, the soil of the nursery should be deeply ploughed.

The grafts are set 5–7 cm apart in the rows and the rows 0,9–1 m apart. All suckers from the rootstocks and all roots from the scions must be broken off before being planted out into the nursery. All operations must be carried out with the greatest care in order to avoid breaking the joints where scions and rootstocks are united with a still very tender callus tissue. The ditches can be made with a plough and deepened with a shovel. Care should be taken to have the grafts of equal length, and the ditch of a uniform depth, so as to have the tops at the same level. Then the most friable topsoil should be carefully put on next to the base of the grafts, and the ditch filled, the first earth being packed so as to avoid 'air-holes'. In banking the grafts after the natural level has been reached, it is the custom to cover the top of the entire graft at first with a layer of sandy soil about 2 cm deep. Burying the canes too deeply is as bad as exposing the tops too much (1, 6, 8, 9, 18).

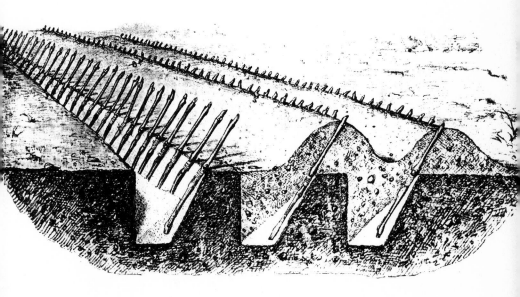

Fig. 7.11. Nursery of grafted cuttings tied with raffia, showing the method of planting and banking. From Hayne (6).

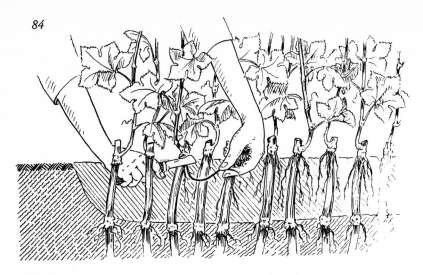

Fig. 7.12. Removing scion-roots in the nursery. From Kozma (8).

Care of the nursery

The nursery is irrigated as often as necessary. If, in a dry region, it becomes necessary to irrigate before the joining is complete, care should be taken that the water does not come into contact with the callus. Downy mildew must be controlled with the greatest care after each irrigation.

The soil between the rows must be kept loose by frequent cultivation. When the shoots are about 20–25 cm long — towards the end of December at the Cape — the soil is removed to just below the joints. Any roots that might have been formed on the scion, must be carefully removed (Fig. 7.12). The grafts are then covered with soil to just above the joint. By mid-January the joints should be well cemented, and shoot growth will help to protect them from being burned by the sun.

Digging, sorting, storing and transporting grafted vines

Grafted vines are dug out as soon as their leaves have fallen. They are immediately sorted and classified.

In sorting out grafted vines, the greatest attention should be paid to whether there is a good graft union. If there is any doubt, the vine should be rejected. It is of the greatest importance to the grower to plant only perfectly grafted vines! It is not the cost of the badly joined and rejected vines that should be considered. This is insignificant when compared with the great amount of actual cash lost by planting, and then cultivating, poorly grafted vines for years before it is discovered that the graft union is so defective that the whole vine must be dug out. This point is especially emphasized because it is of vital importance, and because it is, unfortunately, frequently ignored.

The grafted vine is manually tested by bending it backwards and forwards at the graft union. Only the well-cemented ones, and those that have grown well both above ground and in the roots, are approved.

The canes of the approved vines are usually trimmed to about 20–30 cm, and then tied into bundles of 50. At this stage they must still have their roots unpruned. This is not done until they are to be planted out.

The bundles are heeled-in in a cool, moist place and well covered with soil. Take care to heel-in vines in such a way that loose soil gets in between the bundles and between the roots. Press the soil down firmly on the vines when the trenches are half-filled (9).

2. Cleft-grafting on the spot

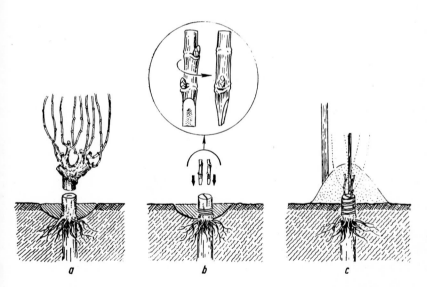

Fig. 7.13. Steps in cleft-grafting: If the rootstocks are 2 cm or less in diameter, one scion with two dormant eyes to each rootstock is sufficient. For larger rootstocks two scions are preferable. If both grow, the weaker is removed. Grafting is carried out in early spring — the beginning of September at the Cape — when the buds of the unpruned rootstocks start budding. If the graft fails, the rootstock will also die. From Kozma (8).

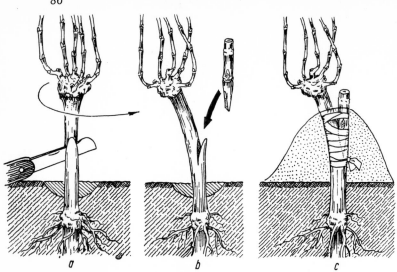

Fig. 7.14. Steps in the Cadillac method of grafting, carried out in autumn (September, early October in Europe). From Kozma (8).

Fig. 7.15. Steps in the mayorquine method of grafting, carried out in autumn. From Kozma (8).

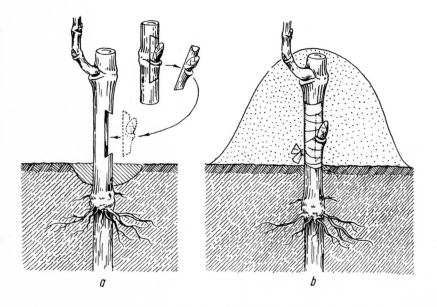

3. Air-grafting

Fig. 7.16. Steps in grafting a dormant scion into a split made through (about) the third internodium of the shoot of an actively growing rootstock. Time: late spring, early summer. (a) Correctly cut scion, ready for insertion; (b) Scion, inserted into the rootstock so that the cambium layers of scion and rootstock will, as nearly as possible coincide; (c) Scion and rootstock shoot wrapped together very firmly with plastic strips, ensuring close contact of the cambium layers until the tissues grow together.

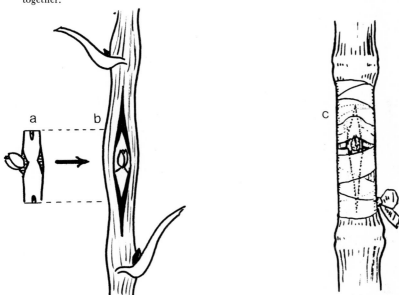

This method of grafting, which was developed by Professor C.J. Orffer of the University of Stellenbosch, is excellently suited to the quick propagation of valuable material from which only small quantities are available; for filling the gaps in established vineyards; and for re-grafting vines in established vineyards to change the variety.

Up to 95 per cent of first-class grafted vines can easily be achieved. If the graft fails, the rootstock does not die and can be grafted again during the next season.

Scions must be preserved in a cold-storage room from early winter at 2 °C. The rootstocks to be grafted must be about three years old. Grafted vines will grow very vigorously and usually reach the development of a three-year-old vine at the end of their first growing season.

After-care. All rootstock suckers, whenever they appear, must be removed weekly during the first three months after grafting; within about three weeks the scions start budding, and soon they leaf out. The shoots of the rootstocks must then be cut off about three leaves above the inserted scions. The bristle scion shoots must be tied to a stake to protect them against being broken off by wind.

5. Green-wood or herbaceous grafting

This method of grafting has been developed in Hungary and it is being used to a considerable extent in south-eastern Europe. It can be carried out as soon as the scion eye is fully developed and the wood (xylem) and diaphragm have a whitish appearance in cross-section, and while the pith is still green and the bark (phloem) is easily detached.

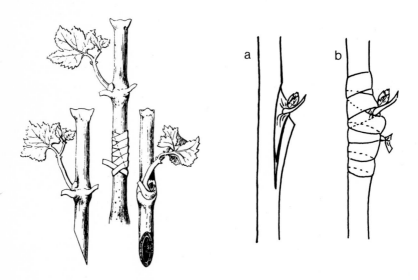

Fig. 7.17. Steps in herbaceous grafting. From Bábó & Mach (1).

Fig. 7.18. Steps in field-budding. (a) Bud in place: fully developed axillary bud of a *V. vinifera* variety inserted into an actively growing shoot of a rootstock at early summer, i.e. at the beginning of December in South Africa. (b) Graft finished and tied securely with a plastic band.

CHAPTER **8**

Establishment of a Vineyard

1. THE IMPORTANCE OF PROPER LAND PLANNING

Viticulture, like any other branch of agriculture is at present dominated by problems of an economic nature. Because of the steadily decreasing labour supply, the increase in wages, and the escalating costs of cultivation, it is generally recognized that in the future viticulture can only be economically practised if land planning takes into account the best possible use of modern power equipment whenever a new vineyard is laid out.

In the huge plantations of the U.S.A., Russia, and the Argentine proper land planning, resulting in very long rows (800–1 500 m) with wide spacing, simple trellising systems, etc., enables one tractor to cope with 70–100 hectares, and one mechanical harvester to cope with up to 150 hectares (5).

In the past, in Europe, grapevines were mostly planted on hillsides. Such vineyards consisted of small blocks, or narrow terraces, making the use of machines very difficult. However, even in mountainous Switzerland, a great deal of success has been achieved during the years 1960–73 in reducing the man-hours per hectare by improved organization of labour, as indicated in Fig. 8.1

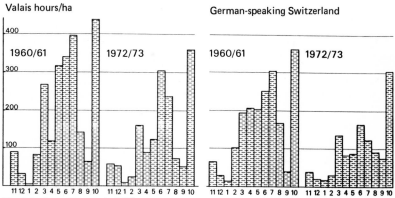

Fig. 8.1. From Simon et al. (8).

In the Valais, the man-hours per hectare per annum were reduced from a total of 2 281 to 1 413. In the German-speaking part of Switzerland, the man-hours per hectare per annum were reduced from 1 986 to 1 094.

The largest savings of man-hours were achieved:

(a) in summer treatment of the vines (suckering, removal of laterals, tying the shoots, topping, etc.), from a total of 846 m-h/ha/a to 572 in the Valais, and from 501 to 294 in German-speaking Switzerland.

(b) in the control of fungoid diseases, from a total of 164 m-h/ha/a to 83 in the Valais, and from 142 to 61 in German-speaking Switzerland.

(c) in harvesting the grapes, from 413 m-h/ha/a to 294 in the Valais, and from 392 to 276 in German Switzerland.

There was no significant saving of man-hours possible in the pruning operation.

2. PREPARATION OF VINEYARD SOILS

A deep and well-distributed root system is necessary to ensure the most effective uptake of plant nutrients. In order to establish this condition, a deep and proper preparation of the soil before planting is necessary. DEEP-PLOUGHING loosens, breaks up and mixes soil layers located below the depth of normal annual cultivation. RIPPERS, or SUBSOILERS, break up hard layers by cracking, without mixing subsoil layers. Ripping is most effective in dry, brittle soils, and least so in moist sands and clays (9, 11). One must always bear in mind that the depth of penetration of roots into the soil to seek for water and nutrients will to a great extent depend upon the degree of aeration of the subsoil. When a soil is not sufficiently aerated to provide for respiration of roots, no root growth occurs (2).

In clearing virgin soils the greatest care must be taken to remove all residues of plant roots, tree-stumps etc. A new vineyard must not be established in the same year that the previous vineyard has been uprooted; it is short-sighted and self-defeating to attempt to save a single crop, when this might have to be paid for over the next 25 years. After the old vines have been uprooted, the soil must be allowed at least one year to rest. During this period a cover-crop should be sown with a heavy application of well-rotted manure, to build up the organic matter in the soil. It is a very good practice to grow lucerne or vegetables for two or three years before the new vineyard is established.

Where there is shallower clay soil, care must be taken during the preparation process not to bring the clay to the topsoil (7).

Where there is shallow stony soil, to rip across the stratification of the underlying rock appears to be the only successful deep-cultivation method. Deep-ploughing would bring too many stones to the surface (7).

If the soil is saline, deep soil preparation must aim at the breaking up of the whole of the soil mass without mixing the layers or bringing the saline subsoil to the surface.

Drainage

Roots below the free-water level cannot respire and will soon die. Therefore, the drainage of vineyard soils, where necessary, must be an integral part of soil preparation. 'By land drainage we understand the removal of the superfluous free water from the upper layers of the soil and thus lowering the water table' (6).

Methods of drainage. There are two fundamentally different ways of removing superfluous water in and on soils: (a) open furrows and (b) closed or underground drains, of which tile drains are the most important (6).

The most important advantages of open ditches are that they are cheaper to construct, and that they more quickly remove water on the surface. Open ditches, however, decrease the area of arable land available and can make mechanical cultivation very difficult if not impossible.

The distance between one row of tiles and the next will depend on the texture of the soil, the depth of the drains, the amount of water to be drained, the fall of the ground, etc.

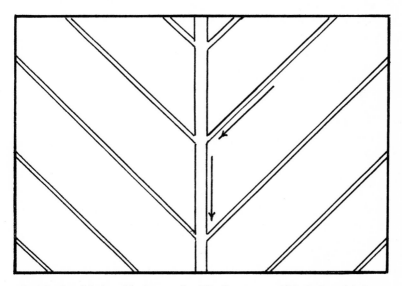

Fig. 8.2. Closed drains with pipes or tiles. The distances at which the lateral drains should be placed are up to 40 metres in deep sandy soil. In heavy loams lateral drains may be 15–20 metres apart.

Fig. 8.3. Implement for the deep-application of lime and phosphatic fertilizers.

Application of lime and fertilizers during the preparation process. The optimum pH for fruit trees and vines is 5,5 for sandy soils, 6,0 for loamy soils, and 6,5 for heavy clayey soils (9). In cases where acidity is below this optimum, it should be rectified as far as possible during the preparation process.

'As most soils are very poorly buffered and have a low cation absorption capacity, lime, for rectifying the pH, should be used very cautiously in order not to induce trace element deficiencies. It is beneficial to apply not more than one ton dolomitic lime (over 50 per cent calcium carbonate and over 40 per cent magnesium carbonate) per morgen [0,8 ha] for every nine inches [18–20 cm] of depth to which the soil is deep-ploughed. One third of the total quantity per morgen is broadcast over the entire surface area and worked in with an off-set disc plough before the soil is deep-ploughed. The balance is applied uniformly from top to bottom on the sloping side of every delf furrow' (9).

The amount of available PHOSPHATE in the vineyard soils of the western Cape is low, especially in the subsoil. As phosphate hardly moves in the soil, it is necessary to supplement the reserve phosphate content in the subsoil during deep preparation of the soil. Any quantity from 500 kg of water-insoluble phosphate for fertile soils, up to 2 000 kg for sandy soils, may be applied per morgen (0,8 ha) (9).

LAYING OUT THE VINEYARD

1. Squaring the land (adapted from Perold, 1926)

In every case we have first to mark a rectangular block of land. Supposing WXYZ (Fig. 8.4) is the block of land we wish to plant, and that one set of rows runs parallel to WX. Put in stakes at W, X, Y and Z. Also put one at P in the line WX. From P measure PQ exactly equal to 9 m. Hold the end of a tape measure at P and describe an arc with centre P and radius equal to 12 m. Do the same with centre Q and radius equal to 15 m. Let the two arcs intersect each other at R; now put a stake at

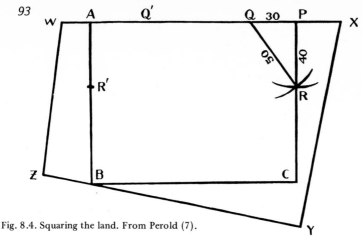

Fig. 8.4. Squaring the land. From Perold (7).

R. Then the angle QPR will be a right-angle, because the sides of the triangle QPR are as 30:40:50, or 3:4:5, and $3^2 + 4^2 = 5^2$.

Test of accuracy: Measure 9 m from P in the direction PX and fix a stake. If the angle QPR is truly a right-angle, the distance from R to the peg in PX will be exactly 15 m. If we find this to be so, then the angle RPQ is a right-angle. Now make a right-angle R'AQ' at A in the same way and fix a stake at B in the line ZY on the continuation AR'. The angle BAP is of course a right-angle. Measure PRC = AB. Now make a right-angle at B, when the line in the direction of C will pass through it. If this is the case, our work is done, and we have the rectangle ABCP.

For locating the position of rows in a block of the future vineyard, and the position of vines in the row, the grower needs a measuring-tape, a planting-line of smooth galvanized cable and a lot of pegs. Assuming that the base lines PA and PX (Fig. 8.5) and the corner X of a block are known, proceed as follows:

(a) Stretch the measuring-tape from peg at point P into the direction of point C. Drive in pegs at the distance where the position of the rows is desired; in this case every 3 m. Repeat this operation from point A to point B. Connect the two corresponding points on lines PC and AB with the planting-line and mark the position of the future rows by making a visible trench with the spade.

(b) Stretch the measuring-tape from point P to point A. Drive in pegs — this time one metre apart — to mark the position of each vine in the row. Repeat this operation between points C and B to mark the position of each vine in this row. Connect the two corresponding points on lines AP and BC and mark the position of each vine in the rows. The holes for the vines all have to be dug on the same side of the point where the

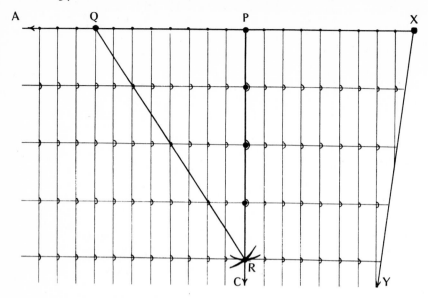

Fig. 8.5. Locating the position of the rows and the position of each vine in the row. Enlarged part of Fig. 8.4 redrawn from Perold (7) and supplemented.

two lines crossed each other. The connecting line must be lengthened to lines XY, WZ, and ZY (Fig. 8.4) to be able to mark the position of lines and vines in the whole block to be planted.

2. Vine spacing

Vine spacing varies greatly in the different grapegrowing countries. In general, when travelling through the world's grapegrowing areas, one will notice that the number of vines per hectare grows smaller as one travels from the colder to the warmer and drier regions (1, 2, 7, 10). In the present era of mechanization and restricted labour supply, by far the most important factor determining vine spacing is cost. 'The most desirable spacing, therefore, is the widest that can be had without reducing the crop of the mature vineyard or upsetting normal vineyard operations' (12).

For the coastal area of the western Cape the generally recommended spacings are 2,7 × 1,2 m for varieties to be cordon-pruned, and 2,7 × 1 m for varieties to be pruned according to Guyot's renewal system. If the soil is deep, and supplementary irrigation is possible, the distances between the rows can be reduced to 2,4 m. On the deep and very fertile soils of the Little Karoo with unlimited water supply, the spacing can be reduced to 2,1 X 1 m.

Experience has shown that the yield per hectare continues to increase with increased density of the plantation even under hot climatic conditions (2).

TABLE 8.1
Number of vines per hectare from different spacings. From *Byvoegsel tot die Wynboer,* October 1973

Distances between the rows (in metres)	Number of vines per hectare corresponding to distances between the vines in the rows (in metres)				
	0,9 m	1 m	1,2 m	1,5 m	1,8 m
1,5	7 407	6 667	5 556	4 444	3 708
1,8	6 173	5 556	4 630	3 704	3 086
2,1	5 291	4 762	3 968	3 175	2 646
2,4	4 630	4 167	3 472	2 777	2 315
2,7	4 115	3 704	3 086	2 469	2 058
3,0	3 704	3 333	2 778	2 222	1 852
3,3	3 367	3 030	2 525	2 020	1 684
3,6	3 086	2 778	2 315	1 852	1 543

On very fertile soils, to restrain too vigorous growth of the vines, thereby improving the fertility of the eyes and the quality of the fruit, the tendency is to decrease spacing in the row, since it is not possible to decrease the distances between the rows owing to the use of modern power equipment. Indications are that at a spacing of 3 X 1 m, i.e. producing 3 333 vines per hectare, all *V. vinifera* grape varieties perform well. For this reason, this spacing, with slight variations, is considered a suitable standard spacing applicable to all grapegrowing countries under intensive cultivation. As density is an important factor from both quantitative and qualitative points of view, gaps in the vineyards should not be tolerated (5).

PLANTING
In South Africa it is best to plant out grafted vines as early during the winter as possible. Only first-class vines with well-cemented graft unions, well-developed root systems and vigorous shoot-growth should be planted.

Depth of planting
(a) In well-drained soils which never get too dry, vines should be planted at a depth of 28–32 cm;

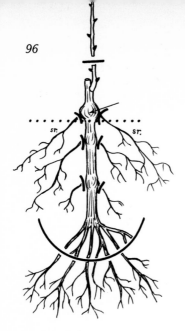

Fig. 8.6. Preparation of grafted vines before being planted. The most erect and if possible the most vigorous cane is cut back to two good eyes. For convenience of planting, the basal roots are cut back to 5 cm. All other roots, especially the scion-roots rising from above the graft-union must be entirely removed. The vines must be carefully protected from drying out during their transfer from the nursery to the vineyard.

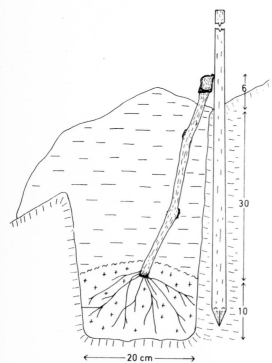

Fig. 8.7. Planting of waxed grafted vines. From Vogt/Götz (10). It is advisable to dig holes for each vine. The hole should be deeper than the vine is long. The vine is dropped into the hole and the hole is filled with moist topsoil, which is packed solidly about the roots. The vine is now raised to its proper height so that the graft-union is just above the level of the ground. Then the hole is filled with topsoil and the top of the vine, if it is not waxed, is covered with a 2–3 cm thick loose-soil layer to prevent drying before growth starts. In the western Cape the tops of the vines, planted early in the winter need not be covered with loose soil. But in this case the vines are not pruned back to two eyes until early spring, when the upper eyes of the canes start leafing out.

97

(b) In arid climatic conditions, the depth at which the vines are planted should be increased to 35 cm;

(c) In very heavy soils or in soils which get too wet, the depth should be decreased to 16–18 cm (4).

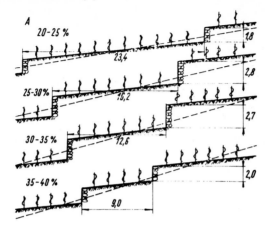

Fig. 8.8. Establishing a vineyard on terraces with varying percentages of slopes. From Kozma (4).

Fig. 8.9. Establishing a vineyard on terraces. Abbreviations: (1) contour-lines of the slope; (2) established terraces; (3) lateral water-collecting furrows; (4) main water-lead-away channel (concrete), and (5) vine rows. From Kozma (4).

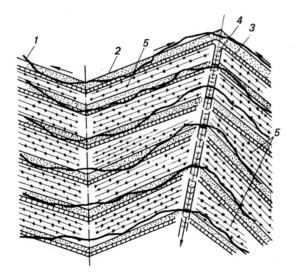

Care of young vines during the first summer

Everything should be done to promote the vigorous development of the newly planted vines. One must bear in mind that, for example, in the Winter Rainfall Area of the western Cape, the last good winter rains usually fall in September and often the young vines do not get any good rain until the beginning of May. For this reason, whenever possible, newly planted vines should receive additional water during their first two summers in the vineyards, even if it has to be done by hand out of water-containing tanks drawn between the rows by tractors. Supplementary irrigation should be applied *before* the young vines begin suffering from drought, and active growth stops.

The first two years are the critical period in the life of a grafted vine. Vines neglected in these first years will never catch up with those which have been well cared for.

THE ESTABLISHMENT OF ROOTSTOCK MOTHER-PLANTATIONS

As it is the aim of nurserymen, as well as of grapegrowers, to produce a large number of canes of medium thickness that are well matured, representing one single variety, rootstocks for the production of canes should be grown in specially established mother-plantations (1, 2, 3, 7, 10).

It is desirable that all larger grapegrowers should have their own rootstock mother-plantations, established with material which has been thoroughly tested on their own farms, not only for its adaptability to soil and climatic conditions but, even more important, for its affinity with the best selections of *V. vinifera* varieties, selected on the farm by the grower or his advisers personally. The grower can each year collect his own cuttings required for grafting and take them together with the selected scion-material to a reliable nurseryman.

Establishment and care

Rootstock mother-plantations should be established on deep, well-drained, warm and fairly fertile soil, well supplied with water.

Recommended spacing depends on the fertility of the soil, availability of irrigation water etc. In South Africa rootstocks are generally spaced at 2,7 X 1,2 m in mother-plantations.

Planting. Rooted one-year-old rootstocks must be cut back to one eye, and not to two eyes as grafted vines before being planted. They should not be planted too deep into the soil, as problems such as suckers on the stem below the soil surface can develop. Plant as early as possible during the winter.

The plantation should be *judiciously* irrigated during the most active growth period of the vines, i.e. from November until mid-February in South Africa.

Rootstock mother-plantations place a heavy demand on the nitrogen and potassium supply of the soil. It is desirable that the *fertilizer application* every third year should be replaced by a liberal dressing of well-rotted stable manure, as cover crops are usually not sown in South Africa.

Trellising systems for rootstock mother-plantations. Rootstock mother-plantations should be trellised and the shoots trained semi-vertically. Although the annual training and tying of shoots is a labour-intensive operation, it is one of the few branches of viticulture which, in Europe,

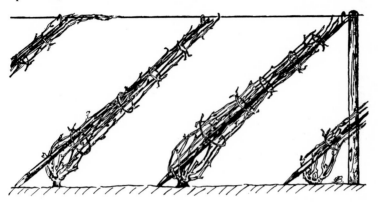

Fig. 8.10. Trellising rootstocks according to Greiner-Decker. From Vogt/Götz (10).

Fig. 8.11. Trellising rootstocks according to Pongrácz. As far as can be ascertained this type of trellising of rootstocks developed by the writer in 1976, has not been described anywhere else.

In each of these two trellising systems a creosoted pole must be planted after every sixth vine to support the upper steel (barbed) wire pulled from corner-post to corner-post.

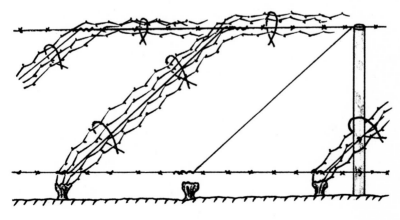

is considered to be absolutely essential. The main reason is that if the growing shoot of a vine is placed in a semi-vertical position its growth will be stimulated by the effect of the well-known physiological phenomenon called POLARITY. When a shoot is untrellised it has to grow horizontally on the ground, which means that the growth of its lateral shoots will be stimulated by polarity, because these shoots are always in an upright position. So the lateral shoots which are mostly too thin for grafting will grow vigorously at the expense of the main shoot, which then becomes too short and too thick for grafting. This happens in South Africa especially with 99 R and Rupestris du Lot, which tend to form numerous and vigorous laterals.

The grower will very soon be compensated for the extra costs of the trellis system by a much higher production of canes which are suitable for grafting, and, even more important, by the much higher quality of the produced canes.

Annual pruning of the mother-vines is very simple as the canes are cut back to the lowest visible eye without an internodium. The trunk should not develop spurs or arms (1, 7).

Crown suckering is of the utmost importance. This will prevent growth where it is not wanted. It is a mistake to leave too many shoots, as they then become too thin. To leave too few is also bad, as the shoots then become too thick. For this reason, when the young shoots have reached a length of about 25–35 cm, all those not wanted should be removed. The number of shoots to be retained depends on the age of the vines, fertility of the soil, etc. Generally one should leave not more than four shoots on two-year-old vines, eight on three-year-old vines, and twelve on fully grown vigorous vines. It is of the utmost importance that laterals be removed from the retained shoots systematically and frequently.

The most vigorous and most erect shoots on the upper part of the trunk should be retained.

Unfortunately crown suckering, as well as trellising of rootstock mother-plantations, is neglected in South Africa.

Tying of the shoots. After suckering, the reserved shoots will develop vigorously. When they reach the length of about 50 cm they should be tied carefully with a soft string to the semi-vertical wire. The tying of the shoots should be repeated until they reach the horizontal upper wire. Most of the shoots will cling by their tendrils to the semi-vertical wire and to each other and usually need little help.

Harvesting the canes. Once the leaves have been shed, the canes can be cut from the mother-vines and immediately cut to a length of 25–30 cm.

The harvesting of trellised rootstocks is simple: (a) cut off all shoots from the trunk; (b) cut off all tendrils from the upper and from the semi-vertical wire of the trellis; (c) pull out the bundle of canes.

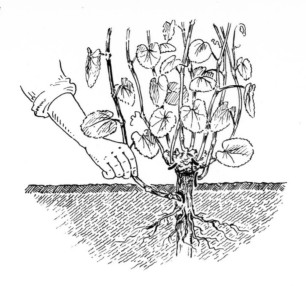

Fig. 8.12. Crown-suckering. From Kozma (4).

Yield per vine. If a mother-plantation is properly maintained, each mother-vine can produce about 100 cuttings suitable for grafting and about 50 thin cuttings suitable for rooting. Untrellised mother-vines usually produce 50 cuttings suitable for grafting, and 100 thin cuttings.

Unfortunately, rootstock mother-plantations are often established on the poorest soil of the farms in South Africa. The growers argue, wrongly, that 'a rootstock is a wild vine, it does not produce grapes and therefore it must grow everywhere'.

CHAPTER 9

Fertilizer Elements Required by the Grapevine

The vine, like any other higher plant, takes all its food out of the soil, with the exception of carbon and oxygen, which are obtained from the air. Cultivated agricultural soils usually contain a sufficient supply of necessary plant food ingredients, with the exception of nitrogen, phosphorus and potassium. Each of these *three critical plant foods* has its specific action on the growth and bearing capacity of the vine.

Since grapevines do not respond to fertilizing as readily as do annual field crops, it is sometimes difficult to determine their plant nutrient requirements. Without an exact knowledge of the amounts of different elements to be applied to vineyard soils, it is a sound policy to return to the soil what is removed by the crop (1, 4, 5, 6).

It must be emphasized that until a soil is in a physically favourable condition (well aerated, well drained, etc), fertilizing of any kind whatsoever cannot give positive results.

Chemical elements essential for plant growth

The soil is usually poor in available nitrogen. Nitrogen is therefore quantitatively the most important single element in fertilizers applied to the soil.

Of the different nitrogen compounds, two forms are of more importance in plant nitrogen supply than the others. Both forms are the extreme phases of reduction and oxidation, namely the *ammonium phase* or maximum reduction state of nitrogen, and the *nitrate phase* or maximum oxidation state, where nitrogen is combined with the maximum number of oxygen atoms (2).

Nitrates are the only water-soluble compounds that may exist in soils in considerable quantity for any length of time without being changed by microbes to other forms (3).

'In nature a *nitrogen cycle* exists in which the stable nitrogen molecules from the atmosphere (the main source of nitrogen on our planet) are broken up by electrical atmospheric processes or by special nitrogen-fixing micro-organisms in the soil and on the roots of leguminous plant

species, to be converted to electrically charged ion compounds. These compounds, which are available to plants, are absorbed by them. The residues of plants are converted to organic humus compounds in the soil after the plants have died and the cycle is completed when decomposition takes place and nitrogen is released back to the atmosphere.'
(2).

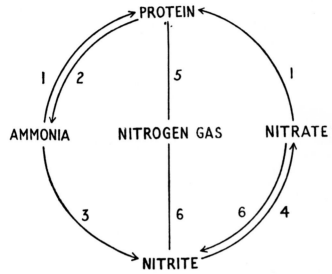

Fig. 9.1. The nitrogen cycle. From Malherbe (3).
1 — Assimilation of ammonium compounds and nitrates (bacteria, fungi, higher plants). 2 — Ammonification (bacteria and fungi). 3 and 4 — Nitrification (bacteria). 5 — Nitrogen fixation (bacteria). 6 — Denitrification (bacteria).

(1) *Nitrogen*
The greatest amount of nitrogen is needed by the vine during early spring growth through the period of flowering. *Nitrogen should be in the root zone when spring growth begins* (1, 3, 8). NITROGEN DEFICIENCY is reflected in reduced growth and general yellowing of the younger leaves. This element is the nutrient most likely to be deficient.

(2) *Phosphorus.* Unlike nitrogen and sulphur, phosphorus is not reduced in plant tissues, but is linked into organic combinations in a highly oxidized form (3).

Phosphate salts are not readily soluble in water. As phosphorus hardly moves in the soil, it is necessary to supplement the reserve phosphate content in the subsoil during the deep preparation of the soil prior to planting (1, 6, 8).

Superphosphate should not be used on acid soils with a pH of less than about 5,5, because the availability of phosphate in such soils is too low, and its residual effect too short. The majority of the vineyard soils of the western Cape fall into this class. As a result, the grower cannot depend on the residual effect of the previous year's application, and therefore phosphatic fertilizers should be applied every year (6).

A DEFICIENCY OF PHOSPHORUS causes reduced growth, dull-green leaves, premature fruit ripening and premature defoliation (9).

3. *Potassium.* Potassium is absorbed by the roots in the form of potassium salts. The two salts that are most commonly used for fertilizing are potassium sulphate and potassium chloride. From the point of view of nutrition, all potassium fertilizers are equally available to plants because all of them are readily soluble in water. For deep-rooted plants such as fruit-trees and vines, it is essential, however, to plough the potassic fertilizer deep into the soil because it moves downward very slightly, except in sandy soils (3).

Vines place a heavy demand on the potassium supply of the soil. High potash dressing should be given to vineyards that receive a high nitrogen dressing and which are irrigated in summer (3).

The visual symptoms of POTASSIUM DEFICIENCY begin to appear in early summer. First the leaf colour fades, beginning at the leaf margin. Upward or downward curling of the leaf edges, and marginal scorching of the leaves, are the typical symptoms of acute deficiency of potassium.

One must always bear in mind that potassium and phosphorus increase the fertility of the eyes, while nitrogen can be considered as 'the engine of growth'. Too vigorous growth always decreases fertility.

4. *Sulphur.* This element is usually absorbed by the roots as SO_4 ions. Sulphates are fairly soluble in water.

Sulphur is not likely to be deficient in soils suitable for grape production. The regular dusting of vineyards with sulphur to control oidium offers further insurance against a deficiency of this element (9).

5. *Magnesium* is the only mineral constituent of the chlorophyll molecule. When available magnesium is deficient in the soil, it causes chlorosis, or the leaves may show brown necrotic patches between the veins (9). In such cases potash magnesia should be applied (3).

6. *Iron.* The amount of iron in the plant tissue is very low. There is usually no lack of iron in the soil, but some soil conditions, such as high lime content, make the iron insoluble and thus unavailable to the vines. Plants that do not absorb sufficient iron salts suffer from CHLOROSIS.

American *Vitis* species are more sensitive to lime-induced chlorosis than *V. vinifera* grape varieties (9).

7. *Calcium.* While mineral fertilizers are applied to remedy any deficiency of plant food, calcium (lime) is applied with a different objective: it makes the soil a more favourable medium for the growth of roots and makes plant nutrients more readily available to the plants (3).

INORGANIC FERTILIZATION OF GRAPEVINES

'The amount of fertilizer to be applied is determined by soil-type, available reserves in the soil, cultivation and irrigation practices and the nutrient requirements of the plant. Therefore no single fertilizer programme can be ideal under all conditions and a general fertilizer programme must be regarded as a guide which must be adjusted to conditions of a particular vineyard.' (6).

What does the vine take out of the soil?

Müntz (4) has for a number of years conducted very complete investigations into the composition of the soil and the annual crops of grapes, wine, canes and leaves in all the principal wine-producing districts of France.

Inter alia, he established how much mineral food the grapevine requires annually to produce one hectolitre of wine and in Table 9.1 he provides the following data:

TABLE 9.1
Mineral food required annually by grapevines

| District | Required to produce one hl. wine | | |
	N kg	P_2O_5 kg	K_2O kg
Midi (South)	0,48	1,12	0,42
Médoc	1,48	0,49	2,06
Champagne	1,69	0,41	1,81
Burgundy	1,02	0,29	1,02

It is evident from the data presented by Müntz (4) that two to four times as much mineral food is required in the districts producing wines of high quality compared with the Midi, where the emphasis is rather on quantity. There are, however, significant differences between the various varieties concerning their mineral food requirements. Grenache for example requires five times as much nitrogen as phosphorus; Chardonnay four times as much and the varieties of the Médoc (the Cabernets and Merlot) only three times as much. If we compare the absorption of nitrogen and phosphorus we can conclude that the noble varieties of the Burgundy (Pinot noir, Chardonnay and Gamay) absorb potassium more readily than nitrogen, while for the fertile and vigorous varieties of the Midi (Carignan and Aramon) the reverse is true.

Amount and frequency of application

Substantial amounts of essential elements are removed from the soil by a cultivated crop. If these are more than those released by the soil, a reduction in yield will occur unless these elements are supplemented artificially (2).

Fig. 9.2 indicates the amount of *Nitrogen, Phosphorus* and *Potassium* removed by one metric ton of seed-bearing grapes under South African climatic and soil conditions.

By using the maximum nutrient removal, indicated on Fig. 9.2, and also taking into consideration the inefficiency of fertilizers (owing to leaching etc.), and the probable amounts of nutrients needed for the yearly increase of permanent woody tissues, for each ton of grapes the fertilizer required is indicated on Fig. 9.4.

Nitrogenous topdressing should be increased or decreased according to the observed balance between crop and vegetative growth. Depending on rainfall or irrigation, topdressing with nitrate-containing fertilizers should, especially on sandy soils, be applied in more than one treatment in order to minimize losses through leaching. (2).

Choice of fertilizer type is mainly determined by the pH of the soil. In all cases where pH is below the optimum, basic-reacting fertilizers should be applied: limestone-ammonium nitrate for nitrogen; basic slag, 'Calmofos', 'Basifos', or rock phosphate for phosphorus, and muriate of potash for potash.

For sweet or alkaline soils, acid-reacting fertilizers should be used: ammonium sulphate for nitrogen, superphosphate for phosphorus, and potassium sulphate for potash (3, 6).

Magnesium deficiency usually occurs in the very acid soils of the western Cape, and magnesium should also be applied regularly each year in the form of dolomitic agricultural lime, which contains over 40 per cent magnesium carbonate (3).

Modern viticulture is a complicated combined operation of viticulture, agro-chemistry and exact calculation, based on economic factors. Extensive fertilization has no place in modern viticulture. What is removed by the crop from the soil must be replaced systematically. The amount of plant nutrients to be applied must be determined by an exact knowledge of the size of the crop of each block of vineyard, on the data of the chemical analysis of the soil of each block, and on visual observations of the annual growth of the vines, i.e. the reaction of the vines to their fertilization during the previous season. To buy the same amount of fertilizer-mixture from year to year, and to apply it by starting to broadcast it from one end of the farm to the other ('gooi van die kant af'), without any consideration of the fertilizer requirements of the various blocks in the vineyard, and without even knowing the exact N, P, K content of the mixtures, is a practice which is anachronistic in modern viticulture.

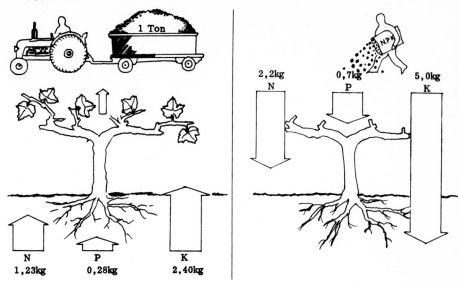

Fig. 9.2. Nutrients removed by the crop. From Saayman (5).

Fig. 9.3. Fertilizer requirement. From Saayman (5).

Fig. 9.4. Fertilizer needed per ton production. From Saayman (5).

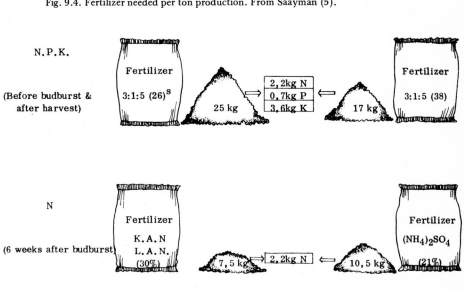

MEANS OF MAINTAINING THE ORGANIC CONTENT OF VINEYARD SOILS

It is well known that the humus content of cultivated soils in South Africa reduces rapidly unless organic matter is regularly applied. In order to maintain a sufficient humus content in the soil, one should frequently apply fresh organic matter in the form of stable-manure, straw, compost or green manure (3).

1. Stable manure

The beneficial effect of stable-manure is threefold:

(a) It contains practically all the plant nutrients that were in the animal feed.

(b) 'It provides the soil with the necessary organic matter to replenish the ever-decreasing humus content of the soil. It is for this reason that chemical fertilizers can never take the place of farm manure in a long-term production system.' (3)

(c) The organic matter has a loosening effect on heavy soils. The result is that the soil becomes well aerated and granular. *Soil structure is one factor of soil fertility which it is not possible to buy!*

Although the N, P, K content of stable manure is relatively low, as shown in Table 9.2, the effect of systematic well-matured manure application on the development of the vine and on the development of natural weeds in the vineyards is so striking in South Africa that no complex statistical analysis is required to demonstrate its desirability.

TABLE 9.2

Composition of stable manures according to German data, quoted by Malherbe (3), converted to metric weights.

From the data presented below it is obvious that the bulk of the phosphate is excreted in the faeces and that the nitrogen and potassium occur largely in the urine. *This shows how important it is to retain all the urine in the manure heap.*

	Cow Faeces	Urine	Horse Faeces	Urine	Sheep Faeces	Urine	Pig Faeces	Urine
	kg	kg	kg	kg	kg	kg	kg	kg
Water	363	420	340	404	308	397	372	426
Organic matter	82	14	104	32	131,5	36,3	72,6	11,3
Nitrogen	1,4	4,5	2,5	5,4	2,7	6,8	2,7	2,3
Phosphoric oxide	0,9	0,5	1,4	0,2	1,4	0,5	2,3	0,2
Potash	0,5	7	1,5	6,8	0,9	8,2	1,8	4,5
Lime	0,5	1,4	1	0,7	1,8	1,4	0,2	0.1
Daily excretion	24	9	16	3,6	1	0,7	2,7	1,6

The moist mixture of faeces, urine, and bedding is excellent for many kinds of microbes because it contains a large amount of food for them. The microbes that we find in a manure heap may be divided into two groups according to their oxygen requirements: AEROBIC MICRO - ORGANISMS which require air, and ANAEROBIC BACTERIA which can decompose carbohydrates or other substances in the absence of air. The substances which undergo changes during the process of decomposition may be divided into two groups: (a) nitrogen-free substances, which constitute the bulk of the solids in dung and bedding, and which consist largely of carbohydrates, mainly cellulose and lignin; and (b) nitrogenous substances (3). Plant roots cannot use organic nitrogen, and the organic matter must first decompose and release nitrogen in the ion form NH_4^+. The ammonium ion is, however, soon oxidized in the soil to the nitrate (NO_3^-) form. The nitrates are very easily absorbed by plant roots (2, 3).

2. Green manuring

Apart from maintaining the humus and nitrogen content of the soil, a green manure crop has the advantage in preventing soil erosion during the rainy season. The roots of a cover crop not only bind the topsoil but also facilitate the penetration of rain-water into the deeper soil layers. The roots die off after the crop has been ploughed under, leaving channels through which water and air can move more freely (3).

Green manure crops should be sown in the western Cape in April, just before the winter-rains start. It is always necessary to apply mineral fertilizers, especially potassic and phosphatic fertilizers, when green manure is sown. A liberal dressing of dry fowl (chicken) manure, instead of inorganic nitrogenous fertilizers, will strikingly stimulate the growth of natural weeds on bare soils.

Fertilizers must be ploughed under as deep as possible between the vine-rows. This will incorporate the essential plant nutrients into the zone where the finest feeding-roots of the vines are situated, and at the same time will facilitate the penetration of the winter rains. Then the cover-crop is sown.

Green manure and natural weeds are disced under during the second half of August, as shallowly as possible, preceded by an application of nitrogen- and potassium-containing fertilizer. We want only to kill the plants to preserve the water-content of the soil for the vines. We do not want to incorporate the green manure deep into the soil, because this would facilitate its quick decomposition, which is undesirable. The aim must be to ensure the formation of a kind of mulch on the surface, which would preserve the moisture in the soil during the dry summer months.

It is necessary that the soil receive a few good showers of rain after the green plant material has been disced under, so that the soil may be restored to its natural structure. This will also allow sufficient time for the organic matter to undergo its initial decomposition, after which nitrogen as nitrate appears in the soil when the vine starts its new growth (3).

3. Compost

'The principle of composting is to encourage the maximum formation of humic acid by microbes and to obtain by addition of clay colloids clay humus complexes, which are further stabilized by combining with calcium and magnesium. These humate clay compounds are the most stable form of humus and only over-cultivation and soil acidity can break up these compounds in due course' (7).

CHAPTER 10

Tillage, Chemical Weed Control, Irrigation

TILLAGE

Once a vineyard has been planted, every possible effort must be made
to maintain and increase the organic content of the soil. The only way
to keep a soil loose and well aerated over a long period is to incorporate
a great amount of organic material into it. The humus that develops
gradually loosens up the soil and keeps it crunchy. Microbial life, which
is so important in soil fertility, flourishes under such conditions, and
roots employ the least amount of energy in order to penetrate the soil.
The importance of suitable physical texture of the soil cannot be overemphasized.

Under South African climatic (very dry and hot) and soil conditions
(very acid, very poor in organic matter and to a great extent structureless
in the coastal region of the western Cape), vineyard soils should be cultivated only as often as is necessary. The first cultivation after the vintage
consists in introducing fertilizers and seed for green manuring into the
soil. In the western Cape this takes place before the first soaking winter
rains fall and the soil becomes too wet. Ploughing must be as deep as
possible to facilitate the penetration of winter rains and the incorporation
of potassium and phosphatic fertilizers into the root zone. A soil must
never be cultivated when it is too wet. It is better to wait until it is dry
enough to work well (5).

If hard, impervious layers (hardpans) occur below the normal depth of
annual cultivation, because the soil was not prepared deeply enough
before the vineyard was planted, such layers must be broken by ripping
very deeply during the driest period of the season.

In order to incorporate stable-manure fairly deeply into the soil, it is
best to draw a furrow 30–40 cm deep between every second row of vines.
The manure is spread in these furrows and the soil ploughed towards them
from both sides. If the vineyard is on a slope, the necessary open drains
for the removal of flowing water should be provided or cleared before
the rains begin.

Otherwise the vineyard soil can be left untouched until it is ploughed towards the end of the winter.

The cover crop is turned when the rainy season is normally at an end, i.e. towards the end of August or the beginning of September in the western Cape. Deep cultivation would be wrong, as it entails an additional loss of water by evaporation. In unirrigated vineyards of the western Cape, the only water available to the vines through most of the growing season is that which was stored in the soil from the winter rains (4).

During the vine's period of growth, and particularly in summer, the vineyard soil should be kept loose and free from weeds. It is sufficient to keep the soil loose to a depth of merely 5 cm, but then this layer of soil must be kept loose all the time. After an unexpected good summer rain, the vineyard must be cultivated with cultivator steels to prevent a hard crust from forming on the surface of the soil. Where the vines are not trellised, cultivation should include cross-cultivation (4).

Loosening the soil between the rows by means of vibrating implements

Tractors are forced to follow the same paths year after year through the vineyard. The soil beneath the wheels inevitably becomes compressed. *It is not the frequency of cultivation by tractors, but the moisture content of the soil which causes compaction of the soil in layers below the wheels of tractors.* Consequently, vine roots find a packed earth-barrier along the row on both sides, which makes it difficult for them to penetrate into the soil layers between the rows. Those layers of the soil which should be kept loose and well aerated by cultivation, and where plant nutrients, originating from fertilizers and from the residues of the cover crop, are available for the vine, are barred from its roots.

It has been found that a ripper (subsoiler), which is generally used to break up and loosen compacted soils towards the end of the summer, tends to slice rather than shatter the soil, leaving a very limited loose zone on both sides of the rows. The beneficial effect of this type of cultivation is very short. When heavy rains fall, the soil will slump again.

A German scientist, H. Schulte-Karring (5), in close cooperation with manufacturers, designed a machine which is reputed to be able to shatter the hardest soils and to have a good potential for deep loosening of compacted vineyard soils.

The machine, which can penetrate to 80 cm, has a fixed shaft with a vertically vibrating shoe. Such vibrating implements claim to be able to do more with less power. It goes without saying that, with wet soil, the tines tend to slice rather than shatter. Where there is a shallow, loose topsoil over a very firm subsoil, there is a tendency for the machine to ride on the top of the subsoil rather than penetrate it.

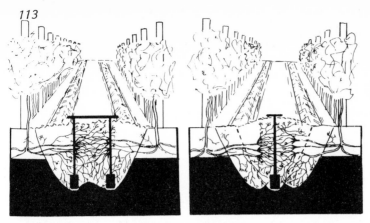

Fig. 10.1. Methods of loosening the soil and rejuvenating the roots between the rows in established vineyards. From Schulte-Karring (5).

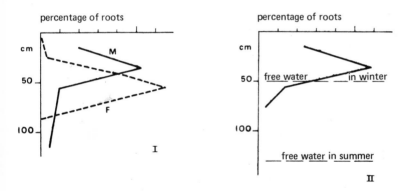

Fig. 10.2 (I). Influence of the *V. vinifera* variety on the depth of the root-system of the same rootstock variety. M: Aramon noir grafted on Rupestris du Lot at Montpellier. F: Carignan grafted on Rupestris du Lot at Fedala, Morocco.

(II). Influence of the level of the free water in the soil on the depth of the root-system of Carignan grafted on Riparia. The depth of the free water-table in winter is about 50 cm below the surface; in summer, 1,3 m. From Branas (1).

HERBICIDE PROGRAMMES

Adapted from 'Spray Programme for Vines 1976–7', Triomf Crop Protection.

It is not possible to recommend a programme which will cover all situations and conditions. The following are examples and should be altered as circumstances dictate.

A. Trellised vineyards (vineyards trellised higher than 60 cm)

Situation	Time of application	Herbicide	Quantity per hectare	Volume of water per hectare	Remarks
1. Perennial weeds	See Remarks in last column	'Roundup'	Common Quick Grass (*Cynodon dactylon*) 6 litres followed by 4 litres	300–600 litres	In the western Cape vine areas, 6 litres applied in autumn, followed by 4 litres in summer on active regrowth has given the best results.
			Couch Paspalum (*Paspalum distichum*) 8 litres followed by 4 litres	300–600 litres	The first application of 8 litres, followed by 4 litres on active regrowth or new regrowth.
			Dallas grass (*Paspalum dilatatum*) 6 litres	300–600 litres	Apply on active growth. A repeat application may be necessary at 3 litres on any new new growth.
			Kikuyu (*Pennisetum clandestinum*) 4 litres	300–600 litres	Apply on active growth. Repeat application, if necessary, at 3 litres to any active regrowth or new growth.
2(a) Annual winter weeds	July/August	'Gramoxone'	5 litres plus 'Agral 90'*	500–1 000 litres	Where Gousblom is predominant, replace half of the 'Gramoxone' with 'Reglone'.
(b) Regrowth of winter weeds and/or germination of spring and early summer weeds	14–21 days after (a)	'Gramoxone'	2,5 litres plus 'Agral 90'*	400–500 litres	Spray at regrowth of winter weeds or at germination of spring and summer weeds.
(c) Annual summer weeds	When summer weeds germinate	'Gramoxone'	2,5 litres plus 'Agral 90'*	200–500 litres	Spray before summer weeds become established. Repeat this spray if necessary.

| 3. Annual summer and winter weeds | July/ August | 'Gramox-one' plus 'Gesatop 80' | 5 litres

2,5–3,75 kg plus 'Agral 90'* | 400–1 000 litres | Use only in vines older than 3 years. The higher 'Gesatop 80' wp rate is used in irrigated vine-yards.
When *Tribulus* spp (Vol-struisdoring) and/or *Digitaria* spp (Kruisgras) germinate after a 'Gesa-top 80' wp application, apply a spot spray of 'Gramoxone' at 2,5 litres per hectare |

* Add 'Agral 90' at 100 millilitres per 100 litres water where indicated above.

B. Bush vines (as well as vineyards *not* trellised higher than 60 cm)

Situation	Time of application	Herbicide	Quantity per hectare	Volume of water per hectare	Remarks
1. Perennial weeds	After 100 per cent natural leaf drop and after pruning	'Roundup'	Common Quick-Grass (*Cynodon dactylon*) 9 litres	300–600 litres	Spray on actively grow-ing Quick-Grass before first frost. If necessary, repeat application as a spot spray the following year after 100 per cent natural leaf drop.
2(a) Annual winter weeds	May/ June	'Gramox-one'	2,5 litres plus 'Agral 90'*	400–500 litres	Where Gousblom is pre-dominant, replace half the 'Gramoxone' with 'Reglone'. Spray when winter weeds have ger-minated. This applica-tion will prevent a dense weed stand when vines are pruned.
(b) Regrowth of winter weeds	July/ August	'Gramox-one'	2,5 litres plus 'Agral 90'*	400–500 litres	
OR					
(c) Regrowth of winter weeds plus summer weeds	July/ August	'Gramox-one' plus 'Gesatop 80' wp	2,5 litres 2,5–3,75 kg plus 'Agral 90'*	400–500 litres	Use only on vines older than 3 years. The higher 'Gesatop 80' wp rate is used in irrigated vine-yards.

3(a) Annual winter weeds	July/ August	'Gramox-one'	5 litres plus 'Agral 90'*	400–1 000 litres	Where Gousblom is predominant, replace half of the 'Gramoxone' with 'Reglone'.
OR					
(b) Annual winter and summer weeds	July/ August	'Gramox-one' plus 'Gesatop 80' wp	5 litres 2,5–3,75 kg plus 'Agral 90'*	400–1 000 litres	Use only on vines older than 3 years. The higher concentration of 'Gesa-top 80' wp is used in irrigated vineyards.

* Add 'Agral 90' at 100 millilitres per 100 litres water where indicated above.

Remarks

In the programme(s) where 'Gramoxone' or 'Gramoxone/Reglone' is used, and plantain (tongblaar), *Plantago lanceolata,* is predominant, either 'Fernimine 4' or 'Weedazol TL' can be used instead of 'Gramoxone' or 'Gramoxone/Reglone'. 'Weedazol TL' is used at the rate of 10 litres per hectare. 'Fernimine 4' is used at the rate of 5 litres per hectare — preferably at 400 litres mixture per hectare.

Important: 'Weedazol TL' can be applied only during the dormant period of the vines; it is preferable to apply 'Fernimine 4' only during this period.

Application

Herbicides can be applied by means of knapsack sprayers or tractor-mounted sprayers. As the amount of herbicide is recommended on a 'per area basis', it is important that the amount of water applied to a given area be determined for each sprayer. Correct calibration will prevent an excessive amount of herbicide being applied, which is costly and could have an adverse effect on the vines. Similarly, too little herbicide applied will give poor control.

IRRIGATION

Irrigation is the artificial application of water to soils in areas where the normal rainfall is insufficient.

Winkler et al. (8) summed up the general principles of vineyard irrigation as follows (abbreviated):

'During the dormant season all parts of the root zone should be wet to the field capacity of the soil by rainfall or irrigation.

'After growth starts in the spring, no additional water is required until some of the soil within the root zone is dried out almost to the permanent wilting percentage. The vines will *not* benefit from earlier application. The change in vine appearance caused by slowed growth is a good

index of when a considerable extent of the soil has reached the permanent wilting percentage. If the vines show evidence of depletion of
available water early in the season, it is exceedingly important that
water be applied soon. Each early irrigation should if possible wet all of
the soil to the depth at which most roots occur, even though the lower
layers still contain some readily available water.

'If there is a hardpan or other impervious layer within 5 or 6 feet of
the surface, just enough water should be applied to wet the soil above
this layer.

'The time to irrigate, the number of irrigations required, and the
amount of water to be applied at each irrigation, are determined by soil
and climate, the kind of grapes grown, and the time of ripening.'

During the second half of November 1976 unexpected heavy rains (up
to 100 mm) fell in the western Cape. The effect of the rain on the development of the vines was strikingly beneficial. This fact should have
opened the eyes of local growers concerning the time when their vines
most need additional irrigation. Unfortunately, it is commonly observed
in the vineyards of the coastal region of the western Cape that growers
irrigate their vineyards from the middle of January up to the harvest. It
does not require a very close look to see that the foliage of the vines is
already scorched by the heat and drought of the preceding weeks, and
the grapes hang lifeless on the nearly defoliated canes.

Judicious irrigation up to the end of the active growing period of the
vines, i.e. until mid-December, is very beneficial in the coastal region of
the western Cape. But irrigating vineyards up to the time of harvesting
means delivering more water into a Cooperative cellar and being paid for
it by weight. Financially it might be profitable for a greedy grower, but
from the viticultural point of view it is barbaric.

Vineyards in South Africa often receive a very heavy irrigation after
the crop has been harvested. The reason given for this is that the vines
must 'recover' before they enter dormancy. I consider this to be unnecessary as it is not practised anywhere else in the world.

(a) Vines that have been well supplied with water up to the end of
their active growing period, and consequently have ripened their grapes
and canes properly, do not need any 'recovery'. If such vines receive an
additional irrigation after harvesting, they will begin to grow again and
produce new shoots just before the winter, which is undesirable.

(b) Vines that, up to harvesting, have lost a great part of their foliage
because they either did not receive enough water during their active
growing season or were overcropped, and consequently could not ripen
their grapes and canes properly, will leaf out again soon after they receive irrigation after the crop has been harvested. Thus such vines,
instead of 'recovering', will waste their meagre reserves for the formation

of leaves which are useless at this time.

With an annual rainfall of about 550 mm in the coastal region of the western Cape, vines should have no difficulty in ripening their grapes. However, in unirrigated vineyards in this area, vines suffer severely from drought from the middle of January, and consequently, the grapes cannot ripen properly. The following factors among others should be considered responsible for this phenomenon:

(1) Owing to human interference through the injudicious use of implements (especially disc-plough, rotavator, repeated shallow irrigation, etc.), root growth in the top 20–25 cm of the soil is excellent, but there are practically no roots lower than this.

(2) Trellised young vines are generally pruned too long. Consequently they overbear during their first 3–7 years. No resources are left for such vines to develop a deep and vigorous root system during the juvenile period of their life, in which the greatest annual increase in length of the individual roots takes place (1).

(3) Jacquez, 101–14 Mgt, and 99 R are the three rootstock varieties which constitute about 90 per cent of all rootstocks used in South Africa. Jacquez, or Lenoir as it is known in America, was abandoned eighty years ago as a direct producer on account of the small quantity and the inferior quality of its wines and because it is not resistant to phylloxera (1, 3). 101–14 Mgt and 99 R are well known in all warm grape-growing countries for their inadequate resistance to drought (2).

(4) Many of the vineyard soils of the coastal region of the western Cape require additional irrigation because soil depth is less than adequate to store a full season's moisture requirement. Subsoil layers that restrict root growth and water movement can often be found at 30–60 cm below the soil surface.

A 'normal' irrigation for a 'deep soil' is usually excessive for these *de facto* shallow soils, drowning the roots by eliminating the air supply to them. The same vine, however, might suffer from lack of water before the next irrigation, because the 'normal' irrigations were applied too infrequently. Consequently, restricting subsoil layers requires careful irrigation management to ensure that grapevines have adequate but not excessive moisture. Wildman et al. (7) made a study to try to find out how variations in soil depth affect the yield and quality of irrigated grapes, and to ascertain the extent to which a compromise in irrigation quantities and timing can compensate for the soil depth variations. They found that both the yield and quality of grapes were improved by irrigating vines according to soil depth and soil moisture measurements instead of calendar date. Light, frequent depth-controlled (LFDC) irrigation with the early cutback did not lower quality even though light irrigations were applied within a few weeks of harvest.

Differences between the two shallow soil-depth areas of the experiment, and those of a greater depth (76–122, 152–213 cm) showed a significant increase in yield and fruit sugars for the latter, indicating that controlled irrigation is related to better regulation of excessive late-season vine growth. Careful monitoring of the soil moisture status and its regulation by the LFDC irrigation was required to achieve optimum balance between vine growth and fruit production. The greater the soil variation within a vineyard block, the greater the degree of compromise required to attain acceptable yield and quality in the majority of the block.

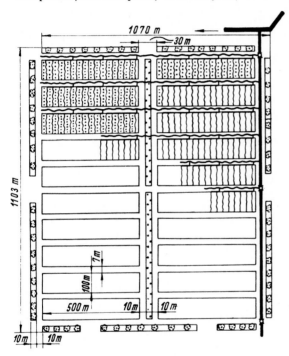

Fig. 10.3. Flood-irrigation scheme with permanent and temporary canals. From Kozma.

CHAPTER **11**

Pruning, Training and Trellising

PRUNING

'The pruning of the vine is the principal operation and the foundation of its cultivation. If one were not to prune it, the vine would develop excessively during its first couple of years, then it would soon exhaust itself and bear no fruit, or if it should produce fruit, this would consist only of small bunches that ripen badly and of which the wine will certainly be bad' — A. d'Armailhacq (1867), quoted by Perold (14).

1. The most important reasons for pruning (2, 6, 10, 12, 14, 15, 20)

(a) To give every young vine a development above ground proportionate to its vigour and to the development of its root system.

(b) To provide new wood, i.e. one-year-old canes, for bearers at the desired places.

(c) To regulate and ensure the production of grapes, as regards both quantity and quality, by leaving the correct number of fruit eyes on the vine according to its capacity.

(d) To establish and maintain vines in a desired shape that will prevent damage during maintenance operations.

(e) To concentrate the activities of the vine into its permanent arms and bearing units.

(f) To remove worn-out and injured parts of old vines.

2. Biological basis of pruning (3, 8, 10, 12, 14, 15, 18, 20)

(a) The fertile eyes of the vine occur on the one-year-old canes that arise from two-year-old wood.

(b) On a cane the fertility of the eyes increases the farther they are removed from the base of the cane.

(c) Excessively vigorous canes are not only less fruitful, but the fruitful eyes are farther up on the canes.

(d) Canes with short internodes usually possess more fertile eyes than those with long internodes.

(e) Only well-ripened canes that have borne well during the previous season should be used as bearers.

(f) *Every vine can properly nourish and ripen only a certain number of bunches and canes, and this is proportional to its vigour. Hence every vine must be pruned on the basis of its own condition.*

3. The response of the vine to pruning

(a) While pruning concentrates the activities of the vine into the parts requisite for a well-shaped vine and for the continued production of grapes and canes, it diminishes the total capacity of the plant for growth and production (3, 7, 18).

(b) Increasing the number of fruit-eyes retained at pruning will result in increased yield and in a sharp decrease in the vigour of the vine (3, 7, 18).

Branas (1946), quoted by Galet (5), furnishes the following data for Aramon noir grafted on Riparia gloire:

TABLE 11.1

Bush-vines with 3 arms	Number of fruit-eyes per vine x (charge)	Yield qx/ha	Pruning weight, i.e. production of canes kg/ha
Each arm 1 eye	3	40,9	3066
2 eyes	6	55,6	2844
2 + 2 eyes	12	106,0	2955
2 + 4 eyes	18	104,1	2444
2 + 10 eyes	36	196,2	1853
2 + 18 eyes	60	209,3	1600

(c) If a vine produces more bunches than it can properly nourish, the crop will be inferior in quality and the vine will be weakened by over-bearing (7, 19, 20).

(d) If a weak vine is pruned too long, many basal eyes will remain dormant and only the eyes farther along the bearers will be stimulated by nature to leaf out. Consequently, fewer shoots and bunches will be produced, to protect the vine against exhaustion.

(e) If a very vigorous vine is pruned too severely, e.g. to one eye per bearing unit, two or even three shoots will arise from one compound bud (eye), and each shoot will bear one or two bunches.

Conclusions (adapted from Winkler [1962])

(a) On a mature vine that has produced a good crop and shows normal vigour, the pruner should leave the same number of bearing units and fruit-eyes as in the previous year.

(b) If a vine seems abnormally vigorous, he should leave more fruit-eyes in order to divert more energy into the production of a crop.

(c) If the vine seems weak; he should prune it more severely than in the year before in order to strengthen it by diverting more of its energy from crop production to growth. Any attempt to make a weak vine bear a large crop by longer pruning without crop thinning can result only in further weakening and in the production of inferior grapes.

(d) *Correct pruning is particularly important for young vines which still have to be formed.* A vine which has had to struggle during its early stages of development, because it has been pruned too long and has had to bear too heavily, recovers only with great difficulty.

4. The best time for pruning

Opinions vary greatly about the best time for pruning. Under South African conditions Perold (14) recommends:

(a) Vigorous varieties that are shy-bearers should be pruned late, i.e. from the beginning of August.

(b) Varieties that are vigorous and productive, and set their berries well, can be pruned early, i.e. from the beginning of July.

(c) Varieties that are vigorous and fertile, but set their berries badly, should be pruned very late, i.e. after 15 August.

(d) Prune very late where spring frosts are to be feared.

(e) Do not prune if the pruning wounds remain dry.

In the viticultural area of the western Cape the vines often get a first pruning when all the canes not required for bearers are removed. This can be done after the first soaking rain has fallen in the autumn and cold weather has set in. Pruning must not commence until the leaves have fallen.

FACTORS WHICH INFLUENCE THE SIZE OF THE CROP PER HECTARE OF A SPECIFIC VARIETY AND THUS DETERMINE THE NUMBER OF FRUIT-EYES TO BE RETAINED

1. Fertility of the eyes

On the cane the maximum fertility lies between the fifth and tenth eyes (1, 8). The number of bunches per shoot may vary from 0 to 5 in some American *Vitis* species (*V. berlandieri, V. labrusca*). On the cultivated *V. vinifera* grape varieties there are generally two bunches per shoot arising from a fruit-eye, i.e. from an eye on a one-year-old cane that is borne on two-year-old wood. Highly significant differences have been established, however, between the different varieties (1, 3, 8).

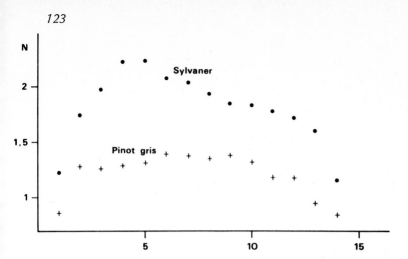

Fig. 11.1. The number of bunches per shoot (N), depending on the position of the eyes on the cane out of which the shoots arose. Data presented indicate that Sylvaner is not only more fertile than Pinot gris (Ruländer), but its maximum fertility lies between its fourth and fifth eyes, while that of Pinot gris lies between its sixth and ninth eyes. Consequently, Sylvaner should be pruned half-long, i.e. to four good eyes, and Pinot gris should be pruned long. From Huglin (8).

2. Size and weight of the bunches of a specific variety

Not only the number of bunches per shoot but also the weight of the bunches decides the size of the crop per vine, and also per hectare of a specific grape variety. Cinsaut, for example, produces a much larger crop than Gamay noir because its bunches are three to four times heavier than those of Gamay noir, although both varieties have fruitful eyes at the bases of their canes. It goes without saying that the size and weight of the bunches depends not only on the variety concerned but also on the vigour of the vine. Larger and heavier bunches will be found on the same variety where it is grown in fertile soil well supplied with water, and grafted on a vigorous rootstock variety.

3. The failure of eyes to leaf-out in spring

A number of studies has shown that the total number of bunches per vine (N) is to some extent also dependent on the total number of fruit-eyes — called the CHARGE (x) of the vine — retained during pruning, because this factor influences the vigour of the vine. Branas et al. (2) gave the following data:

TABLE 11.2

x	N	N/x
3 eyes	9,1 bunches	3,0
6	11,4	1,9
12	12,8	1,0
18	21	1,15
36	24	0,66
58	26	0,44

But the authors did not indicate how many of the retained eyes really developed into bunch-bearing shoots. The effects of the variations of the charge per vine (2 to 42 eyes) on the number of eyes which fail to develop, on the dimension of the bunches, and on the weight of the berries, were reported for the first time by Ravaz (16). *The indication is that it is always nature herself, i.e. the vigour of the vines, that decides the number of eyes which will leaf-out, and the size of the bunches; thus the crop per vine is regulated according to the capacity of the plant.*

A problem of considerable significance in South Africa is that many eyes near the bases of long bearers fail to bud. In some instances the eyes may leaf-out but then have little further growth. In most cases they remain dormant and they do not even swell in the spring. Field observations have often indicated that the phenomenon of 'blind' eyes is greater in the cooler grapegrowing regions of the coastal area. Cabernet Sauvignon, especially when planted on badly aerated, heavy soils, seems to suffer from the failure of eyes to develop.

Kliewer (9) found a highly significant increase in the number of eyes per vine that leafed-out if the root temperatures were increased from 11 °C to 35 °C, even though the aerial parts of the vines were in the optimum temperature range for growth (20–32 °C).

CALCULATING THE SIZE OF THE CROP OF A SPECIFIC VARIETY

The calculation of the size of the crop, based on the number of fruiteyes retained per square metre per hectare, depends on the genetical characteristics of a specific variety, irrespective of the density of the plantation, the system of trellising, etc. (6, 10, 11, 18).

Studies carried out mainly in Germany (4, 6, 7, 18) concluded that the optimum number of fruit-eyes to be retained

(a) for grape varieties that are very fertile and have large bunches is 6 eyes per square metre (60 000 eyes per hectare);

(b) for good clones of Pinot noir is 7 to 8 eyes per square metre;

TABLE 11.3
Number of fruit-eyes per vine depending on the number of eyes per square metre to be retained at pruning. Basic principle: 6, 8, 10 or 12 eyes per square metre. From Hillebrand (6)

Spacing in cm		Surface at the disposal of each vine in sqm	If the number of fruit-eyes/sqm to be retained is:			
			6	8	10	12
			the number of fruit-eyes/vine is:			
150 x 150		2,25	14	18	23	27
200	100	2,00	12	16	20	24
210	100	2,10	13	17	21	25
210	120	2,52	15	20	25	30
240	100	2,40	14	19	24	29
240	120	2,88	17	23	29	35
270	100	2,70	16	22	27	33
270	120	3,24	19	25	32	38
300	100	3,00	18	24	30	36
300	120	3,60	22	28	36	43
330	100	3,30	20	26	33	40
330	120	3,96	24	32	40	48
350	100	3,50	21	28	35	42
350	120	4,20	25	33	42	50

(c) for standard varieties such as Müller-Thurgau, Kerner, Sylvaner (and in South Africa Steen) is 8 to 9 eyes per square metre;

(d) for shy-bearers with small bunches (Riesling, Chardonnay, Sauvignon blanc, etc) is 10–12 eyes per square metre, or 120 000 per hectare, to yield an economically profitable crop.

The well-known morphological characteristic of all premium-quality wine-grape varieties is that they all have small bunches with small berries, which is why they are 'shy-bearers'. But even such shy-bearers, planted in fertile soil and well supplied with water, can produce large crops if they grow vigorously, because it is technically possible to retain a large number of fruit-eyes per square metre. It must be emphasized, however, that long-term and world-wide experience shows that even the most noble wine-grape varieties such as Chardonnay, Cabernet Sauvignon, Pinot noir, Riesling, etc., suffer a sharp decline in the quality of their wines when producing more than 1 kilogram per square metre, i.e. 10 tonnes per hectare.

It cannot be overemphasized that the grower holds in his pruning-scissors: the size of his crop; the quality of his crop; and the longevity of his vines. This fact is often overlooked by greedy growers.

TABLE 11.4
Practical example for calculating the size of the crop of different varieties
based on the fruitfulness of their eyes and the size of their grapes

Variety	*Number of bunches per shoot (N)	*Weight of one bunch in grams	Yield per eye in grams	Number of eyes needed for the production of 1 kg of grapes
Cabernet S.	1,08	80	86	12 (11,6)
Chardonnay	1,20	80	96	10 (10,4)
W. Riesling	1,57	75	118	8 (8,4)
Pinot noir	1,30	95	123	8 (8,1)
Welschriesling	1,80	115	207	5 (4,8)
Merlot	1,50	125	187	5 (5,3)
Aligoté	2,30	120	276	4 (3,6)

The number of fruit-eyes needed for the production of one kilogram of grapes (x)
of the variety W. Riesling can be calculated for example as follows:

$$x= \frac{1\ 000}{1,57 \times 75} = \frac{1\ 000}{118} = 8\ (8,4)$$

* Data adapted from Németh (13).
The calculation was presented by Dr. J. Lászlo during a lecture given on 12 April
1977 at Stellenbosch, Cape.

Perold (14) furnishes the average weight of the bunches of some wine-grape varieties as follows: Stein/Chenin blanc 212,2 g; Hermitage/Cinsaut 342,3 g; White French/Palomino 512,3 g; White Greengrape 270,5 g; and Cabernet Sauvignon 157,8 g. The great difference between the figures for Hungary and South Africa concerning Cabernet Sauvignon could possibly be attributed to different cultural practices, especially irrigation, which is widely practised in South Africa but unknown or even forbidden in Europe in regions producing red wines of premium quality.

SYSTEMS OF PRUNING
Winter pruning is the foundation of the culture of the grape. Yet, in no other facet of viticulture are so many basic blunders made. Substantial profits are lost year after year by grapegrowers, because of the incorrect pruning of vines. We distinguish between SHORT, HALF-LONG and LONG pruning according as we prune to short bearers (spurs), half-long or long bearers (rods, canes). The length of the bearing units is determined by the fruiting habit of the variety.

1. Short pruning (Spur pruning)

On grape varieties which have fruitful eyes at the bases of their canes and bear large bunches, short bearing units with two good eyes are retained. When counting eyes, only those between which distinct internodes may be seen are counted.

In the diagrammatic sketches of this chapter, the age of the wood of the components of a pruning unit is indicated by different shading (Fig. 11.2) in order to clarify the basic principles of the annual pruning of such units. A photograph, generally presented in textbooks, would not be able to distinguish the components as clearly as this graphic representation does. As far as can be ascertained, this method of graphic representation indicating the age of the components of a pruning unit has not been used elsewhere.

Fig. 11.2.

| summer-shoot | one-year-old cane | two-year-old wood | three-year-old wood | four-year-old wood | permanent arm of the cordon |

BASIC PRINCIPLES OF THE ANNUAL PRUNING OF SHORT BEARING UNITS. From Pongrácz/Meissenheimer (15).

Fig. 11.3. Correct. (1) The fruitful eyes occur on one-year-old canes arising from two-year-old wood (horizontally striped). (2) The cane arising from the upper eye of the two-year-old wood, i.e. of the bearer of the previous year, is cut off, together with a segment of the old bearer (A). (3) The cane arising from the lower eye of the old bearer is cut back to two good eyes to serve as the new short bearer (B).

Fig. 11.4. Incorrect. Because the cane arising from the upper eye of the bearer of the previous year is usually more vigorous than the cane arising from the lower eye, owing to the effect of polarity on vine growth, growers are inclined to retain this cane for the new short bearer. The arm with the bearing units must therefore be lengthened annually by about 5 to 7 cm instead of 2 cm.

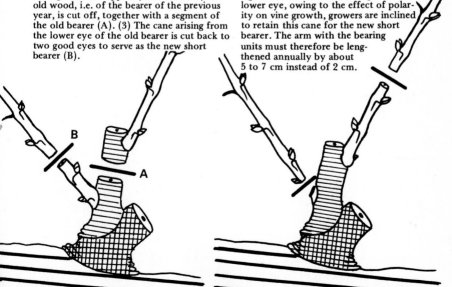

2. Half-long or long pruning according to Guyot's renewal system

This system of pruning was developed in France by Dr. J. Guyot in about 1858 for the pruning of varieties having small bunches or no fruitful eyes on the basal portion of their canes.

The basic principle of this system of pruning is that the vine should always have at least one short bearer with two good eyes and one half-long bearer with four good eyes, or one long bearer with 8 to 12 eyes. The half-long and long bearers are for the production of grapes, and the short bearers are for producing canes to serve as bearers in the following year. For this reason they may be considered as RENEWAL SPURS. If renewal spurs are not provided, the vine's permanent stem and arms will soon become too long, because the eyes near the basal portion of the long bearers either do not bud at all or produce only weak canes that cannot serve as new bearers. For this reason, at least one short bearer must be provided before a half-long or long bearer. If the short bearers do not develop good canes for new long bearers, owing mainly to the poor growth of the vine, the lowest cane of the old long bearer can be used for the new long bearer (14, 15, 18, 20).

STEPS IN THE ANNUAL PRUNING OF HALF-LONG PRUNING UNITS ACCORDING TO GUYOT'S RENEWAL SYSTEM. From Pongrácz/Meissenheimer (15).

Fig. 11.5.

The cane arising from the lower eye of the two-year-old wood, i.e. the bearer of the previous year, is cut back to two good eyes to serve as a renewal spur (1).

The cane arising from the upper eye of the bearer of the previous year is cut to four good eyes to serve as a half-long bearer (2).

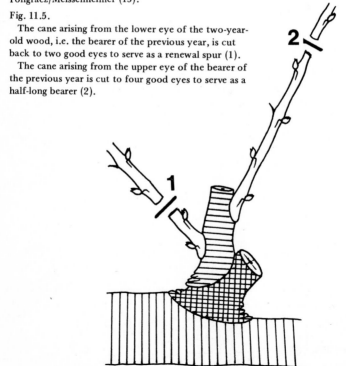

Fig. 11.6.

During the following winter the old half-long bearer is entirely removed (1).

The cane arising from the lower eye of the old renewal spurs, which is now two years old, is cut back to two good eyes to serve as a new renewal spur (2).

The cane arising from the upper eye of the old renewal spur is cut to four good eyes to serve as a new half-long bearer (3).

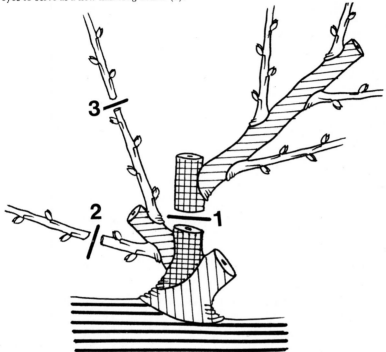

According to this simple and logical principle the vines can also be provided with long bearers. The only difference will be that long bearers are cut back to 8 to 12 eyes, and not to 4, as in the case of half-long bearers.

3. Shortening old arms

As segments of the two-year-old wood of the old short bearers must inevitably be retained during winter pruning, the length of the arms carrying the bearers increases each year, finally becoming too long. They must be then shortened or replaced. This can be done with the help of a conveniently placed WATER-SPROUT rising from the lower part of the arm.

During winter pruning of old vines, about two-thirds of the number of one-year-old canes to be retained should be used as bearers, and one-third for shortening or replacing old arms.

STEPS IN SHORTENING OLD ARMS. From Pongrácz/Meissenheimer (15).

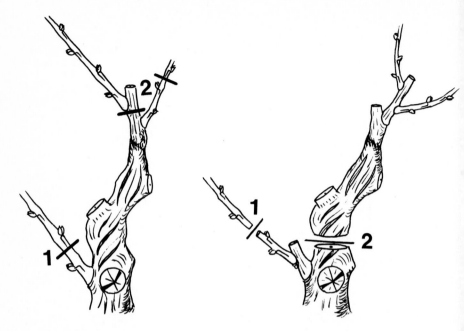

Fig. 11.7. A vigorous water-sprout (ws) arising on the lower part of the old arm is cut back to one eye (1). The bearing units (spurs) on the upper part of the old arm are pruned normally, to bear grapes in the following season (2).

Fig. 11.8. During the following winter the vigorous cane that arose from the one eye of the old water-sprout is cut back to two eyes to serve as a newly created short bearer (1). The old arm just above it can now be cut off and entirely removed (2).

ANNUAL PRUNING AND FORMING OF VINES

1. Unsupported vase-shaped bush vines (Gobelet)

This system is used extensively in most warm grapegrowing regions, and it has certainly been proved that vines can be successfully grown in this way under extremely arid climatic conditions (3, 14).

During the formation of the young vine it is of the utmost importance that the grower should clearly understand what the shape of the future vine must be. Incorrectly formed mature vines can be corrected, but this always requires the removal of thick arms, and such operations always leave large wounds.

STEPS IN DEVELOPING UNSUPPORTED BUSH VINES

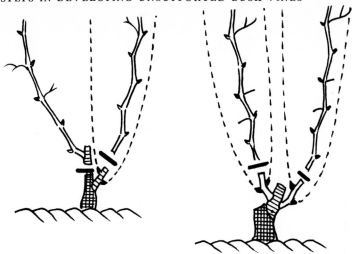

Fig. 11.9(a). First winter after pruning. Select the most erect and if possible, the most vigorous cane and cut it back to two good eyes. (The dotted line indicates the growth during the following season.)

Fig. 11.9(b). Second winter after pruning. If the vine is now sufficiently vigorous, it gets two short bearers, each with two good eyes. The two bearers should be chosen so that they are as nearly as possible opposite each other in the same vertical plane. This is of great importance for the future shape of the vine. Those vines that have not grown sufficiently during the previous season again get only one bearer with two eyes.

Fig. 11.9 (c). Third winter after pruning. Select three to four bearers evenly grouped around the centre of the vine. Only if the bearers and grapes are evenly distributed around the vine will their weight be well balanced and the vine be able to maintain its upright position.

GLEN INNES PUBLIC LIBRARY

According to the fertility of the soil, variety of grape, availability of water, etc., the vine can be given 6 to 10 short bearers in subsequent years. This system of training can also be applied to grape varieties that require half-long or long pruning.

It is evident that grape varieties having usually upright growth-habits, such as Carignan, Grenache, Greengrape, Muscat d'Alexandrie, Furmint, Kadarka, etc., can be grown successfully with this system of training.

2. Untrellised vines supported by stakes

This system is commonly adopted in the grapegrowing regions of Europe. The presence of the stake makes no difference to the pruning. With this system, cross-cultivation and the control of fungoid diseases, especially of downy mildew, can easily be applied. This system is not used at the Cape.

Fig. 11.10. Untrellised vines supported by stakes. From Kozma (10).

3. Cordon-trained vines

The trunk of a cordon-trained vine rises vertically to about 20 cm below the lowest wire of the trellis, called the 'cordon-wire', and then divides horizontally into one branch (UNILATERAL CORDON), or into two branches (BILATERAL CORDONS) that extend in opposite directions along the lowest wire of the trellis to within about 5 cm of the cordon ends of the adjoining vines.

The chief advantage of the bilateral cordon system is that the grapes are well distributed because the bearing units are located at regular intervals (about 20 cm) on the upper side of the horizontally trained cordons. Because the grapes hang at about the same level from the ground, this system of training, especially the four-wire vertical trellis, is well adapted to mechanical harvesting. The spraying of fungicides to control the infection and spread of fungi on crops is greatly facilitated (6, 10, 12, 18. 19).

Overcropping is the most common error committed during the training of young vines. It can lead to permanently weakened vines. Perold (14) summed up the basic principle of proper training of young vines as follows: 'The speed with which we can complete the cordon is determined by the vine's vigour. It is wrong to attempt to proceed faster than the vine's vigour will allow.'

The main goal must always be to make possible a vigorous root system and a well-formed, strong vine framework, by restricting the size of the crop of young vines.

First growing season

No training should be attempted. Attempts to train vigorous vines up to the cordon-wire the same year they are planted leads to disappointing results.

First dormant season

Select the most erect and if possible the most vigorous cane and cut it back to two good eyes. Vines should be trellised and staked.

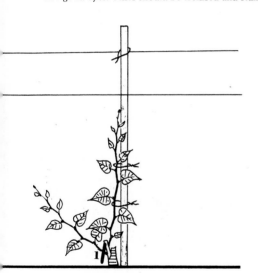
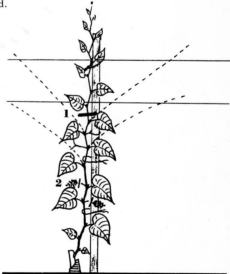

Second growing season. Fig. 11.11(a)

Retain two vigorous shoots that are growing near the stake and thus can easily be tied to it. Once the longest and best-positioned vertically growing shoot is securely tied to the stake, thereby preventing it from being broken off by the wind, the second shoot must be removed (1 on left).

All the growth of the vine is now directed into the development of the selected shoot, which is the future vertical stem (trunk) of the plant. It should be retied

once or twice more until it reaches a height of about 35–40 cm above the cordon
wire. Then it should be topped above the point at which the vertical stem will divide
to develop horizontally trained branches, 20 cm below the cordon-wire (1 on right).

This severe topping of the main shoot will stimulate the vigorous development of
laterals. Retain only 3 or 4 laterals on the upper third of the main shoot (see dotted
lines).

The entire crop, usually two bunches, should be removed early in the season (2).

Second dormant season after pruning. Fig. 11.11(b)

Prune off laterals produced during the previous summer. The vine is thus now
reduced to a vigorous cane, tied vertically to the stake ('Kieriestok'). Remove all
buds (winter eyes) from the future vertical stem of the vine (at positions marked
x), except 2 or 3 on its upper part.

Third growing season. Fig. 11.11(c)

Select two vigorous shoots on opposite sides of the vertical stem 15–20 cm below
the cordon-wire to form the cordon-arms. Rub off all other shoots early in the season.

The two selected shoots are in a position to be attached easily to the cordon-wire.
As growth proceeds, keep them straight by tying them loosely to the wire. Under
no circumstances bend them around the cordon-wire. The shoots must come up to
the cordon-wire in a gradual and not a sharp curve.

When the two selected shoots are about 40–50 cm longer than the desired length
of the future cordon-arms, i.e. halfway to the adjoining vines, they must be cut back
at this point (1). For example, if the vines were planted 1,2 m apart in the rows, the
shoots must be cut to 60 cm.

The horizontally tied position and the severe topping of the shoots during their
most active growing period, i.e. at the beginning of November in South Africa, will
stimulate the very vigorous development of summer laterals (dotted lines). Their
foliage will feed the vine and will especially ensure the thickening of the two shoots
designed for the future cordon-arms of the vine. In this way, through some extra
work in early summer, the grower can enable the cordons to attain their full length
during one growing season.

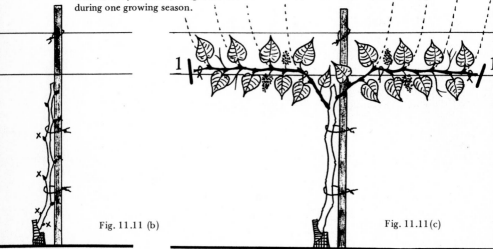

Fig. 11.11 (b)   Fig. 11.11(c)

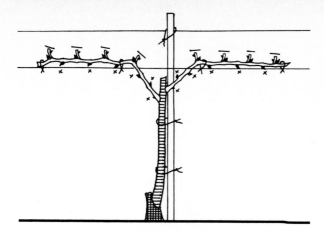

Third dormant season after pruning. Fig. 11.11(d)

Retain bearing units (spurs) at regular intervals, 15–20 cm apart, spaced along the upper side of the cordons. It is extremely important *not* to prune off the laterals, but to cut them back to one eye, especially near the base of the cordons. These eyes will definitely leaf-out during the next spring and will develop into vigorous shoots, thus preventing the formation of blank areas ('ostrich-neck') near the branching-point of the cordons.

Remove all canes arising from within about 15 cm of the point where the trunk was divided, thus leaving here a spur-free area. Remove also all canes below the point of branching, and rub off all buds on the underside of the cordons (at positions marked **x**).

Remember: Overcropping must be prevented during the following growing season!

Fourth dormant season after pruning. Fig. 11.11(e)

The short-bearing units (spurs) are now cut back to two good eyes, thus providing 16 fruit-eyes per vine. Try to select only those spurs that are growing upright. Try also to maintain the arms at uniform vigour by a balanced pruning.

During summer remove all water-sprouts on the vertical trunk and on the bends of the arms.

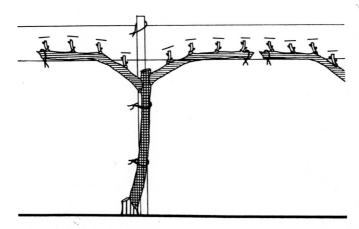

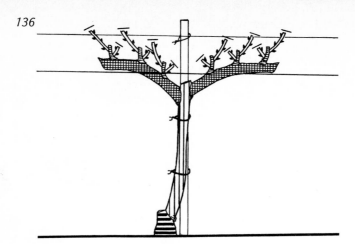

Fifth dormant season after pruning. Fig. 11.11(f)

Convert the short-bearing units into half-long-bearing units, according to the basic principle explained under Fig. 11.5. By this method of pruning each vine can be provided with 36 eyes: six half-long bearers with four eyes, and six short bearers with two eyes to serve as renewal spurs.

A further advantage of this method of training and pruning is that it allows the cordons to be considerably shorter and sturdier. Every observer of the vine knows that long cordons tend to produce poor growth and 'blind' eyes that fail to develop, especially near the point of branching, resulting in bare spaces on the cordons — unfortunately a well-known phenomenon in our trellised vineyards.

STEPS IN DEVELOPING A CORDON-TRAINED EXTREMELY VIGOROUS VINE FROM ITS SECOND GROWING SEASON

Second growing season. Fig. 11.12(a)

As soon as the main shoot has grown 30–40 cm beyond the cordon-wire, it should be topped, about 15 cm below the cordon-wire (1). The severe topping of the main shoot will stimulate the vigorous development of primary laterals. Select two top lateral shoots for the development of the cordons and remove all the other laterals on the vertical stem (trunk) below the point of branching. Remove the entire crop (2).

Tie the two vigorous laterals selected for the development of the cordons, as they develop along the cordon wire, and keep them straight. Do not tie the apical portion of the shoots that are elongating.

As soon as the shoots grow (25–30 cm beyond the desired length of the cordons, they are topped at this point to check their growth in length (3). This will result in the vigorous development of secondary laterals (see dotted lines). The foliage of these laterals will feed the plant and will strengthen it to the extent that the grower will usually be able to complete the development of the cordons of such vines in one season.

Second dormant season after pruning. Fig. 11.12(b)

Secondary laterals near the point of branching are cut back to one eye to ensure uniform budding during the next spring. All buds from the vertical stem as well as from the underside of the cordons should be removed (x).

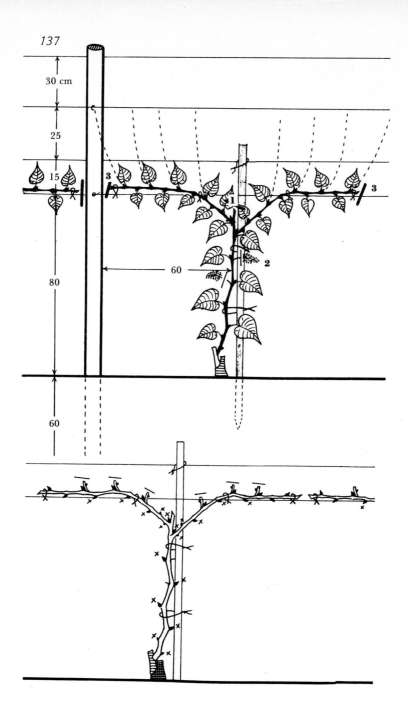

30 cm

25

15

3

3

1

60

2

80

60

During the following growing season the main objective is to develop a strong and well-formed framework for the vine as well as a vigorous root system. For this reason, about half of the crop should be removed.

Remember: First comes the development of a vigorous vine and only then the crop. If the canes selected for the cordons are not vigorous enough, cut them back to four eyes and extend them to their full length only during the following growing season.

If the cordon is completed faster than the vigour of the vine allows, the vine will divert all its energies into the development of the eyes farthest from the base of the canes and cordon-arms, resulting in bare spaces on the cordons.

4. Training of trellised vines pruned according to Guyot's renewal system

In this system of training the vine is given a vertical trunk similar to that used for cordon-trained vines.

Vines to be long-pruned according to Guyot's renewal system are treated in the same way as cordon-trained vines to the end of their third growing season.

Guyot's system of pruning, called 'cane pruning' in California, is the least severe system of pruning now in general use. Consequently it allows the greatest development of the vine (20). The greatest advantage of this system of pruning is the possibility of obtaining full crops on varieties whose eyes are fruitless near the base of the canes.

Third winter after pruning. Fig. 11.13(a)

The vine consists now of a well-developed vertical stem bearing on its upper part four vigorous, well-matured canes.

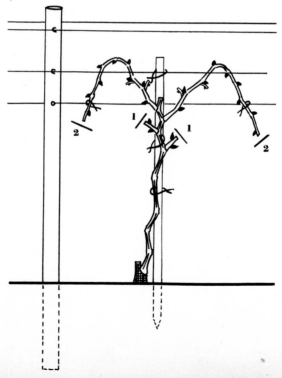

The two lower canes are cut back to two good eyes to serve as renewal spurs (1).

The two other canes *above* them are cut back to 6–8 eyes to serve as fruit-bearing long bearers (2).

Bending of long bearers: A sharp downward bending of the cane causes a certain amount of injury to the tissues of the cane, which tends to check the flow of sap towards the ends. The sap pressure thus increases in the lower eyes of the cane and forces them out into strong shoots, thus distributing fruit-bearing shoots along the long bearers at suitable intervals instead of producing only a few vigorous shoots at the tips of the long bearers. The well-known tendency of the vine to expend the principal part of its vigour on the development of the shoots farthest from the base of the canes can thus be overcome by bending or twisting the long bearers (6, 14, 18).

Fourth winter after pruning. Fig. 11.13(b)

The old long bearers are now entirely removed (1).

The canes arising from the upper eyes of the old renewal spurs are cut back to 8–10 eyes to serve as the new long bearers (2).

The canes arising from the lower eyes of the old renewal spurs are cut back to two good eyes to serve as the new renewal spurs (3).

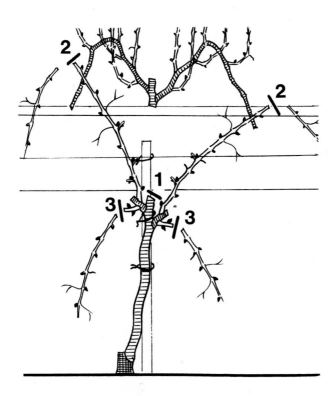

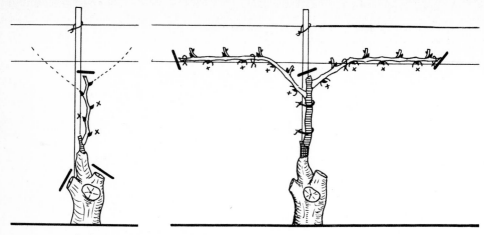

5. Conversion of bush-vines (Gobelet) to bilateral cordon-trained vines

First winter after pruning. Fig. 11.14(a)

(a) Remove all arms except one in the middle of the trunk and in line with the row.

(b) Select one vigorous and straight cane from this retained arm, cut it off about 15 cm below the cordon-wire, and tie it firmly to a stake.

(c) Remove all buds on the lower part of the cane (at positions marked x). Retain only two buds on the upper part, out of which two shoots will arise (dotted lines) during the following spring. These two vigorous shoots will be used to develop the cordons during the growing season.

Second winter after pruning. Fig. 11.14(b)

If the vines are vigorous enough, the development of the cordons can be completed, provided that nearly the entire crop is removed early in the season (19).

(a) Summer laterals situated on the upper part of the cordons are cut back to one eye to ensure that they will leaf-out during the following spring. This is very important because, if the laterals are entirely cut off or are not present, only the eyes on the farthest end of the main cane will leaf-out — owing to the effect of polarity — resulting in a bare space on the cordons.

(b) Remove all buds on the lower part of the cordons (at positions marked x).

Note: It is extremely important not to try to complete the cordons with thin canes. Cut back the canes to a point where they are at least 10 mm thick, and complete the conversion during the following season.

TRELLISING

Grapevines are naturally climbing plants, but in modern viticulture they are trained on trellises for economic reasons. The only difference between untrellised and trellised vines is that the trellised plant is a vine that has an elongated trunk with horizontally trained arms.

Vines are trellised to keep the bunches off the ground, to keep the shoots constantly in a more or less vertical position, thus facilitating the control of fungoid diseases, and to stimulate their growth by making use of the effect of polarity. The vertical position of the shoots will also facilitate tilling, harvesting and pruning.

A higher production per hectare can only be obtained by means of maximum root development through intensive soil preparation, followed by maximum aerial development of the vines by means of appropriate trellising systems (11).

In trellising grapevines one must always bear in mind that the trunk of a vine is first of all a conducting organ. For this reason it must be as straight, and as short, as possible. Twisted or sharply bent trunks hinder the vascular tissues of the plant in their biological function.

Elongation of the height of the trunk above 1,4 m will diminish the fertility as well as the drought-resistance of the vine (2, 3). The basic requirements for an effective and economical trellising system are that it must be as simple as possible, as inexpensive as possible, and adapted to the existing environmental conditions as well as to the grape variety concerned.

Establishing a trellis

It is of the utmost importance that corner posts should be well fixed. They have to be anchored to the ground by means of thick galvanized wire, which passes through a hole near the top and is attached firmly to a concrete block placed in a hole near the corner post. The depth of this hole, the weight of the concrete block, and the distance of the concrete block from the corner post, are largely dependent on the height of the trellis (Fig. 11.15).

Fig. 11.15. From Kozma (10), indicating the height of the trellis above the surface of the ground (sz), the length of the anchoring galvanized wire (h), and the distance of the concrete block from the base of the corner post.

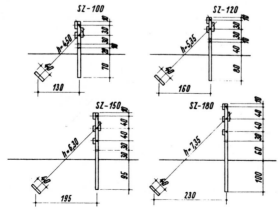

Requirements of poles. Properly trellised vines must be supported by a pole every 5–7 metres. For example, in establishing the number of wire-supporting poles required for a vineyard where the vines are planted 2,7 m × 1 m, 3 703 vines will be planted per hectare; i.e. 740 poles (3 703 divided by 5) are required per hectare if a pole is placed after every fifth vine. If the vineyard has 50 rows, 100 corner posts must be added. These corner posts should always be considerably thicker in diameter and planted at least 30 cm deeper into the soil than wire-supporting poles in the rows.

Trellising systems

Trellis sizes must always be adapted to the differing capacities of the vines to support shoots and leaves. In the shallow soil categories a two-wire vertical trellis with wires 20–25 cm apart is sufficient. Vines grown in deep soils could produce longer shoots and a larger canopy, which would need a higher vertical trellis to prevent shading and Botrytis attack. Trellising systems such as gable, factory, slanting, pergolas, Y- and V-trellis, etc., are not used extensively for the production of wine-grape varieties.

The main disadvantages of such systems are:

(a) Establishing costs are high.

(b) They are unsuitable for mechanical harvesting.

(c) The pruning of the vines requires highly skilled labourers.

(d) The grapes are sheltered under very dense foliage and are never exposed to the sun or to air circulation; consequently, such trellis systems favour the development of fungus diseases, especially *Botrytis cinerea*.

(e) The control of fungus diseases is extremely difficult.

(f) The large vines grown on such trellises require very fertile soils well supplied with water; if water is not available, the vines will exhaust very rapidly.

(g) Not only the grapes, but also the basal portion of the shoots is seldom exposed to the sunshine; consequently, the eyes on such vigorous shoots are always less fertile, and in very dense foliage the shoots do not even ripen properly.

Trellising systems widely used in the world, and recommended

(1) Four-wire vertical trellis, called FENCE-SYSTEM in South Africa, cheap, purposeful, excellently suited to cordon-trained vines and to mechanical harvesting. See Fig. 11.12(a).

(2) ROYAT-CORDON, the oldest system of trellising vines, developed in France in about 1860 (Fig. 11.17). From Kozma (10).

(3) CAZENAVE-CORDON, developed in France (La Réole) in about

Fig. 11.17   Fig. 11.18

1860 by the grower Cazenave, and modified by Guyot (Fig. 11.18). From
Kozma (10).

(4) SYLVOZ-CORDON, developed by the grower Carlo Sylvoz in
Italy (Savoy) and excellently suited for the training of vines which have
been provided with long bearers (Fig. 11.19). From Vogt/Götz (18).

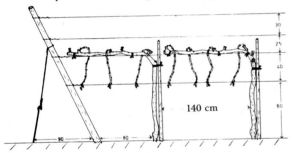

Fig. 11.19

(5) MOSER-CORDON and its annual pruning, developed by the
Austrian grower Lenz Moser (Rohrendorf) during the early thirties
(Fig. 11.20). From Kozma (10).

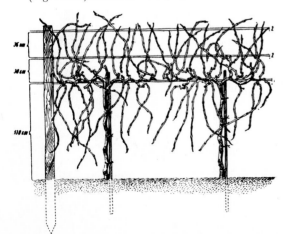

Fig. 11.20

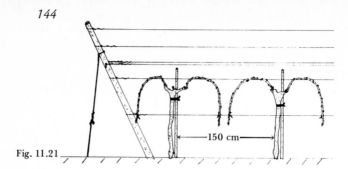

Fig. 11.21

(6) Training of vines along the Rhine (Fig. 11.21). From Vogt/Götz (18).

(7) Training of vines cultivated with wide spacing (Fig. 11.22). From Vogt/Götz (18).

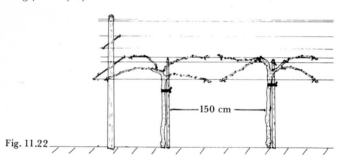

Fig. 11.22

SUMMER TREATMENT OF VINES

Suckering

Vines usually produce shoots either in excess quantities or in places where they are not wanted. SUCKERING is the removal of such shoots from the trunk early in the growing season. It should be performed several times each year when the vines are young.

CROWN-SUCKERING is the removal of unwanted shoots from the bends of the cordons as well as from the undersides of the cordons. This procedure not only controls the size of the crop during the training of young vines, but also reduces the costs of winter pruning.

The proper development of cordon-trained young vines is impossible without systematic suckering. If this is not done, the unwanted shoots will grow vigorously, and divert the energy of the vine into the development of shoots that are not needed for the permanent framework of the plant. This is particularly true in the 'brushy' varieties, i.e. varieties that tend to produce numerous and vigorous water-sprouts, such as Chenin blanc, Cabernet Sauvignon, Pinot noir, Chardonnay, Sauvignon blanc, etc. As we have seen in this chapter dealing with the training of young vines, judicious suckering is one of the most important operations the grower has to perform in the vineyard. Unfortunately it is often greatly neglected.

Topping

TOPPING consists of the removal of the end (apical meristem) of the growing shoot.

Advantages: (a) it strengthens the brittle young shoot so that it can withstand the strong spring winds; (b) it diminishes bad setting of the berries. The effect of topping is the most beneficial when done at the end of blooming (3).

Disadvantages: vines severely topped for a number of years often show signs of deterioration (3, 10).

Topping, like all other operations in the vineyard, must be decided by the grapegrower, taking into consideration the fertility of the soil, the vigour of the vines, the prevailing weather conditions, the trellising systems, etc.

Removing mature leaves

Under unfavourable climatic conditions grapes often do not ripen properly or they are susceptible to fungus diseases, especially to *Botrytis cinerea,* the most dangerous for ripe grapes. In such cases it is advisable to remove the lower leaves on the shoots so as to expose the bunches to air circulation and to the beneficial action of the sun. This operation should be carried out only after the ripening stage of the grapes is well advanced (3, 10, 14, 18).

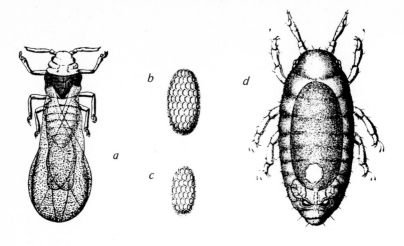

Fig. 12.1. *Phylloxera vastatrix*. Different stages in the development of the insect. From Viala (23).

(a) winged insect; (b) egg laid by the winged insect out of which the larger female insect will hatch; (c) egg laid by the winged insect out of which the male insect will hatch; (d) female insect viewed from the dorsal side; (e) male insect viewed from the dorsal side; (f) winter egg laid by the female insect; (g) leaf form (gallicola) of the insect; (h) root form (radicicola) of the insect, originating from the nymph (i).

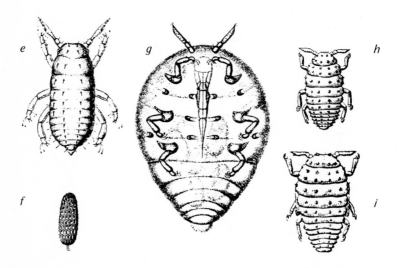

CHAPTER 12

Parasitology of the Vine

INSECTS THAT ATTACK THE VINE

1. Phylloxera

Historical

The name phylloxera is derived from the Greek words *phyllon*, leaf, and *xeros*, dry (17).

This insect lives only on the vine and cannot live on any other host. Phylloxera occurs on the leaves and on the roots. The leaf form has been termed *Phylloxera vastatrix gallicola*, and the root form *Phylloxera vastatrix radicicola*.

The insect is indigenous to the eastern states of the United States of America, and was probably brought from there to England and France between 1854 and 1860 on the roots of imported American direct producers. The insects then spread rapidly over the whole of Europe and before the end of the 19th century had destroyed two-thirds of the established vineyards of the continent (14, 16, 23).

At the Cape it was discovered in patches of sick vines in Constantia and in Moddergat (Helderberg) in 1886 and spread from there with devastating effect (16).

Life cycle of phylloxera

Viala (23) classifies the different stages in the development of the insect as follows: (1) the sexual form; (2) the leaf form; (3) the root form, and (4) the winged form.

(1) The SEXUAL FORM originates from the eggs laid by the winged insect on the lower surface of the young leaves between the nerves. The eggs are of two sizes. The males hatch out of the small eggs, the females out of the large ones. Both sexes are devoid of sucking and digestive organs. After they have mated, the male dies. The female lays just one large egg, the winter egg, in the dead bark of the trunk (5, 14, 16, 23).

(2) The LEAF FORM. In spring one insect hatches out of the winter

egg. It crawls up the young shoot and begins to suck the lower surface of the young leaf. In phylloxera-susceptible *Vitis* species the feeding puncture inhibits cell division and enlargement in the immediate area. 'About 15 cells distant from the puncture, periclinal divisions in layers II and III produce a hollow gall which surrounds the insect and is open at the top. Veins in the area enlarge by cambial activity' (18). In this gall the insect lays a number of eggs out of which insects are again hatched. This propagation is parthenogenetic (the Greek word *parthenos* means virgin or maiden).

In more or less phylloxera-resistant *Vitis* species the punctured cells are deformed and die, and a wound meristem develops around them (18).

According to Winkler (25) the sexual forms of phylloxera do not

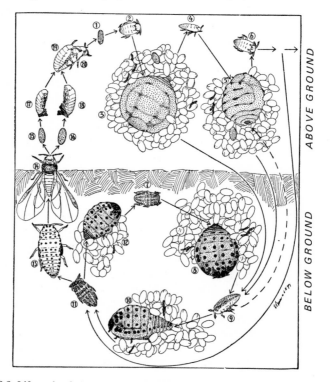

Fig. 12.2. Life-cycle of phylloxera. From Braun & Riem (4).

(1) fertilized winter egg; (2) young louse hatched out of 1; (2–6) successive generations of leaf-form; (6) Young larvae which return below the ground; (7–12) successive radicicole generations; (7) hibernal radicicole form; (13) nymph; (14) winged migrant; (15–16) eggs of the winged insect; (15) male eggs; (16) female eggs.

mature in California and consequently the above-ground forms of the life-cycle of the insect do not occur there.

(3) The ROOT FORM. These are the insects that are hatched in the leaf galls, whence they emerge especially in autumn to enter the soil and reach the roots, which they puncture and suck for nourishment. *It is here that they do great damage.* These root-lice can propagate themselves directly on the roots in several generations during the year and from year to year without passing into the other form. This is what mainly happens at the Cape (16). The adult insects are oval in shape, have a yellow to brown colour and are very small, but can be seen with the naked eye. The eggs are lemon yellow. The late autumn eggs hatch into larvae which hibernate under the bark of thick roots. When in spring the temperature rises by about 10 °C, the hibernating larvae develop to maturity and produce the first generation of the year.

(4) The WINGED FORM. Many of the young root-lice of each generation leave the roots through soil cracks in search of new vines. Some of the insects appearing from midsummer to the end of autumn are winged. They begin to fly to other vines and lay the two kinds of eggs that were referred to above (16, 23).

Phylloxera gall on the root

The swellings formed by the feeding of the root lice are of two kinds: NODOSITIES if they occur near the root tip; and TUBEROSITIES if they occur in older parts of the root covered by periderm. Wherever tuberosities are found, there are also nodosities, but the reverse is not true (5, 14, 16).

These nodosities are whitish or yellowish, resembling somewhat the head and neck of a long-billed bird. The insect causing the swelling is, as a rule, to be found in the acute angle formed where the head joins the neck (5, 9, 14, 23). The cells punctured by the root louse die, and adjacent cells, including those of the endodermis, are inhibited from further development. The cells enlarge and divide more rapidly on the side opposite the puncture than on the punctured side, until the tip curves and encloses the feeding louse (18).

The mere presence of a few of these nodosities on the roots of a vine does not indicate that the vine is not sufficiently resistant. In fact, there are but few of the American *Vitis* species on which nodosities are not found (3, 9, 14, 23).

In *Vitis* species and hybrids of such species that are resistant to phylloxera, a periderm develops in the swellings which limits the spread of the decay into the root interior. The characteristics said to favour resistance are rapid growth, early differentiation of the endodermis, early development of the secondary vascular tissues, narrow vascular rays, and

the development of sequent periderms (10, 11, 19, 24). If, however, can-
cerous patches of decomposition are found on the older roots, something
more serious than the nodosities is threatened, namely the tuberosities.
This indicates that the resistance of the vine is less than where only nodosities were found (4, 9, 10, 14, 23, 24).

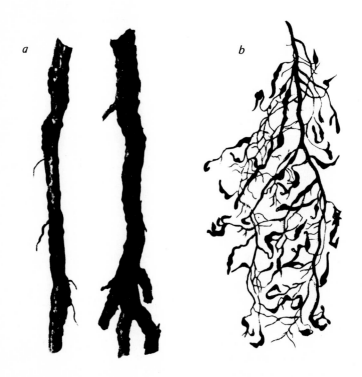

Fig. 12.3. Effects of phylloxera on the roots of the vine: (a) tuberosities,
(b) nodosities. The nodosities are first yellow, then golden yellow, then brown.
From Viala (23).

A PHYLLOXERA PATCH is easily detected in a vineyard. The first
sign of the damage inflicted by the insects on the roots, is that the
affected vines stop summer growth sooner than healthy ones. Their
leaves at first have a dull green colour, then they turn yellowish later in
the summer and drop early. The following year the patches enlarge and
one can also notice new patches in the vineyard. In three or four years
a large vineyard on clay soil will have only odd patches of vines that are

still alive (16). When the attacked vines are so weakened that they cannot form new roots, the insects leave them for more healthy vines. For this reason, the roots of very weak vines need not be examined for root lice.

The spreading of phylloxera happens in a natural way or by the agency of man. The insect crawls slowly in and on the ground from vine to vine. When infected vines are carried away by floods and end up far away, phylloxera can spread rapidly over a great distance. Man can spread it by his boots and implements when going from an infected into a non-infected vineyard, and also by sending rooted vines into non-infected areas.

Control

(1) GRAFTING. Once phylloxera is established in the soil, the only effective control is to graft the susceptible *V. vinifera* grape varieties onto rootstocks that resist it (3, 25).

(2) PLANTING VINES IN SAND. From the beginning of the invasion of the phylloxera it was noticed that vines in certain sandy soils were hardly damaged by the insects, while vines on clay soils perished quickly (3, 9, 14, 16, 24). There must be at least 85 per cent pure sand in the soil that is to be relied on as a phylloxera-proof soil.

(3) SUBMERSION IN WINTER. This is done in parts of France. The vines must be absolutely dormant when submerged. While it is perfectly true that, under certain conditions, submersion is effective and economical, yet the conditions under which submersion is possible are so special that few can avail themselves of this means of combating the phylloxera. In the first place, the vineyard must be perfectly or almost level. Then the soil must be neither too porous nor too compact. The submersion must be continuous, and not interrupted even for an hour. The duration of the submersion depends, to a certain extent, upon the climate. In very cold countries the duration of the complete submersion may be considerably shortened (3, 9). According to Hayne (9) the time required to kill the phylloxera in a Californian vineyard by submersion in water varies from 55–60 days in very slightly permeable soils to 90 days in very permeable soils.

2. Root eelworms or nematodes

Injury to vines caused by nematodes was first reported by Perold (16) and identified somewhat later in California (25).

Damage and species

(1) ROOT-KNOT NEMATODES cause abnormal cell growth that results in characteristic swellings or galls which may sometimes be con-

fused with those caused by phylloxera (25). The swellings caused by root-knot nematodes are, however, usually much larger and softer than those caused by phylloxera (16). In California the most widely distributed nematode pest of vines is the root-knot nematode *Meloidogyne incognita* var. *acrita* Chitwood (25). Boubals (2) observed that *Meloidogyne marioni* was almost exclusively located in sandy soils of southern France.

(2) ROOT-LESION NEMATODES: *Pratylenchus nulnus* Allen & Jensen causes poor growth of vines and reduced yields in California. In contrast to root-knot nematodes, it does not produce swellings on the roots (25).

Control

(a) Although destroyed by desiccation, nematodes will survive in a soil that is apparently dry. In cool weather they are less active (25).

(b) Fumigation with DD or Telone has provided new plantings with favourable conditions for becoming established; no control measure, however, has yet eradicated nematodes on a field scale (25).

(c) The best control is the use of nematode-resistant rootstocks (25), provided such rootstock varieties are sufficiently resistant to phylloxera.

Snyder (21) reported that all *V. vinifera* varieties are susceptible to injury by nematodes, but a few species of *Vitis,* such as *V. solonis, V. champini* and *V. doaniana* showed moderate to high resistance. It must be emphasized again that the resistance of *V. solonis* and *V. champini* to phylloxera is indicated by the number 15, i.e. it is highly questionable (3, 9, 19).

Boubals (2) recommends the use of the rootstocks SO 4, 5 BB, 1616 C, 44–53 M, and 99 R for nematode-infested soils.

3. Calandra

This insect, *Phlyctinus calloses* Bohem., is indigenous to the Cape. The calandra attacks a number of plants. It is usually worst in clay soils and during the first year after the soil has been deeply ploughed and planted with vines. The insect eats all the green parts of the plant. The beetles eat mainly at night. During the day they hide in the soil under the clods of earth, beneath old bark, and under the foliage. If they are touched they drop to the ground and feign death. As their colour corresponds closely to that of the soil, they cannot easily be detected on the ground (16).

Control

Apply 10 per cent DDT-powder around the trunk of the vines.

4. Erinosis

The injury caused by the erineum mite, *Eriophyes vitis* Pgst., appears as a swelling on the upper surface of the leaf and forms a sort of blister, which when small has a reddish colour, but gradually turns yellowish to greenish as it grows larger. Underneath these blisters a white felty mass of hairs develops out of the lower epidermis cells where the leaf was punctured. The mites can be seen amongst the hairs by means of a microscope (16, 25).

Control

If the vines are regularly sulphured early in the season, the disease will soon disappear completely. The full-grown leaves are hardly ever attacked (16).

5. Grape-bud mite

By feeding on the tissues in the dormant buds and on the expanding very young shoots, the bud mites cause a dwarfing and stunting of young shoots. Such affected shoots produce no grapes. The mites live in the buds and produce many generations a year. The population is the highest on the basal portion of the shoot.

Control

According to Winkler (25) no chemical control has been found successful.

FUNGOID DISEASES OF THE VINE

1. Downy mildew or Peronospora

Causal organism

Downy mildew is indigenous to North America, where it was reported and described for the first time by Schweinitz in 1834 (10). In 1863 de Barry carefully studied this disease and the fungus causing it, which he named *Peronospora viticola*. In 1888 Berlese and de Titoni called it *Plasmopara viticola*. In France it was discovered in 1878 by Planchon. Downy mildew is by far the most dangerous fungoid disease of the grapevine. Its seriousness in any region depends on the humidity of the air and on the frequency and duration of summer rains or heavy dews (1, 3, 11, 12, 14, 16, 23).

External characteristics of downy mildew (adapted from Perold 1926)

The fungus attacks all the green parts of the vine.

(a) *Leaves*. The first evidence of infection is the appearance of light-yellow translucent spots on the upper surface of the leaf, which the French call *taches d'huile*, i.e. oil patches, while a white downy mass is formed on the lower surface of the leaf. The white mass consists of the CONIDIOPHORES and CONIDIA or SUMMER SPORES of the fungus. The emerging of the conidiophores through the stomata on the lower surface of the leaves is so sudden that the Germans call it *Ausbruch*, which may be best translated into English as the 'outbreak' of the disease. This stage marks an intensive development of the fungus, which now kills the cells of the infected leaf. In the centre of the oil patches the leaves begin to turn brown. In serious cases the leaves drop. Vines that are poorly cared for may be completely defoliated by late summer.

(b) *Shoots.* On the shoots the disease causes dark-brown patches on or near the nodes. Here it causes little damage.

(c) *Bunches.* The young bunches are attacked by the fungus on the stalk, pedicels, flower clusters and later the berries. The mycelium filaments of the germinating spores enter the berries through the stomata, which are fairly numerous on the bourrelet, i.e. the thickened portion of the pedicel near where it enters the berry. Under the influence of the fungus the berries turn brown. This is why the disease in this case is called *rot brun* (brown rot) in French. The infected berries shrivel and drop. Once the berries have changed colour (véraison), the danger of downy mildew infection is over.

Fig. 12.4. (a) Penetration of the mycelium filament of downy mildew into the berry via the bourrelet. (b) Berries destroyed by the fungus. From Lüstner (14).

Life-cycle and control of the fungus

Towards the end of summer and in autumn the fungus forms its WINTER SPORES *or* OOSPORES. These spores are dark-brown, round bodies and have a diameter of 25–30 microns. The winter spores occur in large numbers in the infected leaves and they are liberated when the leaves rot in the soil. They can remain alive for some years. After a good rain early in the spring, the germinating winter spores produce one to three conidia, which correspond to the summer conidia, except that they are larger. Ravaz (20) called them macroconidia. From the ground, where the winter-spores germinate, the macroconidia are carried to the leaves by wind or rain. As soon as they enter a drop of water their content undergoes a change and they become ZOOSPORANGIA. Within about two hours the cell-wall bursts and on average 5 to 6 (sometimes up to 15) zoospores emerge from one conidium. The zoospores are naked masses of protoplasm, which swarm for about a quarter of an hour, and then under favourable conditions they begin to germinate. The mycelium filament thus formed enters the green organs of the vine through their stomata, and the first infection of the season from the winter-spores takes place. This infection is called PRIMARY INFECTION.

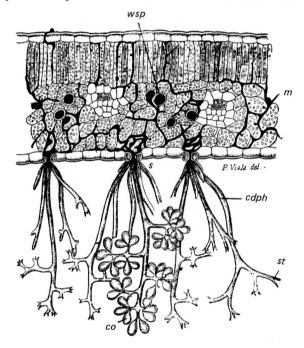

Fig. 12.5. Diagrammatic transverse section of a mature leaf severely infected with *Plasmopara viticola.* From Viala (23).

Abbreviations: wsp — winter spores; m — intercellular mycelium of the fungus; s — stomata; cdph — conidiophores; co — conidia or summer spores; st — sterigmata whose conidia have dropped.

The prerequisites for primary infection are: (a) at least 15 mm rain to wet the soil thoroughly; (b) minimum temperature of 10 °C; (c) young leaves of a minimum of 2 cm in diameter; and (d) the green parts of the vine must remain wet for about four to six hours (1, 3, 11, 12, 23).

Once the mycelium has penetrated the green tissues of the vine, none of the fungicides available for the control of downy mildew are effective. Thus it cannot be emphasized enough that control of the disease is preventive and not curative. Preventive measures have to be taken by covering the surface of the green parts of the vine with a protective film of water-soluble fungicide which will kill the conidia before they can germinate. *What we try to achieve is in reality to poison the water, the only medium in which the spores can germinate* (11, 14, 16, 20, 23, 24).

If the primary infection has not been prevented and the mycelium of the fungus has penetrated into the tissues of the green parts of the vine, its further development inside the tissues needs several days. This is called the INCUBATION PERIOD. The length of this period depends on the season, daily temperature, and humidity of the air (11, 12, 20, 23, 24).

In the grape-growing regions of central Europe it is as follows: 15 to 18 days during mid-May; 12 to 15 days at the end of May; 11 to 14 days during mid-June; 6 to 7 days at the end of June; and 5 to 6 days during July and August (11).

SECONDARY INFECTION. If downy mildew is not checked by control measures or by dry weather, after the lapse of the incubation period the conidiophores emerge through the stomata on the lower surface of the leaves. They emerge in numbers of 1 to 10 through one stoma. To the extremities of their branches the CONIDIA, or SUMMER SPORES, are attached. They drop from the conidiophores, are scattered by the wind, and if they enter a drop of water their further development (zoosporangia, zoospores, germination, etc.) is identical to that of the macroconidia which emerge from the germinating winter spores (3, 11, 12, 14, 16, 20, 23).

The zoospores begin to germinate within the next quarter of an hour at optimum temperatures. As soon as the mycelium filament penetrates the green parts of the vine, a new infection takes place. This infection is the second of the season, but the first from the summer spores of the fungus, and it is called secondary infection.

The conidia retain their germinating power for at the most five days in very moist air. Fortunately, however, they are very sensitive to dry air and to high temperatures, which explains why dry winds and high temperatures check downy mildew so effectively (12, 16, 20, 23).

Optimum temperature for the development of the fungus is considered to be between 22 and 24 °C. Temperatures above 32 °C kill the fungus (11, 12, 14, 16, 20, 23).

The prerequisites for secondary infection are (a) a minimum of 4 to 5 mm rain or even heavy dew; (b) a minimum temperature of 12 °C; (c) the green parts of the vine must remain wet for about half an hour to two hours (1, 11, 24). If secondary infection is not checked, a third (tertiary) will occur after the incubation period has elapsed, provided that the weather is favourable (rainfall or heavy dew) for the development of the fungus. If this tertiary infection is not checked after the following rain or heavy dew, a fourth infection, and perhaps further infections, will occur until the tissues mature; thus the disease can assume epidemic proportions.

From the preceding it must be clear that the whole success of control of downy mildew depends on a strict adherence to the so-called incubation calendar, based on the knowledge of the incubation periods. To begin spraying the vines when the light-brown translucent patches appear on the upper surface of the leaves, is already too late.

It must be categorically stated that there is no *V. vinifera* grape variety which is resistant to downy mildew.

Control

It is recommended that the disease be controlled with organic fungicides until the end of the active growing season, because copper has an inhibiting effect on the growth of the meristematic tissues. At a later stage mixtures in which copper is present in a very slightly soluble combination may be used.

2. Powdery mildew, or oidium

Causal organism

The disease is indigenous to North America. It came to Europe in the first half of the previous century. Tucker observed its presence in England, and Berkeley described the fungus as *Oidium tuckeri.* Unlike most other fungus diseases of the grapevine, which are favoured by moist conditions, oidium grows well in a dry climate. It is the most common vine disease in the western Cape (16).

Fig. 12.6. Spots caused by oidium on the canes. From Lüstner (14).

Symptoms and development of the fungus

The fungus causing this desease grows on the surface of all green parts of the vine. A white, powdery mycelium appears on shoots, upper surfaces of leaves and young berries. Unripe berries crack and become very susceptible to rot. Oidium thus causes the greatest damage to the grapes. Once the grapes have turned colour (véraison) they are seldom attacked by the disease (3, 14, 16, 23, 24).

The mycelium threads grow on the surface of the green parts of the vine, drawing sap from the epidermis cells by means of suckers, or haustoria, which grow into these cells. Out of the mycelium arise the more or less erect conidiophores, at the ends of which are formed the conidia, which can immediately propagate the disease. The fungus may survive the winter in two ways: in the bud-scales of infected canes or free in the soils (14, 16, 23, 25).

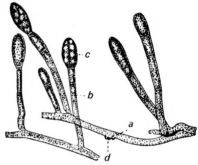

Fig. 12.7. The organs of *Oidium tuckeri*:(a) mycelium; (b) fully developed conidiophora; (c) conidium nearly separated; (d) sucker, or haustorium. From Viala (23).

Temperature is one of the most important factors limiting the development of oidium. As long as the weather remains cool, there is no danger of the disease developing to any dangerous extent. Oidium develops far more abundantly in shade than in bright light, indeed long exposure to the direct sun may destroy the fungus. For this reason, the trellising of vines reduces the development of the disease (25).

Under identical conditions the different *V. vinifera* grape varieties differ greatly in their susceptibility to oidium. In the western Cape the varieties Steen/Chenin blanc, Sauvignon blanc, Furmint, Cabernet Sauvignon and Cabernet franc are among the most susceptible varieties.

Sémillon, White greengrape, Clairette, White French/Palomino/Listan, Grenache, Merlot, Pinot noir, etc., are not affected seriously by oidium.

Control

Oidium is most successfully controlled by dusting the green parts of the vine with sulphur. It is well known that sulphur is much more effective against the disease when it is hot than when it is cool (16).

3. Anthracnose

Causal organism

Anthracnose is one of the oldest European grapevine diseases. In 1873 de Barry recognized a fungus as the cause of the disease and described it

under the name *Sphaceloma ampelium*. In 1877 Saccardo gave the disease
its present name *Gloesporium ampelophagum* Sacc. (3, 14, 16).

Symptoms and development of the fungus

The disease is a particular problem early in the season during wet conditions in the higher rainfall areas of the western Cape. On young shoots
and leaves the fungus causes, at first, light-red spots with brown margins,
which later turn brown and black. On young berries they remain circular,
becoming greyish in the centre, the border remaining dark (3, 11, 14, 16,
25).

The fungus hibernates in the diseased tissues in the form of mycelium
on special fruit-bodies called PYCNIDIA, which open during spring and
liberate large numbers of spores which germinate in water (16). The
different *V. vinifera* grape varieties differ considerably in their susceptibility to anthracnose.

Very susceptible are Sultana, Hanepoot/Muscat d'Alexandrie, White
French/Palomino/Listan, Grenache, Alicant Bouschet, etc. (16).

Control

For control of anthracnose the vines are sprayed during the dormant
season with lime-sulphur solution diluted 1 to 8 parts in water.

During the growing season Winkler (25) recommends spraying the
vines five times with 4–4–100 Bordeaux mixture: (1) when the shoots
are 14–20 cm long; (2) just before blooming; (3) immediately after
blooming; (4) seven to ten days later; and (5) when the berries are about
half grown.

4. Dead arm

Causal organism

The geographical origin of the disease is uncertain. It is possible that
it was always present in Eastern Europe but its symptoms were confused
with those of anthracnose. The English name of the disease derives from
the effect of the killing of spurs and arms (3, 16, 24).

Dead arm is caused by the fungus *Phomopsis viticola* Sacc.

Symptoms and development of the fungus

On the lower part of the shoots small dark-brown spots with black
centres develop. Often many of these spots run together and form
irregular black crusty areas that crack. The many black spots on the
diseased tissues are the spore-producing bodies called pycnidia. When
wet, the pycnidia release great numbers of spores that are dispersed by
rain or wind. Infection takes place only while the green parts of the vine
are wet (25).

Control

Early pruning is recommended. Pruning wood should be burned. Spraying with captan when the shoots are about 2–3 cm has been an effective control measure (25).

FUNGI ATTACKING THE FRUIT

1. Botrytis (grey-mould) rot

Causal organism

According to its degree of development and the variety of grapes, *Sclerotinia fuckeliana* Fuckel/*Botrytis cinerea* Pers. can cause grey or noble rot (3, 11, 14, 16, 23, 24).

Symptoms and development of the fungus

If it rains when the grapes begin to ripen or are already ripe, the fungus causes the grapes to rot. The berries then become soft, they rot, and we see a grey powder on them. Areas of skin that slip freely from the grapes characterize early stages of Botrytis rot. The grey powder on the berries consists of the oval conidia of the fungus. They are formed on conidiophores that are branched like the grape bunch. The conidia can be transported to sound berries by wind and insects. Although infection will take place in an atmosphere of very high humidity, berries with free moisture on the surface, or cracked berries (from oidium), are most conducive to infection. On germination of the conidia the mycelium enters the berry through a split or through the lenticels on the berry or through the soft skin of the ripe berry (3, 14, 16, 25). The disease will end as soon as dry weather sets in and the grapes can get properly dry.

Under moderately warm weather conditions with a fair amount of moisture in the air, grapegrowers purposely leave the grapes of the varieties W. Riesling, Sauvignon blanc, Sémillon, Furmint and Hárslevelü on

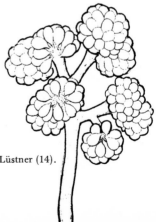

Fig. 12.8. Conidiophores of *Botrytis cinerea.* From Lüstner (14).

the vines till fairly late in order to develop the NOBLE ROT (in German *Edelfäule,* in French *pourriture noble*). The fungus causes little cracks in the skin of the ripe berry through which a good deal of water evaporates, thus gradually converting the berry into a sort of noble-rot raisin. This is *not* a dry raisin, but a kind of moist raisin which is covered with the characteristic grey powder, the conidia of *Botrytis cinerea.* Such bunches are gathered one by one, producing a thick, brown must containing 35–40 per cent sugar, with low acid and low nitrogen content. Such musts produce the delicious and highly aromatic wines of the Rhine, Moselle, Sauternes and Tokaj.

TABLE 12.1
Change in the chemical composition of the berry under the influence of *Botrytis cinerea* developing noble rot. From Kádár (13).

Date and rate of development of the fungus	weight of 1 000 berries (grams)	sugar (grams)	acidity (grams)	ashes (grams)
17.9 healthy berries	1 444,3	266,3	13,7	6,8
5.10 healthy berries	1 634,8	276,4	13,3	9,4
12.10 moist Botrytis berries	1 259,2	234,6	11,9	7,5
22.10 shrivelled Botrytis berries	1 045,2	186,7	6,2	5,6

Control
The best remedy is to remove a number of leaves from the inside of the vine as soon as one notices that rotting has begun. This will expose the grapes directly to the rays of the sun. For the chemical control of botrytis see Table 12.2.

2. Black rot

Causal organism
It is principally due to this disease that *V. vinifera* grape varieties are seldom grown in the United States of America east of the Rocky Mountains. In Europe it is particularly dreaded in the Gironde. Black rot occurs in Natal and the eastern Cape, but is unknown in the viticultural areas of the western Cape (16). Viala and Ravaz studied this disease and gave the fungus causing the disease its present name *Guignardia bidwelli* Viala et Ravaz in 1892 (3, 16).

Symptoms and development of the fungus
Black rot principally attacks the grapes. The berries are usually attacked when they are almost turning colour. From a small round spot the whole berry can develop a reddish-brown colour within 24–48 hours. After

fungus diseases	dormancy	budding	gm/ 100 l	pre-bloom	gm/ 100 l
dead-arm (Anthracnose)	lime-sulphur diluted 1 to 8 parts in water	'Folpet'	200	'Folpet'	200
powdery mildew (Oidium)				'Bayleton' 5% w.p. or vine-sulphur dust 20 to 30 kg/ha	125
downy mildew (Peronospora)				'Antracol' 70 % w.p. or 'Mancozeb' ('Diathane' M–45) or 'Pomuran' or 'Basfungin' or 'Polyram-Combi' 'Folpet'	200 200 250 200 200
grey mould-rot (Botrytis)					

TABLE 12.2
Chemical control of the most common fungoid diseases of the vine.

three to four days the infected berries are dry and pitch black. The skins remain intact. Later the berries drop. A severe attack can destroy practically the whole crop (14, 16). The black pustules on the berries and shoots consist of pycnidia and spermogonia, in which conidia are formed. Under favourable conditions the conidia germinate. In autumn we find also sclerotia, which are formed out of the mycelium and empty pycnidia. During the following spring they develop conidiophores on which conidia are formed (14, 16, 23).

blooming	gm/ 100 l	berry-set and berry growth	gm/ 100 l	véraison gm/ 100 l
		'Bayleton' 5% w.p.	125	'Bayleton'
		or 'Benomil' ('Benlate')	50	5% w.p. 125
		or vine-sulphur dust 20 to 30 kg/ha		
ntracol' 70% w.p.	200	'Pomuran'	250	'Pomuran' 250
Mancozeb' ('Diathane' M–45)	200	or 'Antracol' 70% w.p.	200	'Cupravit'
olyram-Combi'	200	or 'Cupravit' 85% w.p.	500	85% w.p. 500
'Pomuran'	250	or 'Mancozeb'('Diathane' M–45)	200	'Bordeaux-
olpet'	200			mixture' 400
				to
				500
asfungin'	200	'Basfungin'	200	'Basfungin' 200
onilan'	100	'Ronilan'	100	'Ronilan' 100

Fig. 12.9. Berry infected and destroyed by black rot.
From Lüstner (14).

FUNGI ATTACKING THE ROOT OF THE VINE

1. Dematophora root rot

Causal organism

This disease can develop wherever the soil is too wet, especially when there is stagnant water in the subsoil. The disease is caused by the fungus *Dematophora necatrix* Hart., as it was called by R. Hartig, who first studied it, and is now known as *Rosellinia necatrix* (Hart.) Berl. Under favourable conditions the fungus attacks large and small roots (16, 25).

Symptoms and development of the fungus

The mycelium that develops on the surface of affected roots is at first white and cobwebby, later turning black. During wet weather a delicate, pure-white mould growth may be seen on the surface of the bark and in the soil around the base of the vine (25). The mycelium propagates the fungus and spreads it in the soil. The fungus can be both a parasite and a saprophyte. It shows its fructifications only when acting as a saprophyte on dead parts of the vine (25). (The word saprophyte is derived from the Greek words *sapros,* rotten, and *phyton,* plant.)

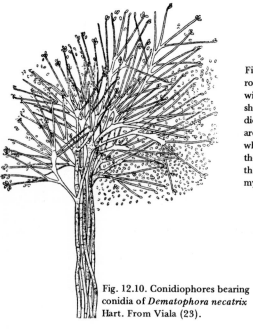

Fig. 12.11. Fragment of a dead root of a vine severely infected with *Dematophora necatrix* showing sclerotia bearing conidiophores. The conidiophores are inserted into the sclerotia, which are produced always by the internal mycelium, never by the white cobwebby external mycelium. From Viala (23).

Fig. 12.10. Conidiophores bearing conidia of *Dematophora necatrix* Hart. From Viala (23).

Control

The most effective control of dematophora root rot is removal of the conditions favouring this disease, i.e. energetic drainage of the soil (16, 25).

2. Collar rot (stem girdling)

Causal organism and symptoms

Young vines are occasionally attacked in the spring by a species of *Pythium* that causes a wet, sour-smelling lesion on the stem just below the surface of the soil. Under cool, wet conditions, the lesion enlarges rapidly and may destroy the phloem and the cambium layers girdling the vine. Completely girdled young vines suddenly wilt and die in late spring. Old vines are seldom affected (25).

FUNGI ATTACKING THE WOOD OF THE VINE

1. Black measles

This disease is known by various names such as *apoplexy* in France, *esca* in Spain, *iska* in Greece, etc. It has existed since ancient times in Europe and in Asia (3).

Causal organism

According to Winkler et al. (25), Chiarippa found (1959) that the soft, spongy decay of the wood of older vines seemed to be caused by *Fomes igniarius* (L. ex Fr.), one of the most destructive of wood-rotting fungi.

Various fungi were found in the decayed wood of affected vines in France and it is possible that fungi such as *Stereum necator* Viala, *Polyporus versicolor* (L.) Fr., *Stereum hirsutum* (Wild) Pers., etc., may coexist on the same vine (3).

Symptoms

Leaf symptoms vary; sometimes there are small chlorotic areas between the main nerves, which enlarge and become necrotic. In red grape varieties the interveinal necrotic areas have a dark margin. Symptoms on the berries consist of dark purple spots on the surface. There is no correlation between symptoms on leaves and those on the fruit (25).

A longitudinal cut through the trunk reveals a continuous brown band which contrasts sharply with the light colour of the healthy tissues of the wood. The infected wood is spongy and decayed. The brown band is always connected with a large wound on the trunk, stopping at the joint in the case of grafted vines. Ungrafted vines may show symptoms down to their roots.

Black measles is most prevalent amongst the older vines (15 years and older). The frequency as well as the severity of the disease increases with the age of the vines (3, 16, 23, 25).

Control

The treatment for black measles is to spray the trunk and the arms of affected vines, after they have been winter-pruned, with a solution of 3 litres of prepared sodium arsenite solution to 450 litres of water. Special care should be taken to wet all old wounds thoroughly (25).

VIRUS DISEASES OF THE VINE

About virology and the virus and virus-like diseases of the vine, more is written in English than in all the other languages together. For this reason virus and virus-like diseases will not be discussed in this book. The reader is referred to the work of Winkler et al. (25) and the extensive bibliography which it provides.

BACTERIAL DISEASES AND DISEASES OF DISPUTED ORIGIN

1. Crown gall

Causal organism and symptoms

Tumours or galls formed on the trunk and arms of the vines are caused by the organism *Agrobacterium tumefaciens* (S. and T) Conn., which is ever present in the soil (3, 25). The infection enters the tissues through injuries or wounds. Rains splash soil laden with the bacteria into these

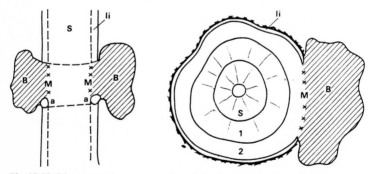

Fig. 12.12. Diagrammatic representation of the damage caused by *Ph. tumefaciens* on the trunk of the vine. From Branas (3).

Abbreviations: li — phloem; S — xylem; B — desiccation of the tumour, which makes an incision in the phloem, interrupting the transport of plant nutrients through the phloem at M, which brings about the death of the xylem (S), while the bacteria remain alive at (a).

wounds. Bacteria may also be washed into wounds from other galls. Infection usually occurs only during the winter. Gall development becomes apparent in the wounds when growth begins in the spring. When young, the galls are soft and greenish in colour. As they age, the tissue darkens to brown, and the surface of the gall becomes very rough (3, 25).

Control

Avoid cutting into the galls with pruning-tools. Surgical treatment of the trunk removing affected parts is required. Most of the galls disappear after several years if left alone (25).

2. Bacterial blight

Causal organism and symptoms

The *mal nero* of Italy and *la maladie d'Oleron* of France seem to be the same as the 'bacterial blight' ('vlamsiekte') of South Africa. Du Plessis (7) reported on the causative organism of the disease, classifying the bacterium as *Erwinia vitivora* (Bacc.) Du P. Because none of the research workers who continued the work of Du Plessis could achieve artificial infection, the existence of such a 'bacterium' was doubted, especially in the U.S.A. Their assertions were confirmed by the fact that Dowson (6) identified a culture of *Erwinia vitivora* from South Africa as *Erwinia lathyri*, a general saprophyte of the vine. Panagopulus isolated in 1939 the bacterium *Xanthomonas ampelina* and used it successfully for artificial inoculations. His method was recently used in South Africa; inoculations with *Xanthomonas ampelina* culture were successful and 'bacterial blight' symptoms were easily reproduced (15).

The disease attacks leaves, bunches and shoots. Infection usually occurs on the lower two to three nodes and spreads slowly upwards. On infected shoots more or less lens-shaped, small, yellowish green spots develop. The spots soon become greyish black. Very young shoots may be killed before they are more than 10 cm long (7, 15). The importance of the disease varies with the susceptibility of the variety. Most American *Vitis* species are believed to be resistant. Among varieties regarded to be very susceptible to the disease are Sultanina, Muscat d'Alexandrie/Hanepoot, White French/Palomino/Listan, Alicante Bouschet, Dattier/Waltham Cross, and Queen of the Vineyards (25).

Control

As a result of the outbreak of downy mildew in South Africa in 1968, copper compounds are used regularly early in the growing season to control this disease. This may lead to the complete disappearance of 'bacterial blight' alias 'vlamsiekte' (15).

3. Flavescence dorée

Causal organism

The disease appeared in Armagnac for the first time in 1949 on Baco 22 A. Since 1951 it has been known as *flavescence dorée, maladie de Chardonnay,* and was reported from the Chablis and Burgundy, as well as from Germany, Switzerland, Rumania, Israel, Chile and Italy (3, 8).

The disease was studied by Caudwell, who found the cicadelle *Scaphoideus littoralis* Ball., to be the responsible aerial vector which transfers flavescence dorée (3, 8).

Recent investigations by Giannotti, Vago, Caudwell and Duthoit, quoted by Galet (8), have shown that flavescence dorée is caused by a form of mycoplasm, type L, which causes necrosis in the phloem, interrupting it in its function.

Various other factors, such as suffocation of the roots, defective structure of the soil (the disease can assume epidemic proportions on badly aerated, heavy clay soils), are also being considered as possible causes of flavescence dorée (3).

Symptoms

The first symptoms of flavescence dorée generally appear after blooming and are characterized by a bright, irregular, golden-yellow coloration of the young leaves. The flower clusters dry up. Later the leaves become rigid and breakable with downward-rolling leaf margins. Above the nodes and at the base of the petioles, small necrotic depressions can be observed.

During the second cycle of the disease, budding is retarded and becomes irregular. Growth is very poor, diseased vines do not ripen their canes, and they retain their leaves until early winter. The shoots remain green, soft and bent downwards, resembling a weeping-willow tree. Hence the French name *port pleureur,* literally 'weeping growth-habit'. Affected vines usually perish during the following winter (3, 8).

Anatomically, flavescence dorée is characterized by the total absence of secondary phloem fibres and by the very poor development of the xylem in affected canes (8).

Control

Flavescence dorée is a very serious disease of the vine. To date no preventive or curative methods are known (3, 8).

NONPARASITIC DISORDER

1. Apoplexy or stroke

Symptoms

As the name suggests, the symptoms of this phenomenon appear suddenly. The leaves at the end of a shoot wilt suddenly. Within a few days such shoots and the whole vine may be dead.

Perold (16) emphasized that there is a totally different disease also called apoplexy in France, which Viala named *maladie de l'esca,* and which is caused by a fungus, *Stereum necator.*

'The disease is caused through the vine evaporating more water than is taken up in the same time from the soil. Thus it occurs when dry hot weather suddenly follows upon a cool, rainy, early summer. It is of most common occurrence where the subsoil is wet. It is always only a few vigorous vines that are affected here and there in the vineyard. What has thus far been described is a kind of apoplexy also known as *folletage* in France.'

The words of the late Professor A. I. Perold (16) are cited because his description of the symptoms of this phenomenon coincide closely with the symptoms of the sudden death of vines grafted on 99 R or ungrafted 99 R rootstocks, occurring at present mainly in the coastal region of the western Cape. The fungus *Phytophtora cinnamoni* has recently been considered to be the causal organism of the phenomenon in South Africa. 'This soil-borne fungus forms different spore types of which the sporangium stage is the most important for infection. Water is required for the production of sporangia, as well as the liberation, movement and spread of the zoospores which mainly infect the finer roots, just behind the root tip' (22).

Although the fungus was isolated from the crown and roots of affected vines, the following observations seem to indicate that *Phytophtora c.* might not be the primary cause of the sudden death of young, vigorous 99 R vines:

(a) Dormant vines are so insensitive to water in their root-zone, that in some viticultural regions of the world ungrafted vines are submerged in water during the winter for up to three months in order to kill the phylloxera on their roots.

(b) In the winter rainfall area of the western Cape it is only during the winter months (May–September) that stagnant water might be present in the root-zone of vines. The sudden death of unirrigated, young, vigorous vines is, however, often observed during January or February, i.e. during the hottest and driest period of their first growing season. The root-tips of these vines could not have been infected by the zoospores of the fungus during the winter months, because they had only been planted at this time of the year, thus did not have any roots at all. It would also be difficult to believe that a fungus could suddenly kill a vine which did not show any symptoms of a disease at all, and that it would select the most vigorous vines in a vineyard to 'kill'.

(c) The sudden death of young *V. vinifera* grape varieties grafted mainly on 99 R occur mostly on well-drained, dry slopes, the subsoil of which has never been too wet. This phenomenon was always limited to a few vines here and there in a vineyard. It has never occurred in patches in the past.

(d) In recent years, however, some 'virus-tested' clones of 99 R were supplied to nurserymen by an official scheme for the establishment of rootstock mother plantations. Some of these vines died on an unprecedentedly large scale even on well-drained alluvial soils, where no vines have previously been planted. Rootstock varieties genetically closely related to 99 R (110 R, 101-14 Mgt, Metallica) performed normally alongside the dying 'virus-tested' 99 R. This should have been a clear indication that the material itself, and not the fungus *Phytophtora c.* must have been responsible for the poor performance of this particular 99 R. Plant pathologists, however, discovered *Phytophtora c.* in the water of irrigation dams in the area, as well as in the soil of the nursery of the central propagation scheme, from where the rooted 99 R vines were supplied. And so, a new 'deadly danger' for the South African nursery industry, *Phytophtora c.,* was born. This fungus is not even mentioned as a possible vine-parasite in the book of Professor J. Branas (3), the most up to date and one of the most elaborate works ever written on viticulture.

While the author does not wish to dispute the possibility that *Phytophtora c.* might be one of the factors contributing to the death of young vines which live under unfavourable conditions ('wet-feet', compaction of the soil, overcropping, drought conditions during a heatwave, etc.), he refuses to believe that this fungus could play such a destructive role in viticulture as it plays in the culture of avocados and proteas.

CHAPTER 13

General Ampelography

The first concern in the description and identification of a variety is its proper name. Most varieties are known under different names in the various countries where they are being cultivated. We should describe a French variety under its French name, a German under its German name and so on, adding to each, as synonyms, all other names under which the particular variety is grown elsewhere. It is of the greatest importance that there should be no confusion of true varietal names.

The word ampelography is derived from the Greek words *ampelos,* vine, and *graphein,* to write, describe; it is the science concerned with the study and description of the various species of *Vitis,* as well as the cultivated varieties and hybrids of such species (7, 8, 9).

The first descriptive notes of cultivated *V. vinifera* grape varieties are found in the works of Roman writers, *Naturalis historiae* by Pliny, and *De re rustica* by Columella (7). The foundation that led to the nomenclature, classification, and systematic description of *Vitis* species was laid only during the second half of the nineteenth century. H. Goethe's *Ampelographisches Wörterbuch* appeared in 1876 and in 1874 Pulliat classified the principal *V. vinifera* grape varieties in five groups according to the order in which they ripen in comparison with the Chasselas.

According to Németh (7), it was Ravaz who first showed how one can express the most important ampelographic characteristics of the leaf by means of numbers obtained by ampelometric measurements. Galet (4) completed and simplified Ravaz's ampelometry. The voluminous works of Molon (6), Dalmasso (3), Viala and Vermorel (9), Németh (7) and the Soviet ampelography (2) must be regarded as the standard studies in modern ampelography.

From the preceding it is evident that there are no comparable complete works on ampelography in English. Consequently, only in English-speaking grapegrowing countries are the names of the most noble *V. vinifera* grape varieties used (or rather, misused) for second-grade 'cultivars', which they do not even resemble.

1. The tip of the growing shoot

The growing tip, which includes the apical meristem of the developing shoot, like any other organ of the vine, can be *glabrous, cobwebby, downy, woolly* and *felt-like, pubescent* or covered with *brush-like* hairs.

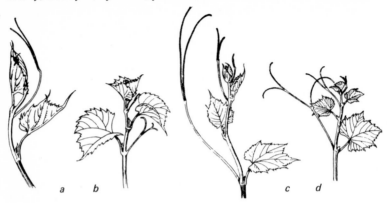

Fig. 13.1. The four main shapes of the growing tip. From Németh (7). (a) *V. riparia* type: the growing tip is completely enclosed by the unfolding small leaves; (b) *V. rupestris* type: the growing tip is very small, triangular, flattened and half-enclosed by the unfolding small leaves; (c) *V. berlandieri* rupestris-riparia type: an intermediate type, and (d) *V. vinifera* type: an 'open type' because the growing tip is not enclosed by the unfolding small leaves.

2. The young leaves

The colour of the developing young leaves provides a very good ampelographic characteristic for the identification of a variety, because it often differs from the colour of the fully grown leaves of the same variety. It can be green in its various shades, yellowish, red, rose, bronze-coloured, etc. Young leaves are usually more pubescent and deeper lobed than fully grown leaves.

3. The fully grown leaves

Once the leaf is fully grown its form remains constant and each variety can be recognised by the characteristics of the leaf alone. Because the shape of the lowest, middle, and uppermost leaves on the same shoot can differ markedly, only the sixth to tenth leaves from the base of the shoot are used for descriptive purposes.

(i) Size of the leaf

There are noticeable differences in the sizes of the leaves of various species of *Vitis* and its various varieties. Galet (4, 5) classifies the possible variations in the size of the leaves as follows:

Class 0: very small leaves, surface less than 50 sq. centimetres (*V. embergeri, V. flexuosa, V. rubra,* etc.).

Class 1: small leaves, surface less than 100 sq. centimetres (*V. rupestris*).

Class 9: very large leaves, surface more than 450 sq. centimetres (*V. coignetiae,* some varieties of *V. vinifera* and *V. riparia*).

Fig. 13.2. The five main types of leaf forms: b, d and e from Galet (5).

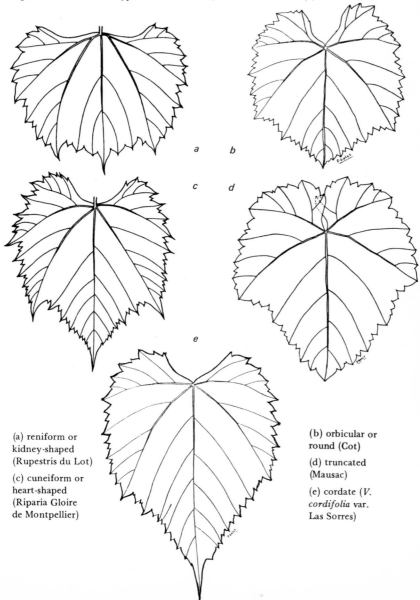

(a) reniform or
kidney-shaped
(Rupestris du Lot)

(c) cuneiform or
heart-shaped
(Riparia Gloire
de Montpellier)

(b) orbicular or
round (Cot)

(d) truncated
(Mausac)

(e) cordate (*V.
cordifolia* var.
Las Sorres)

(ii) Shape of the leaves

As well as the five main types of leaf forms shown in Fig. 13.2, there are intermediate forms, such as orbiculo-reniform, cuneo-truncated etc.

(iii) Lobing of the leaves

The general leaf form is in no way affected by the fact that some of them are entire, whereas others are more or less deeply cut up into 3, 5 or even 7 lobes by LATERAL SINUSES.

(iv) Shape of the petiolar sinus

The petiolar sinus is formed and bordered by the petiolar lobes. Great ampelographic value is attached to its shape. It can be open, closed, partly open, overlapped, lyre-shaped, U-shaped, V-shaped etc.

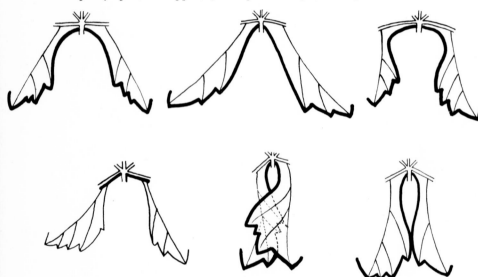

Fig. 13.3. Some frequently occurring variations in the shape of the petiolar sinus. From Németh (7).

(v) Ampelographic measurements of the leaf

Galet (4, 5) worked out a simple open scale by which the most important ampelographic measurements of the leaf (Fig. 13.4) can be indicated by groups of code numbers as follows:

(a) The ratio of the length of each of the nerves L 2, L 3 and L 4, to the length of L 1, each indicated on a scale from 0 to 9.

(b) The ratio of the maximum length to the maximum breadth of the

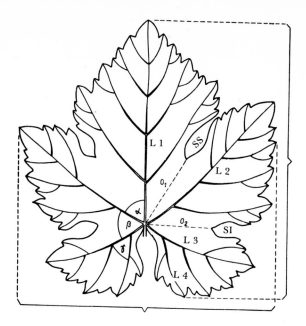

Fig. 13.4. Ampelographic characteristics to be measured. From Németh (7).

leaf, indicated on a scale from 0 to 6.

(c) The sum of the angles alpha, beta, gamma between the main nerves, each indicated by one code number on a scale from 0 to 9.

(d) The depths of the lateral sinuses: SI and SS (dotted line)

(vi) Surface of the leaves

This can be glossy or dull, even or uneven. If the unevenness affects the parenchyma between the last branchings of the veins (nerves) the leaf is BULLATE; if the unevenness measures one cm or more in diameter, the leaf is CRINKLED (*gaufrée*); if the unevenness occurs between the principal nerves parallel to their direction, the leaf is UNDULATING.

Like the tip of the growing shoot, leaves can be GLABROUS or PUBESCENT in varying degrees.

(vii) Dentition of the leaves

Dentition can be even or uneven. The TEETH can be pointed or rounded off. Their form varies with different species and varieties, ANGULAR, CONCAVE and CONVEX (ogivale) being the most commonly occurring forms.

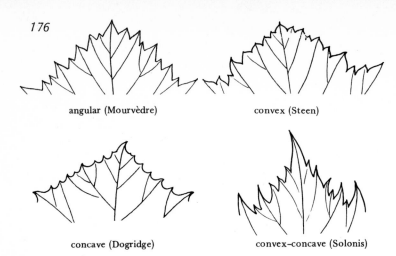

angular (Mourvèdre) convex (Steen)

concave (Dogridge) convex–concave (Solonis)

Fig. 13.5. Variations in the sizes and forms of dentition of the leaves.

4. Shoots (canes when mature)

(a) The growth-habit of vines can be indicated as UPRIGHT (Carignan, Grenache, Rupestris du Lot, etc.); SEMI-UPRIGHT (99 R, Colombard, etc.); SPREADING (110 R, Chenin bl, Cinsaut, etc.); or CREEPING (Riparia gloire etc.).

(b) The length of the internodes depends to some extent on the progress of vine growth. Vines grown in fertile soil well supplied with water will always have longer internodes. There are, however, also genetically based differences between the various species and varieties of *Vitis*. Some varieties, for example Rupestris du Lot, Carignan, Grenache, have short internodes, although all of them are very vigorous growers. The varieties of *V. riparia* characterized by poor growth have thin canes with long internodes (4, 5, 9).

(c) The surface of the shoots and canes can be SMOOTH, ANGULAR or RIBBED. It can be glabrous or pubescent. Glabrous canes are often pubescent at their nodes.

(d) The size and shape of the dormant buds are of great ampelographic value in identifying rootstocks. All pure Americo–American hybrids have small buds, while those of *Vinifera* × American hybrids have distinctly larger buds.

5. The bunch

The size, form and compactness of the bunch are specific for a variety, although there are sometimes marked variations owing to the emergence of sub-varieties and environmental conditions. Classification of the bunches according to their sizes by Galet (4, 5) is as follows (page 178):

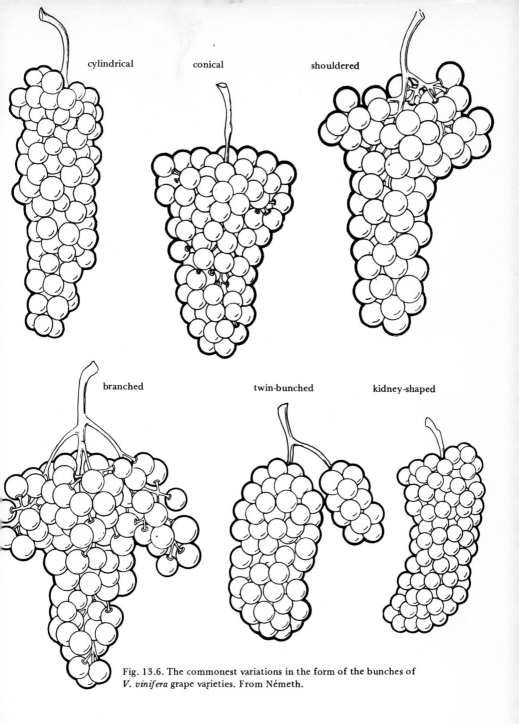

cylindrical

conical

shouldered

branched

twin-bunched

kidney-shaped

Fig. 13.6. The commonest variations in the form of the bunches of
V. vinifera grape varieties. From Németh.

very small	length less than	6 cm
small		6–12 cm
medium		12–18 cm
large		18–24 cm
very large		more than 24 cm

The commonest variations in the form of the bunches of *V. vinifera* grape varieties are shown in Fig. 13.6.

6. The berry

Galet (5) classifies berries according to their diameter and the weight of 100 berries as follows:

Classification	Size	Weight of 100 berries
very small	less than 8 mm	less than 35 g
small	8–12 mm	35–110 g
medium	12–18 mm	110–330 g
large	18–24 mm	330–700 g
very large	more than 24 mm	more than 700 g

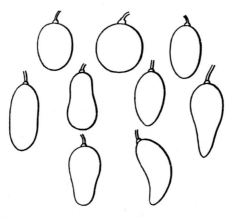

Fig. 13.7. The commonest variations in the shape of grape of *V. vinifera* grape varieties. From Bábó & Mach (1).

The size and form of the grape seed varies considerably in the various species and varieties of *Vitis*. The differences can best be expressed by indicating the relation between the weight of 100 or 1 000 berries and the weight of the seed in them. It is about 15 per cent in *V. vinifera* and up to 80 per cent in *V. berlandieri* (5).

The physical composition of ripe grapes is not only important from the ampelographic point of view, but also from the economic point of view. For the South African grower and wine-maker the most valuable information is given in the table below, abridged from Perold (8):

Kind of determination	Cabernet Sauvignon	Riesling*	White French	Steen	White Green-grape	Hermi-tage
Weight of bunch in grams	157,8	212,2	512,3	212,0	270,5	342,3
Average weight per stalk in grams	5,02	8,20	15,31	6,52	7,30	6,75
Average number of berries per bunch	113	153	228	141	103	96
Ratio of bunch : stalk	28,1	25,5	32,5	32,4	37,0	56,0
Ratio of berry : seeds	24,0	26,2	36,1	24,2	36,6	59,0
Percentage of weight of berries in bunch	96,44	96,00	96,91	90,92	97,30	98,03
Percentage of weight of stalk in bunch	3,56	3,91	3,09	3,08	2,70	1,97
Percentage of weight of seeds in berries	4,01	3,81	2,31	4,09	2,71	1,70

*The 'Riesling' referred to is not Riesling proper but the inferior unknown variety cultivated in South Africa under that name.

CHAPTER 14

Special Ampelography

PURE AMERICAN VITIS SPECIES AND VARIETIES

There are about 21 species of the genus *Vitis* which are indigenous to North America. Because of their inherent resistance to phylloxera, the grape root louse that is native to the Mississippi Valley, some of these American *Vitis* species were used as parent plants for interspecific hybridization in the creation of phylloxera-resistant rootstocks. Of much the greatest importance are *V. riparia, V. rupestris* and *V. berlandieri* (1, 3, 8, 14, 15, 16).

1. Vitis riparia Michaux

Synonyms. — *V. vulpina* var. riparia RGL, *V. missouriensis* PR, *V. illionensis* V., Riverside grape, etc. (4, 10).

Varieties. — Riparia Gloire de Montpellier, Riparia tomenteuse, Riparia glabre, etc. Ravaz (14) described 42 varieties of *V. riparia*.

Description

Tip of the growing shoot is enclosed by the unfolding small leaves.

Leaves large, cuneiform, 246-4-24 (4), slightly trilobed, dull light green, very thin, undulate, nerves pubescent below; petiolar sinus widely open; teeth convex–concave, sharply pointed; at the ends of L 1 and L 2 nerves are strikingly long and hooked, which is very typical for the species, called 'riparia teeth'.

Shoots thin, with long internodes, smooth and glabrous.

Geographical distribution. — *V. riparia* has been discovered in parts of Canada north of Quebec and southward to the Gulf of Mexico. It is the most widely distributed of any American *Vitis* species.

Cultural characteristics. — In its natural habitat it grows usually on river banks and on islands in deep, moist, fertile river soils. For reconstituting the French and the central and south-eastern European vineyards on phylloxera-resistant rootstocks, varieties of *V. riparia,* especially Riparia Gloire de Montpellier, were used very extensively. It is highly resistant to phylloxera, 18, and responds best in a temperate climate, provided that the soil does not contain more than 10 per cent lime (6, 10, 14). Riparia cuttings root and graft easily. In poor soils it gives grafted vines with thin stem, because the riparia stem remains thinner than that of the vinifera vine grafted on it (10).

2. Vitis rupestris Scheele

Synonyms. — Rock grape, Mountain grape etc.

Varieties. — Rupestris du Lot, Rupestris Ganzin, Rupestris Martin, Rupestris métallique, Rupestris Metallica, etc.

Description. — See Rupestris du Lot.

Geographical distribution and cultural characteristics. — *V. rupestris* is indigenous to south-western Texas, extending eastward and westward. Its name, derived from the Latin word *rupes*, stone, indicates its common occurrence in stony soils in its natural state. This species is highly resistant to phylloxera, 16–18, although its rootlets show numerous nodosities. *V. rupestris* is sensitive to lime and soon perishes in soils that are too wet or too dry (3, 10, 14). Ungrafted varieties of *V. rupestris,* as well as some of its hybrids, frequently show an alarming number of dark brown spots on the leaves, so abundant in some cases as to cause their early dropping. This phenomenon is due to the MELANOSE caused by the fungus *Septoria ampelina* Berk u. Curt. This disease of rootstocks should alarm no one; as soon as the vines are grafted, the symptoms will disappear, as the disease does not live on *V. vinifera* grape varieties (6).

3. Vitis berlandieri Planchon

Synonyms. — Mountain grape.

Varieties. — Berlandieri Rességuier Nos. 1 and 2, Berlandieri Las Sorres, Berlandieri Lafont, etc.

Description

Tip of the growing shoot white — woolly.

Leaves medium, cuneiform, slightly trilobed, cobwebby pubescence below; petiolar sinus lyre-shaped, narrow; *teeth* broad but shallow, convex.

Shoots long, thin, green to reddish-violet, ribbed, pubescent with short internodes and thick diaphragms (4, 10).

Geographical distribution. — *V. berlandieri* is a native of the limestone hills of south-west Texas (3, 6, 10). Planchon described this species in 1880, naming it after the Swiss botanist Berlandier, who discovered it in Texas between 1834 and 1836 and brought it to Europe in his herbarium (4, 10).

Cultural characteristics. — *V. berlandieri* is a vine for the hot climate. Its wood ripens only in hot regions. The greatest drawback of *V. berlandieri* is that its cuttings strike roots only with great difficulty. For this reason, only its hybrids with easily rooting species such as *V. riparia* and *V. rupestris* can be used as rootstocks. They belong to the best rootstocks available in viticulture. *V. berlandieri* is most highly resistant to lime in the soil, and its thick, fleshy roots are highly resistant to phylloxera. Vines grafted on berlandieri hybrids grow much more underground than above ground during the first years. After about 5–7 years they are equal to the other rootstocks, and the grafted vines bear well and ripen their grapes well (3, 4, 6, 10).

GLEN INNES PUBLIC LIBRARY

TABLE 14.1.
Genetical origin ('family tree') of the most widely cultivated rootstocks

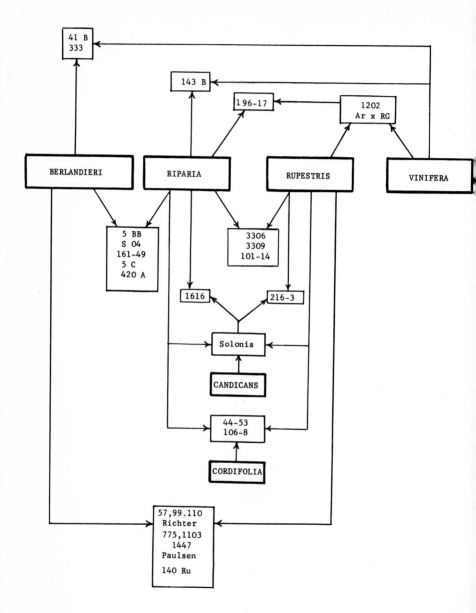

PHYLLOXERA-RESISTANT ROOTSTOCKS

1. Rupestris du Lot

Synonyms. — Rupestris Saint George, Rupestris monticola, Rupestris Sijas, Lot, etc.

Origin. — Variety of *V. rupestris.*

Description

Tip of the growing shoot small, flattened, half-enclosed by the developing little leaves.

Young leaves brilliant, copper-coloured, glabrous.

Leaves small, reniform, 025-1-00 (4), entire, glabrous, dull, fatty, somewhat bluish-green, veins violet-red near the point where the leaf is attached to the petiole; petiolar sinus strikingly wide open, shallow; *teeth* convex, quite large.

Male plant.

Shoots dark carmine-red, glabrous, cobwebby pubescence near the growing point; *canes* reddish-brown, angular with short internodes; *buds* very small, pointed.

Growth habit strikingly erect, canes with numerous and very vigorous secondary and tertiary ramifications.

Geographical distribution. — In the Mediterranean countries most vine-yards were reconstituted on Rupestris du Lot. It is still the second most important rootstock in France (2, 5), but is being increasingly replaced by 110 R, 99 R, 1103 P, 140 Ru, SO 4, 161–49, etc. Vines grafted on these rootstocks bear better, ripen their grapes better and are less sensitive to drought and to wet-feet than vines grafted on Rupestris du Lot (2, 3, 8).

BERLANDIERI X RUPESTRIS GROUP OF ROOTSTOCKS

2. 99 Richter

Origin. — Berlandieri Las Sorres X Rupestris du Lot, obtained by Franz Richter in 1889.

Description

Tip of the growing shoot flattened, bronze-coloured, cobwebby.

Young leaves shiny, dark violet-red, cobwebby below.

Leaves small, reniform, 136-2-12 (4), entire, even, dull light bluish-green, thick, slightly pubescent below; petiolar sinus wide open, resembling Rupestris du Lot, its father; *teeth* convex, medium-sized.

Flowers hermaphrodites, unisexual male by abortion. No fruit is borne.

Shoots dark violet-red, shaded darker and pubescent at the nodes, ribbed; semi-upright in growth; *canes* light brown with fairly long internodes and vigorous secondary ramifications; wood hard with small pith (11); dormant *buds* small, pointed.

Geographical distribution. —99 R was the most widely cultivated berlandieri X rupestris hybrid in France, Spain and Morocco, but it is being replaced by 110 R, SO 4, 1103 P and 140 Ru. These latter rootstock varieties are not as sensitive to wet-feet, resist drought better and perform better on shallow, clay soils than 99 R (2, 4, 5, 8).

According to Winkler (16), 99 R performed better in California than

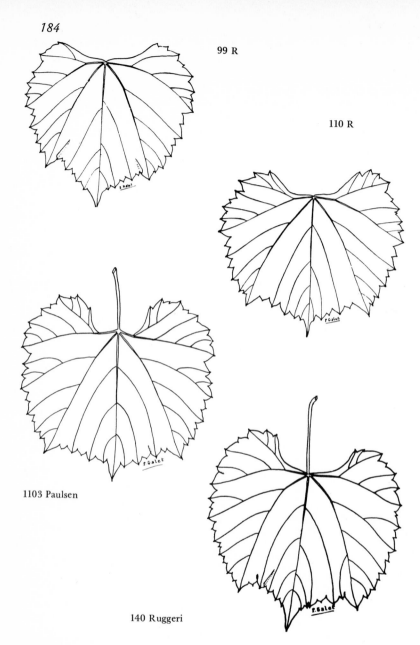

Fig. 14.1. Leaves of the four most important rootstocks of the berlandieri x rupestris group. From Galet (4).

44, 57 and 110 R. However, 'virus-free 99 R' vines, imported to South Africa from the Foundation block at Davis, turned out not to be 99 R at all.

99 R is the third most important rootstock in South Africa.

Cultural characteristics. — 99 R is a very vigorous grower. Its cuttings root and graft very well, and it has an excellent affinity with all *V. vinifera* grape varieties cultivated in South Africa. It is an excellent rootstock for deep, well drained, fertile soils well supplied with water. 99 R is, however, very sensitive to stagnant water in the subsoil and to drought. Without supplementary irrigation, especially on sandy soil, varieties grafted on 99 R do not ripen their grapes properly (3, 4, 8, 13).

It has been observed in South Africa that young 99 R vines, as well as young vines grafted on 99 R, die suddenly, especially when dry, hot weather suddenly follows a cool, rainy summer. This phenomenon is usually limited to a few very vigorous vines here and there in the unirrigated vineyards of the coastal region (13).

3. 110 Richter

Origin. — Berlandieri Rességuier No. 2 X Rupestris Martin, obtained by Franz Richter in 1889.

Description

Tip of the growing shoot flattened, reddish, cobwebby, Berlandieri-type.

Young leaves brilliant, dark copper-coloured, cobwebby.

Leaves small, reniform, 025-1-11 (4), entire, bullate, shiny, dark green, thick, glabrous; petiolar sinus U-shaped, open; *teeth* small, convex, very pointed.

Male plant.

Shoots dark brownish-red, glabrous, semi-erect in growth habit with poorly developed secondary ramifications; *canes* dark brown, ribbed, thick with fairly long internodes; dormant *buds* small, pointed; wood hard with medium-sized pith.

110 R vines defoliate very late (11).

Geographical distribution. — Although 110 R showed its superiority in the field-trials of the École de Montpellier, created by Ravaz (4), it was not propagated on a large scale until after the end of the last war. It became the sixth most important rootstock in France, surpassing 99 R, and it is also one of the most important rootstocks in Spain, Algeria, Greece, and Israel (4, 8).

110 R was imported to South Africa in the early 1930s. However, it was excluded from field-trials laid out on the experimental farms before 1963. It was practically unknown to the growers. The author could not accept the allegations of earlier research workers that the performance of 110 R was inferior to Jacquez (the 'greatest saboteur' of South African viticulture) and to 99 R, because the allegations were not supported by collected data, and were indeed contrary to all experience gained throughout the world with the same three rootstock varieties. Consequently, he

multiplied 110 R, included it in field-trials and recommended its use as a rootstock whenever possible.

Cultural characteristics. – 110 R is a very vigorous grower. Its cuttings root and graft well with all *V. vinifera* grape varieties cultivated in South Africa. Vines grafted on 110 R are vigorous, fertile and ripen their grapes well. It is much less sensitive to drought and to wet-feet than 99 R (4, 8). It is an excellent rootstock in all warm grapegrowing regions, especially for shallow clay soils. It should be used as a rootstock on a much larger scale in South Africa.

During the past fifteen years, some highly placed officials have attempted to encourage the use of the rootstocks Jacquez and 101–14 Mgt by attributing to them cultural characteristics which they did not in fact possess. Simultaneously, the use of 110 R was discouraged by the attribution of bad cultural characteristics. With the exception of Metallica (recommended by the author since 1968), no other rootstock has been attacked to the same extent as 110 R. During the last two or three years, however, the demand for 110 R in the South African nursery industry suddenly increased dramatically, while the demand for Jacquez and 101–14 Mgt not only decreased drastically, but in many areas growers would not even accept them as gifts. This sudden 'discovery' of 110 R is due to the excellent performance of this rootstock in the vineyards of numerous growers who were prepared to test it in comparative field-trials on the recommendation of the author, notwithstanding the continuous negative criticism of various 'experts'.

4. 1103 Paulsen

Origin. – Berlandieri Rességuier No. 2 X Rupestris du Lot, obtained by F. Paulsen in 1895.

Description

Tip of the growing shoot flattened, reddish, cobwebby.

Young leaves shiny, bronze-coloured, glabrous.

Leaves small, reniform, 025-2-23 (4), nearly entire, lateral sinuses 20, slightly bullate, dull green, nerves violet and slightly pubescent below; petiolar sinus U-shaped, open, bordered at its base by nerves L 3; *teeth* convex, fairly broad.

Male plant.

Shoots violet-red on the side exposed to the sun, semi-erect in growth habit with fairly vigorous secondary ramifications; slightly pubescent at the nodes; *canes* chocolate-brown, ribbed, pubescent at the nodes with medium-long internodes; dormant *buds* small, pointed.

Geographical distribution. – Introduced from Sicily, where it is an important rootstock, 1103 P is highly appreciated in Tunisia and Algeria. Since the repatriation of French grapegrowers from Algeria, 1103 P is being planted on an ever-increasing scale in France (5, 8).

Cultural aptitudes. – 1103 P is a vigorous grower, and its cuttings root and graft well. In field-trials at Montpellier its performance was superior to 99 R but inferior to 110 R (4). It does not seem to be superior to 99 R in South Africa. 1103 P adapts better than 99 R to stagnant water in the subsoil, and its tolerance to slightly saline soils has also been reported (4, 8).

5. 140 Ruggeri

Origin. — Berlandieri Rességuier No. 2 X Rupestris du Lot, obtained by Ruggeri.

Description

Tip of the growing shoot Rupestris-type, bronze-coloured, cobwebby.
Young leaves green, brilliant, slightly bronze-tinted.
Leaves below medium, reniform, 015-1-24 (4), entire, finely bullate, dark, shiny green resembling 110 R but finer in texture and L 1 nerve markedly longer, glabrous; petiolar sinus U-shaped, wide open; *teeth* convex with broad base, pointed.
Male plant.
Shoots dark violet at the nodes, semi-erect in growth habit, slightly pubescent; *canes* dark brown, ribbed with medium-long internodes; dormant *buds* small, pointed.

Geographical distribution. — As well as in Sicily, its country of origin, 140 Ru is a highly regarded rootstock in North Africa and is being planted on an increasing scale in France (2, 4, 8).

Cultural characteristics. — 140 Ru is a very vigorous grower and for this reason is not to be recommended for deep, fertile soils. It adapts well on heavy loam and clay soils under very dry conditions. The cuttings of 140 Ru root and graft well and no problem of affinity is reported with *V. vinifera* varieties. Together with 110 R it is probably one of the most promising rootstocks for shallow, heavy soils, where drought and compactness of the soil are problems.

BERLANDIERI X RIPARIA GROUP OF ROOTSTOCKS

Historical

The existence and development of the most important varieties of this group will always be connected with the name of Zsigmond Teleki, a Hungarian viticulturist. In 1896 Teleki went to France and brought 10 kilograms of 'Berlandieri' seed from M. Rességuier for the reconstitution of the vineyards on his estate at Villány. He obtained about 40 000 seedlings from the 10 kilograms of seed and, to his great astonishment and disappointment, the seedlings consisted of a mixture of different varieties. During the years Teleki succeeded in selecting and classifying ten different groups of the material. Three of them were morphologically pure *berlandieri;* six *berlandieri* X *riparia,* and one *riparia* X *rupestris.* After a tremendous work of systematic selection Teleki found two types to be very promising and propagated them under the names 5 A and 5 B.

They proved to be very good rootstocks and were further selected in Austria, Germany and later Italy. In 1904 Herr Kober of Klosterneuburg in Austria selected the famous 5 BB from Teleki's 5 A. The agricultural school at Oppenheim in Germany selected SO 4, and in 1924 Teleki's son Alexander selected his 5 C from his father's 5 A. These rootstock varieties became the most widely used rootstocks of northern France, the German-speaking countries, and central and south-eastern Europe. The only 'non-Teleki' *berlandieri* X *riparia* hybrid which plays a fairly important role as a rootstock is Couderc's 161-49.

Morphological characteristics. — All *berlandieri* X *riparia* hybrids have large leaves, resembling *V. riparia* in shape but thick and leathery in structure, a characteristic inherited from *V. berlandieri*. They are very vigorous growers, having long and thick canes with long internodes. Their wood is hard with small pith. Lack of affinity with numerous *V. vinifera* grape varieties has been experienced, especially in grape-growing areas with a warm climate.

Fig. 14.2. SO 4.

OTHER ROOTSTOCKS OF CONSIDERABLE IMPORTANCE IN WARM GRAPEGROWING COUNTRIES

1. 44-53 Malègue

Origin. – This rootstock is a complex hybrid of Riparia grand glabre X 144 Malègue (cordifolia X rupestris).

Characteristics. – 44-53 M is a vigorous grower and its cuttings root and graft well. Because of its resistance to drought and to nematodes it was widely planted in southern France after the last war. The drawback of 44-53 M is its sensitivity to the lack of magnesium in the soil (4, 8).

Fig. 14.3. Malègue.

2. 41 B

Origin. – Chasselas X Berlandieri hybrid, obtained by Millardet in 1882.

Characteristics. – Because of its resistance to drought and its extreme resistance to lime chlorosis, 41 B is still one of the most widely used rootstocks in France, especially in the Champagne and in Charantes. It is also an important rootstock in Greece and in North Africa. 41 B is a vigorous grower and its cuttings root and graft well. Its resistance to phylloxera is sufficient.

Fig. 14.4. 41 B.

TABLE 14.2
The development of the areas of rootstock mother plantations in France.
From Galet (5).

Class	Variety	Area in production (ha)				Total area in 1972
		1946	1959	1965	1972	
1	41 B	229	405	519	693	841
2	Rup. du Lot	762,8	785	728	638	641
3	SO 4	2	41	141	487	543
4	3309 C	584,1	501	456	404	426
5	110 Richter	36,6	100	219	302	381
6	5 BB	80,4	294	272	350	371
7	161-49 C	276,8	356	335	271	284
8	99 Richter	79,5	197	403	253	255
9	1103 Paulsen	–	2	24	174	200
10	140 Ruggeri	–	1	22	74	123
11	44-53 Malègue	11,9	142	155	99	107
12	420 A Mgt	83,2	86	81	73	76
13	101-14 Mgt	37,3	45	40	45	50
14	Vialla	7,8	30	28	36	47
15	Riparia Gloire	180	178	111	41	45
16	333 EM	2,8	5	11	16	28
17	G 1	0,4	0,1	0,04	23	23
18	196-17 Cl	6,5	4	10	16	18
19	5 C	0,2	1	6	13	16
20	R.S.B. 1	–	–	–	1	5,8
Total		2 474	3 274	3 756	4 041	4 513

In addition to the 20 rootstock varieties of Table 14.2 the following rootstocks are authorized by law, dated 10 April 1968, for the establishment of officially recognized rootstock mother plantations: 8 B, 216-3 Cl, 34 E.M., 1616 C, 4010 Cl, 1447 P and BC 2. It will be noted that the nematode-resistant Californian rootstocks Salt Creek, Dogridge and 1613 C are *not* among the authorized rootstocks in France. The reasons given by Branas (2) are that the cuttings of Salt Creek and Dogridge root and graft with great difficulty and their resistance to phylloxera was seriously questioned. 1613 C, a hybrid of Solonis X Othello, called 'Fairy' in South Africa, is not resistant to phylloxera.

The need to graft the varieties of *V. vinifera* on Californian nematode-

---

T A B L E 14.3
The most important cultural characteristics, other than resistance to phylloxera, of commercially cultivated rootstock varieties.
Summarized after Branas (2), Galet (3, 4), Mottard et al. (8).

rootstock variety	vigour	affinity	adaptation to high lime content	drought resistance	adaptation to wet feet	adaptation to saline soils	resistance to nematodes
Riparia Gloire	**	**	*	*	**	*	**
Rupestris du Lot	***	***	**	**	*	*	*
3309 C	*	**	**	*	***	*	*
99 Richter	***	****	***	**	*	*	**
110 Richter	***	***	***	****	**	*	**
161-49 C	**	*	***	*	*	*	*
5 BB	***	*	***	**	***	*	**
SO 4	**	*	***	**	***	*	**
41 B	**	**	****	***	*	*	*
1103 Paulsen	***	***	***	***	**	**	?
140 Ruggeri	***	***	***	****	**	*	?
1616 C	*	*	*	*	***	***	**
44-53 Malègue	***	***	*	***	**	*	***
196-17 Cl	****	**	*	***	**	?	*

For saline soils:
(a) not infested with phylloxera: varieties of *V. vinifera* ***
(b) slightly infested with phylloxera: Solonis * to **
(c) infested with phylloxera: 0–11 per cent active lime: 1616 C, 216-3 Cl, Gl,
more than 11 per cent active lime: 1103 P

Abbreviations: * weak, bad, poor
      ** mediocre
      *** vigorous, good
      **** very vigorous, very good

resistant rootstocks is so overemphasized by research workers in the English-speaking grapegrowing countries that anyone knowing very little about viticulture could conclude that the main purpose of grafting is not to graft *V. vinifera* grape varieties onto American rootstocks in order to prevent their being destroyed by the phylloxera but to prevent their being destroyed by nematodes. While the names of new hybrids are constantly being added to the list of possible 'saviours' (Harmony, Schwarzman), the name of a French rootstock 44-53 Malègue is never mentioned. This hybrid of riparia X cordifolia X rupestris is not only highly resistant to phylloxera, but it is also resistant to nematodes. For this reason it is extensively used in France in soils where the reinfection of newly planted vines with court noué ('fanleaf'), a soil-borne virus disease, is a serious problem (2, 4, 8).

Laying out comparative rootstock trials

The depth and physical structure of the soil is a decisive factor in determining the cultural value of a specific rootstock variety. There is no 'ideal' rootstock for all types of soil and for all *V. vinifera* grape varieties. For this reason, scientifically laid-out rootstock trials on experimental farms may satisfy the statisticians with their computers, but the collected data of such trials is of little value for a grapegrower who wants to establish a vineyard on a completely different type of soil, in a completely different climatic region and grafting a different *V. vinifera* grape variety onto the rootstocks.

A tremendous variability of the soil is characteristic of the viticultural regions of South Africa. It is difficult to find a block of vineyard with homogeneous soil. For this reason, grapegrowers should try to establish for themselves what the most suitable rootstock variety will be by planting comparative rootstock trials on their own farms. This can be easily done as follows: in establishing a new vineyard on a commercially cultivated rootstock, such as 99 R and 101-14 Mgt, in South Africa, one should plant into this vineyard vines grafted on different rootstock varieties which, according to the literature or to local experience, perform well under similar soil and climatic conditions. Sixty to eighty vines, grafted on 110 R, Rupestris du Lot, 140 Ru, 1103 P, 44-53 M, Metallica, and in deep, fertile virgin soils on 41 B and Jacquez can be recommended for the grapegrowers of South Africa. Vines grafted on the mentioned rootstock varieties should be planted in three or four repetitions with the commercial rootstock on which the vineyard is grafted. It is absolutely essential that for scion stock homogenous, i.e. clonal material, be used.

Such privately laid-out comparative rootstock trials should be planted in the various viticultural regions of the country on all predominant soil-types. The exact location, the depth and type of the soil as well as the collected data of such trials should be made public for the benefit of all grapegrowers.

DIRECT PRODUCERS

The grapes of American *Vitis* species all have to some extent a characteristically musky flavour, generally called 'foxy taste'. While this is more or less acceptable for table-grapes, it becomes unpalatable when fermentation vinifies the must. However, American *Vitis* species are usually resistant to phylloxera, to downy mildew, to oidium and to Black rot, diseases of the vine which are indigenous to the north-eastern states of the United States of America. The presence of these diseases, together with low winter temperatures, made the culture of *V. vinifera* grape varieties impossible in regions east of the Rocky Mountains (6. 15).

For this reason, the Americans were forced to improve their wild vines by hybridization. What was wanted was a vine that had all the qualities of the American species in resistance to indigenous diseases, and some qualities of the European vine as regards the quality of the grapes. Although great progress has been made, the goal has not yet been reached (6).

When phylloxera began to destroy the vineyards in France, the French grapegrowers began to grow certain varieties of American origin which were planted out directly without grafting, and therefore called DIRECT PRODUCERS or SELF-BEARERS. They included Lenoir, or Jacquez as it is known in France, Herbemont, Isabella, Clinton, and a little later Othello (10, 14).

Later French viticulturists took up the hybridization of American and European varieties in order to obtain hybrids which would sufficiently resist the fungoid diseases and insect pests of *V. vinifera* grape varieties, and yet produce grapes of fairly good quality for wine-making. Notwithstanding the progress that has been made by breeders like Seibel, Couderc, Seyve-Villard, Baco, Oberlin, etc. the ideal direct producer has not yet been obtained. For viticultural areas like the western Cape, where the fungoid diseases of *V. vinifera* are not so bad, the whole question of direct producers is of little interest. *Direct producers are hardly ever grown at the Cape, as there is no good reason why they should be.*

TABLE 14.4

Technical data of noble red and white wine-grape varieties, collected in Hungary. Adapted from Németh (9).

Variety	bunches			berries						
	weight/g	length/cm	breadth/cm	weight/g	length/mm	breadth/mm	number of seeds	number of berries in the bunch	sugar-grade at full maturity	total acidity g/l
Cabernet Sauvignon	80	13,9	7,5	1,2	13,7	12,8	1,5	66,4	21,5	8,0
Cabernet franc	125	14,2	9,5	1,4	15,1	13,9	1,8	87,5	21,5	7,5
Merlot	125	12,9	8,5	1,5	13,1	12,6	1,8	71,3	20,5	7,5
Pinot noir	105	11,5	8,0	1,5	14,0	13,0	1,7	66,8	22,0	8,5
Weisser Riesling	85	10,9	7,7	1,5	13,0	12,5	2,1	53,5	20,5	9,5
Welsch-riesling	115	13,3	8,6	1,3	12,3	11,9	2,5	85,2	21,0	8,5
Chardon-nay	69	11,6	8,1	1,5	14,0	13,7	1,7	55,4	21,5	9,0
Sémillon	145	14,5	10,6	2,1	16,1	15,5	2,1	70,0	20,5	8,0
Sauvignon blanc	100	11,8	7,6	1,4	14,2	13,3	1,3	62,6	21,0	9,0
Furmint	180	18,2	9,1	2,0	16,2	14,6	1,4	91,9	20,5	9,5
Hárslevelü	200	23,5	10,9	1,8	14,2	14,2	1,8	103,8	20,0	10,0

Remarks: Although no similar data are available in South Africa, the author's observations and measurements of the weight of the bunches of the same varieties indicate that:

(a) Good clones of Weisser Riesling, Ruländer, Pinot noir, Furmint, Hárslevelü, etc., are much more fertile in South Africa when grafted on 99 R.

(b) In South Africa the corresponding varieties all bear considerably larger bunches than indicated by Németh in this table.

Variety	number of bunches per shoot	wine						
		alcoholic degree vol per cent	total extract g/l	invert sugar g/l	acidity g/l tartaric acid	pH value	total per cent of juice recovered	sugar-free extract g/l
Cabernet Sauvignon	1,08	11,8	34,5	2,61	5,8	3,82	67,8	31,9
Cabernet franc	1,20	11,6	34,7	2,65	5,0	3,75	72,8	32,0
Merlot	1,50	12,9	37,9	3,21	5,7	3,58	73,3	34,7
Pinot noir	1,30	13,6	35,9	3,29	6,7	3,61	77,6	32,6
Weisser Riesling	1,57	13,1	30,4	2,02	7,5	3,43	69,3	28,4
Welsch-riesling	1,80	12,4	30,5	3,86	7,6	3,34	75,4	26,6
Chardon-nay	1,28	13,5	38,2	3,04	7,9	3,47	77,4	35,2
Sémillon	1,26	13,5	34,4	4,87	7,0	3,35	81,1	36,6
Sauvignon blanc	1,21	14,2	37,0	4,62	8,0	3,50	75,2	32,4
Furmint	1,55	13,1	35,4	4,82	8,2	3,33	78,4	30,6
Hárslevelü	1,73	11,5	34,1	2,95	9,1	3,25	75,9	32,1

V. VINIFERA WINE GRAPE VARIETIES

'Good wine and a beautiful woman are two sweet poisons' — old Persian proverb.

WHITE WINE GRAPE VARIETIES

1. Weisser Riesling

Synonyms. — White Riesling, Riesling rhenan, Riesling renano, Risling rynski, Rheingauer Riesling, Johannisberger, etc. Actually the name 'Rhine Riesling' would be more appropriate in English for this variety than 'White Riesling'. Such a name would also clearly distinguish this noble variety from the numerous inferior varieties (Grey Riesling, Emerald Riesling, Clare Riesling, S.A. Riesling, etc.) which are also called 'Riesling'.

Origin. — Riesling has been grown along the Rhine probably from as long ago as the Roman conquest of Germania. Typical *convarietas occidentalis.*

Description

Tip of the growing shoot greenish-white, woolly.

Young leaves yellowish with copper tint, dense downy pubescence.

Leaves below medium, round, 036-3-69 (4), five-lobed, lower lateral sinuses usually much less marked, bullate, crinkled near the petiolar sinus, grass-green, dull, downy pubescence below; petiolar sinus always closed with overlapped edges; dentition regular, convex, pointed.

Bunches small, cylindro-conical, compact with short peduncles; *berries* small, spherical; skin fine but tough, greenish-yellow with brown spots; pulp juicy with a pronounced and characteristic varietal flavour.

Shoots half-erect, cylindrical, strikingly red and pubescent towards the end of the growing shoot, fairly vigorous with medium-long internodes and pronounced nodes; *canes* light brown, ribbed; wood hard with a small pith.

Cultural characteristics. — Good German clones of Riesling, such as 64, 110, 198, 239 Geisenheim, 90 Neustadt, 356 Trautwein, are vigorous growers and fertile. Owing to the small size of its bunches Riesling vines are, however, long or half-long pruned, as the crop will otherwise be too light. It is easy to graft Riesling and no problems with affinity have been experienced. Riesling is not very susceptible to the fungoid diseases of the grapevine, but its ripe grapes rot easily when rains fall late in the season. It ripens mid-season.

'The breed of the German fine wines is the result of the struggle for life in the most northerly climate at which the vine can grow. The cost of producing is twice that of wine-production of France, four times as great as in Spain. But the yield per hectare is very much higher than in such fine regions of France as Burgundy and Bordeaux.' This statement by Professor Steinberg, quoted by Lichine (7), summarizes the story of Riesling.

Fig. 14.5. Riesling. From Németh (9).

Wine. — Weisser Riesling is one of the finest grape varieties of the world. In the valleys of the Rhine and Moselle, it produces a wine of the highest quality. A delicate bouquet and a well-balanced, fruity, elegant, steely aristocracy are the outstanding characteristics of the German Riesling wines. If it is taken away from its natural habitat and planted abroad, something happens to its wines. Although above average in quality, they lack the fine bouquet and delicacy of the Riesling wines of Germany. On favourable sites, when conditions during late autumn are favourable, the grapes of Riesling develop noble-rot under the influence of the fungus *Botrytis cinerea,* which turns them into half-raisins, resulting in a very sweet must (over 30 per cent sugar) from which the world-famous 'Trockenbeerenauslese' wines are made.

Geographical distribution. — White Riesling is not planted extensively outside Germany and Alsace. It constitutes over 20 per cent of the total area planted by vines in Germany. W. Riesling is cultivated successfully in California and in Australia.

2. Chardonnay

Synonyms. — Chardonnay blanc, Epinette, Pinot blanc Chardonnay, etc.

Origin. — Very old French variety. The name 'Pinot blanc Chardonnay' given it mainly in the English-speaking countries is misleading because Chardonnay does not belong to the Pinot family. By 1872 it had already been officially separated from the Pinot group.

Fig. 14.6. Chardonnay.
From Németh (9).

Description

Tip of the growing shoot reddish white-woolly.

Young leaves yellowish-green, slightly bronze-coloured, downy pubescence below.

Leaves small, round, 035-2-57 (4), slightly trilobed, lateral sinuses deep in degener-ated clones, bullate, dark green, shiny, quite thin but tough structure, nerves slightly pubescent below; petiolar sinus lyre-shaped, open, its base is bordered by L 3 nerves typical of the variety, but never occurring in the Pinot group; dentition uneven, small, angular, pointed.

Bunches small, cylindro-conical, compact; *berries* small, spherical, light green with golden colour on the sunny side; skin fairly thick, pulp firm, juicy, with a special varietal flavour.

Shoots thin, reddish-brown striped on the side exposed to the sun and darkened at the nodes; *canes* brown with short internodes; wood very hard with small pith.

Subvarieties. — Chardonnay rose and Chardonnay musqué (4).

Cultural characteristics. — Chardonnay is a very degenerated old variety and only carefully selected material should be propagated. It has been extensively and successfully selected in France. Like the Riesling, it is fertile, i.e. has two bunches on the shoots arising from fruiting eyes, but because of the small size of its bunches it should be half-long, or long pruned. Chardonnay should be planted only in fertile, well-drained and lime-rich soils. It adapts well to warm climatic conditions. Chardonnay is very susceptible to millerandage. The variety is not particularly sensi-tive to the fungoid diseases of the grape vine. The affinity of Chardonnay is good in South Africa for the berlandieri X rupestris rootstocks, but un-satisfactory for 101-14 Mgt, and for the berlandieri X riparia group of rootstocks, especially for 5 BB (13).

It ripens early.

Wine. — Young Chardonnay wines are light greenish-yellow in colour, delicate, well balanced with a high acidity and rather neutral flavour. Its wines gain tremendously with maturity. Chardonnay is one of the greatest revelations of the recent decades, and its wines represent one of the noblest white wines of the world. Together with Pinot noir, Chardonnay supplies the best sparkling-wines of the world.

Geographical distribution. — Chardonnay produces the famous wines of the Chablis, Montrachet and Mersault. In the Champagne it is mainly planted near Épernay. Recently it has been planted on an ever-increasing scale in California and Rumania.

3. Sauvignon blanc

Synonyms. — Sauvignon, Sauvignon bianco, Muscat Sylvaner, Feigentraube, etc.

Origin. — Sauvignon blanc and its colour-mutation **Sauvignon rose** have been planted in France since the beginning of the eighteenth century.

Description

Tip of the growing shoot white-woolly, light rose-coloured around the border of the unfolding small leaves.

Young leaves yellowish-green with some brownish tint, downy above, white felt-like pubescence below.

Leaves medium to small, round, 035-2-57 (4), tri- or five-lobed, lateral sinuses always less marked by good selections, bullate, light green, dull, fairly thick and

Fig. 14.7. Sauvignon blanc. From Németh (9).

tough in structure, main nerves lighter green and cobwebby pubescence below; petiolar sinus V-shaped, narrow, dentition quite even, distinctly convex.

Bunches small, cylindro-conical, compact; *berries* medium, greenish-golden when full-ripe, slightly oval with corky spots; skin fairly thick; pulp greenish, juicy, very sweet with a special aromatic flavour.

Shoots semi-erect, long but not very thick in diameter, light green; *canes* yellowish light brown, darker shaded at the nodes, ribbed; wood very hard with small pith.

Subvarieties. — Petit Sauvignon and Gros Sauvignon.

Cultural characteristics. — Sauvignon blanc is a fairly vigorous grower and sufficiently productive when pruned half-long. It is susceptible to oidium, and its ripe grapes rot quite easily if rain falls. Sauvignon blanc adapts itself to all kind of soils, and it can be grown even on dry sandy soils (9).

Its affinity is very good and it grafts easily.

It ripens very early.

According to Perold (10) Sauvignon blanc did well in the Cape and produced wines of very high quality. The variety, however, has now practically disappeared from cultivation, mainly because local viticulturists and wine-makers considered its productivity and the quality of its wines to be inferior to Steen/Chenin blanc, a kind of 'sacred cow' of South African viticulture. Because this was contrary to all experience gained with the two varieties throughout the world, the author propagated every available eye of it in 1963, included it in field-trials on the experimental farms in 1964, and from about 1967 recommended planting it for the production of high-quality wines.

In recent years, growers, especially estate-wine producers, have begun to plant Sauvignon blanc on an ever-increasing scale. This late renaissance of Sauvignon blanc in South Africa can only be welcomed.

Wine. — Sauvignon blanc is the finest grape in the Sauternes district, which produces, together with Sémillon and a little Muscadelle, the world-famous Sauternes wines. In a mild, misty autumn the fungus *Botryis cinerea* engineers the escape of a proportion of water in the berries, leaving the sugar and aromatic compounds in the juice very concentrated, which requires the grapes to be picked as they shrivel. Bad weather in October can rob the grower of all chance of making a sweet wine, and sometimes of his whole crop.

Sauvignon blanc is extensively planted in warm grapegrowing regions such as California, Australia, Israel and Rumania.

4. Furmint

Synonyms. — Gelber Mosler, Zapfner, Furmint bianco, Moslavac bijeli, etc.

Origin. — The name of Furmint appeared in Hungary for the first time in the middle of the eighteenth century. Although it is considered to be an old Hungarian variety, its morphology indicates that it came to Hungary from the Balkan peninsula or more probably from Asia Minor. Németh (9) classified it as *convarietas pontica — subconvarietas balcanica.*

Description

Tip of the growing shoot white, felt-like pubescence with a slight faint red.
Young leaves grass-green, felt-like pubescence below.

Leaves rather large, round, entire or tri- or five-lobed depending on the phenotypes, crinkled, dull green of leathery structure, dense cobwebby pubescence below; petiolar sinus lyre-shaped, open but narrow; dentition uneven, convex.

Bunches large for a high-quality wine grape variety, cylindrical, fairly loose; *berries* medium, slightly oval, soft; skin is thin and bursts easily; pulp juicy with a pleasant neutral flavour.

Shoots erect, very thick, brownish-green, pubescent towards ends; *canes* rusty-brown, finely ribbed, with prominent nodes and fairly long internodes; wood hard.

Subvarieties. — Rosa Furmint, Nemes Furmint, Hólyagos Furmint, etc.

Cultural characteristics. — Furmint is a very vigorous grower with thick, erect canes. Good Hungarian clones, such as Pécs 1, 2 and 26, bear well with short pruning. It adapts well to all kinds of soils, but produces its best quality on loamy soils. Furmint is fairly drought-resistant (9). It is quite susceptible to oidium, and its ripe grapes are inclined to rot if rain falls late in the season.

Furmint grafts easily and has an excellent affinity with the berlandieri X rupestris group.

It ripens fairly late.

Fig. 14.8. Furmint. From Németh (9).

Wine. – Furmint gives full-bodied, wonderfully balanced, dry or semi-sweet wines with good acidity and very fine flavour. It is also the main component of the world-famous 'Tokaji aszu' wines, made from over-ripe, shrivelled grapes which have undergone 'noble rot', as do the grapes of the Sauternes and of the Rhine. The vines are grown on hills facing south, and the soil is the lava of ancient volcanoes covered with sandy loam (7, 9).

Tokaji aszu wine is unparalleled in its velvety grapiness and flavour. Voltaire, quoted by Lichine (7), said of it, 'This wine invigorates every fibre of the brain and brings forth an enchanting sparkle of wit and good cheer from the depth of the soul.'

Geographical distribution. – Furmint is cultivated extensively in the countries of the Carpath–Danube basin.

5. Welschriesling

Synonyms. – Riesling italien, Riesling italico, Olaszrizling, Taljanskaja rizling, etc.

Origin. – The Welschriesling probably came to Heidelberg (Germany) from France. *Convarietas occidentalis.*

Fig. 14.9. Welschriesling.

Description

Tip of the growing shoot white-woolly, tinted a light rose colour around the border of the unfolding small leaves.

Young leaves deeply lobed, light green, woolly pubescence below.

Leaves medium, round, five-lobed, finely bullate, dull light green, thin but tough in structure, downy pubescence below; petiolar sinus U-shaped, nearly closed; dentition uneven, angular, pointed.

Bunches medium, conical, winged, fairly compact with long peduncles; *berries* small, spherical, yellowish, spotted; skin thin; pulp juicy with a rather neutral, pleasant flavour.

Shoots long but rather thin, light green glabrous; *canes* finely ribbed, light yellowish-brown, shaded darker at the nodes, with medium-long internodes; wood hard.

Subvarieties. — Many have been selected and evaluated by Németh (9). The best clones are Olaszrizling Pécs 2 and 10.

Cultural characteristics. — Welschriesling is a fairly vigorous grower and a good, and very regular, bearer. It is one of the most reliable wine grape varieties. This variety should occupy a prominent place in South African viticulture. It grafts very well and no problems with affinity have been reported. Welschriesling is fairly susceptible to oidium, but its ripe grapes do not rot easily. In South Alrica it is sensitive to the lack of magnesium in the soil. Although Welschriesling accommodates well to all kinds of soils, it should not be planted in sandy soils under dry conditions (9).

It ripens late mid-season.

Wines. — The wines of Welschriesling are light greenish-yellow, with a delicate varietal flavour, well-balanced, full-bodied, smooth with sometimes rather low acidity. They gain with maturity and are the most highly appreciated white quality wines of central and south-eastern Europe.

Geographical distribution. — Welschriesling is one of the most widely grown noble white wine grape varieties in central and south-eastern Europe. On the other hand, Weisser Riesling of the Rhine and the Moselle does not accommodate itself well to the warmer climatic conditions of these viticultural regions.

6. Ruländer

Synonyms. — Pinot gris, Grauer Burgunder, Tokayer, etc. The Alsatian synonym 'Tokayer' is misleading and often leads to confusing the Ruländer with the Furmint.

Origin. — Ruländer is a spontaneous mutation of Pinot noir and, except for the greyish colour of its berries, it is identical to Pinot noir and Pinot blanc. Although of Burgundian origin, the variety is better known under its German name Ruländer, derived from the name of Ruländ, a merchant from the Burgundy who brought it from France to Germany. Baron von Basserman-Jordan identified and described it in Speyer in 1711.

Wine and geographical distribution. — Ruländer gives wonderfully balanced, full-bodied, delicate, fruity wines on the volcanic soils of the

Kaiserstuhl near Freiburg in Germany, on the opposite bank of the Rhine in Alsace, and on the northern shore of Lake Balaton in Hungary. It requires warm slopes with well-aerated lime-rich, loamy soil (9).

Cultural characteristics similar to Pinot noir.

7. Sémillon

Synonyms. – Sémillon blanc, Gros Sémillon, Colombier, etc.

Origin. – This old French variety spread from the Gironde during the eighteenth century into the other grapegrowing regions of Europe.

Description

Leaves medium, round, 035-3-46 (4), tri- to five-lobed, light grass-green, leaf edges always curled downward.

Bunches short, cylindro-conical, compact; *berries* above medium size, spherical, pretty golden-coloured when ripe; skin thick; pulp firm, very sweet, with its special varietal flavour.

Cultural aptitudes. – Sémillon is a fairly vigorous grower but for good crops it must be pruned half-long. It adapts well to all kinds of soils, and to warm climatic conditions, but it should not be grown under too dry conditions. Sémillon is not very susceptible to sunburn or to the fungoid diseases of the vine.

It ripens mid-season.

Sémillon is confused in South Africa with a variety called White Green-grape. The two varieties can easily be distinguished from each other by the petiolar sinus of Greengrape which is bordered by nerves L 3, and

Fig. 14.10. Sémillon.
From Németh (9).

by the berries of Sémillon which are fairly large, golden-yellowish and firm. The quality of the wines of Sémillon is superior to those of Green-grape.

Geographical distribution. —Outside France, Sémillon is extensively planted in California, Australia and Israel.

8. Hárslevelü

Synonyms. — Lindenblätter, Lipovina, Feuilles de tilleul, etc.

Origin. — Very old Hungarian variety. It is classified as *convarietas pontica — subconvarietas balcanica* (9).

Description

Leaves small, orbiculo-reniform, entire or slightly trilobed, light dull green, crinkled, tough structure, downy pubescence below.

Bunches very long, cylindro-conical, loose; *berries* small, round, soft, golden-yellow when full-ripe, skin tough, pulp juicy with neutral flavour.

Subvarieties. — Many are described by Németh (9).

Cultural characteristics. — Hárslevelü is a very vigorous grower and good bearer. Its best clone is Pécs 41, selected by Németh. It is a robust, healthy variety, well adapted to all kinds of soils and to a dry climate. The grapes of Hárslevelü are highly resistant to sunburning and its ripe grapes do not rot easily (9). It grafts easily and no problems with affinity have been experienced.

Hárslevelü ripens fairly late. Owing to its very vigorous growth, high fertility, the high acidity content of its wines coupled with good quality,

Fig. 14.11. Hárslevelü.

and its resistance to oidium and botrytis, Hárslevelü might be the variety which could replace Steen/Chenin blanc in certain grapegrowing regions of South Africa, where Steen is a complete failure due to its susceptibility to oidium and especially to botrytis.

Wine. — Hárslevelü produces in Europe full-bodied wines with a fine varietal flavour with somewhat too high acidity. Under favourable climatic conditions its grapes undergo noble-rot, and together with Furmint and a little Sárga Muskotály (Yellow Muscadelle) it is a component of the famous natural sweet wines of the Tokaj.

Geographical distribution. — Hárslevelü is not cultivated extensively outside the Carpath–Danube basin.

RED WINE GRAPE VARIETIES

'Music is a greater revelation than all wisdom of philosophy of the world. It is the wine which awakens creative forces; while I'm Bacchus who pours out this inestimable wine to mankind, intoxicating its spirit.' — Beethoven.

1. Cabernet Sauvignon

Synonyms. —Petit Cabernet, Carbonet, Petite Vidure, Sauvignon nero, etc.

Origin. — The cabernets (Cabernet Sauvignon and Cabernet franc) are not only the noblest but also among the oldest varieties of the Médoc. Their wines were already famous at the beginning of the eighteenth century. Morphologically they are classified as *convarietas occidentalis-subconvarietas gallica* (9).

Description

Tip of the growing shoot greenish-white woolly, carmine-red coloured around the edges of the unfolding small leaves.

Young leaves deeply lobed, bronze-coloured, shiny, downy pubescence.

Leaves medium, round, 035-3-58 (4), five-lobed with very deep lateral sinuses with edges superposed, showing five round holes, which is typical for the variety, bullate, dark green, glabrous above with a cobwebby pubescence below; petiolar sinus lyre-shaped, superposed, bordered by nerves L 3 on its base; dentition very broad-based, distinctly convex, blunt.

Bunches small, conical, somewhat shouldered, loose with long peduncle; *berries* small, spherical; skin thick and very tough; pulp juicy with a pronounced flavour characteristic of the Cabernets. This flavour is unusual in *V. vinifera* grape varieties, and it is possible that the name 'Sauvignon', derived from the French word *sauvage*, wild, was given to the variety for this reason.

Shoots erect, very vigorous, green with red stripes on the side exposed to the sun; *canes* light brown darkened reddish at the nodes, strongly ribbed with medium-long internodes; wood very hard with small pith.

No *subvarieties* or morphologically different clones of Cabernet Sauvignon are known.

Fig. 14.12. Cabernet Sauvignon. From Németh (9).

Cultural aptitudes. — Cabernet Sauvignon is a very vigorous grower but only a shy-bearer due to the infertility of the eyes on the basal portion of its canes and to the small size of its bunches. It should be pruned according to Guyot's renewal system and, being a very vigorous grower can be made to retain up to four long bearers per vine, provided that the person who does the pruning understands his job.

Cabernet Sauvignon grafts well and possesses a good affinity for practically all rootstocks. Only on 'virus-free' 5 BB, flown in from Davis, California, was it a complete failure in South Africa. It often failed on 101-14 Mgt, but never on 99, 110 R, Rupestris du Lot or Metallica.

Cabernet Sauvignon is immune to anthrachnose but its leaves are very sensitive to oidium. It should therefore be sulphured. Fortunately it would require a great deal of rain to cause its berries to rot.

It ripens late.

Wine. — Cabernet Sauvignon gives a beautiful, dark, full-bodied red wine with a peculiar and typical flavour. Pure Cabernet wines are, however, too astringent and too rich in tannin, and they take too long to mature. For this reason not only in the Médoc but in all famous Cabernet-producing regions of the world (Chile, Italy, Rumania, etc.) the most famous Cabernet Sauvignon wines are blended with about 40 per cent Cabernet franc and 20 per cent Merlot. These well-matured wines are indescribably delicate and harmonious. Médoc wines are long-vatted and pick up more tannin from the skins, seeds and stalks than Burgundian wines. This makes them harder at the outset but allows them to reach a greater character with longevity. Only with age do the great Cabernet wines achieve their full glory.

Geographical distribution. — The Cabernets are the characteristic varieties of the Médoc, the area north of the city of Bordeaux contributing with Merlot to the famous wines of the area. In the northern part of the region around St. Estèphe the varieties Cot (Malbec) and Petit Verdot are used plentifully in the ordinary red wines of Bordeaux. No other varieties are permitted, and no white wine has the right to be called Médoc (7).

Cabernet Sauvignon is also cultivated extensively in the Midi (southern France), Italy, south-eastern Europe (especially Rumania), Chile, California, South Africa and Australia. Only in the last-mentioned three English-speaking wine-producing countries is Cabernet Sauvignon not blended with Cabernet franc and Merlot. It is either vinified pure or blended with varieties (Syrah, Cinsaut, etc.) not cultivated in the great Cabernet-producing regions of the world.

2. Cabernet franc

Synonyms. — Gros Cabernet, Carmenet, Gros Vidure, etc.

Origin. — Similar to that of Cabernet Sauvignon.

Description

Tip of the growing shoot white-woolly, violet-red coloured around the edges of the unfolding small leaves.

Young leaves deeply lobed, bronze-coloured, downy pubescence.

Leaves medium, round, 036-2-57 (4), five-lobed with deep lateral sinuses pointed at their bases, in contrast to the lateral sinuses of Cabernet Sauvignon, which are always round at their bases with superposed edges, bullate, light green, glabrous above with a cobwebby pubescence below; petiolar sinus lyre-shaped, open but narrow, dentition uneven, small, angular, very pointed.

Bunches below medium, cylindro-conical, shouldered, sometimes branched, loose with fairly long peduncles; *berries* slightly larger than those of Cabernet Sauvignon, spherical; skins fairly thin, pulp juicy, less pronounced Cabernet flavour than Cabernet Sauvignon.

It ripens about two weeks before Cabernet Sauvignon.

Shoots half-erect, light green slightly brown-striped on the side exposed to the sun; *canes* light brown, ribbed with medium-long internodes, thinner in diameter than those of Cabernet Sauvignon.

Cultural aptitudes. — Cabernet franc is less vigorous but much more fertile than Cabernet Sauvignon. It bears well when pruned half-long. It does not graft as easily as Cabernet Sauvignon and seems to be unhappy on 101-14 Mgt in South Africa.

The susceptibility of Cabernet franc to the fungus diseases of the grapevine is similar to that of Cabernet Sauvignon.

Wine. — Young Cabernet franc wines are finer, less astringent and lighter coloured than those of Cabernet Sauvignon. They age sooner.

Fig. 14.13. Cabernet franc.

Geographical distribution. – Cabernet franc is grown extensively in France in the Médoc, in the Midi, and in the Loire Valley, as well as in north Italy and in south-eastern Europe.

By comparing the leaves, Cabernet franc can easily be distinguished from Cabernet Sauvignon (12), but it can easily be confused with Merlot (4, 9).

3. Merlot noir

Synonyms. – Merlot, Merlau, Merlan, Merlo, etc.

Origin. – The name of this variety appears for the first time in France in 1783. It is derived from the French *merle,* thrush, because these birds especially like its early, small and very sweet berries (1).

Description

Tip of the growing shoot greenish, white-woolly.

Young leaves deeply lobed, light green, downy pubescence below.

Leaves medium, cuneiform, 135-3-46 (4), five-lobed with deep lateral sinuses which are pointed at their bases, very dark dull green, almost smooth, cobwebby pubescence below; petiolar sinus U-shaped, wide open; dentition small, convex, pointed.

Full-grown leaves of Merlot resemble closely those of Cabernet franc. They can, however, be easily distinguished from each other by the U-shaped and wide-open petiolar sinus, and the much darker-green colour of Merlot leaves (4, 9).

Bunches medium, cylindro-conical, branched, loose with long peduncles; *berries* small, round; skin fairly thick and tough; pulp very juicy, sweet, pleasant but neutral flavour.

Shoots half-erect, green, glabrous; *canes* brownish, ribbed with fairly short internodes and prominent nodes; wood hard with a very small pith.

Subvariety. — Merlot blanc.

Cultural aptitudes. — Merlot is a variety of medium vigour and its good selections bear well and regularly. It is a degenerated old variety and only carefully tested French and Italian selections should be propagated.

Merlot is one of the noblest red wine grape varieties. It is also well known for its very good grafting capabilities.

In France Merlot is pruned long, but it has been observed in South Africa that, when vines grafted on 99 R are pruned long, they bear too much, which affects the growth of the vines unfavourably. Merlot is slightly subject to oidium and anthracnose, and its ripe grapes are inclined to rot when rains fall at late summer.

It ripens mid-season.

Wine. — Merlot gives beautifully coloured, full-bodied, well-balanced, velvety wines which blend magnificently with the Cabernets. Its wine makes the wine of the Cabernets softer and fit for consumption earlier. For this reason Merlot is a component of the most famous wines of the Haut-Médoc.

Although Merlot has been in South Africa at least since the beginning of the century, the variety is hardly cultivated at all. The recommendation of the late Professor Perold in 1926 (10), according to which the best red wines of the claret class can be obtained 'by growing at least one-third as many vines of the two Cabernets as of Hermitage (Cinsaut) and other similar varieties giving less quality but more abundant yields', might have been correct for the marketing possibilities of South African

Fig. 14.14. Merlot noir.

red wines of his time. *To follow it today would be suicidal for our Cabernet wines.* In no other wine-producing country have the wines of the Cabernets ever been blended with the wines of Cinsaut. The deplorable fact that in South Africa nearly three times as many Cinsaut vines are planted as all the other red wine grape varieties together, can be considered as the 'cancer' of our red wine industry.

Geographical distribution. — Merlot is grown extensively in northern Italy, Switzerland, Rumania, Bulgaria, Russia and Chile.

It has recently been planted in California, where it seemed to have been previously unknown, as it is not even mentioned by Winkler (16).

4. Pinot noir

Synonyms. — Blauer Burgunder, Blauer Clevner, Pineau noir, Pinot nero, Pinot cernij, etc.

Origin. — Pinot noir is one of the oldest cultivated varieties and is considered to be indigenous to Burgundy. It has been established that the Romans found vines in Burgundy when they conquered Gaul. These vines were most probably planted by Greek settlers who founded Marseilles in 600 B.C., i.e. shortly after the legendary founders of Rome, Romulus and Remus, the sons of Mars, were set afloat on the river Tiber and were found under a figtree by a she-wolf who suckled and sheltered them.

Description
Tip of the growing shoot white-woolly.
Young leaves pale yellowish-green, dense downy pubescence below.
Leaves medium, nearly round, 035-2-57 (4), with markedly long L 2 nerves, entire or trilobed in degenerated material, dark green, shiny, bullate, thin but tough structure, cobwebby pubescence below; petiolar sinus lyre-shaped, open but not wide; dentition quite even, small, convex, pointed.
Bunches rather small, cylindro-conical, compact with short peduncles; *berries* small, round; skins thick and tough; pulp very juicy, sweet with a pleasant simple flavour and high acidity.
Shoots spreading in growth habit, grass-green, rose-coloured at the nodes exposed to the sun; *canes* vigorous, long but not thick in diameter, with medium-long internodes, dark grey-brown, ribbed; wood hard.

Subvarieties. — Pinot gris (Ruländer), Pinot blanc, Pinot précoce.

Cultural aptitudes. — Good clones of Pinot noir, imported from Wädenswil, Switzerland, in 1964 to South Africa are vigorous growers and bear well if pruned half-long. They graft well and possess good affinity for all rootstocks.

Pinot noir is highly resistant to anthracnose, and not severely attacked by oidium, but its ripe grapes are inclined to rot easily when rains fall early in the season. According to European experience, Pinot noir produces its best wine on well-aerated, deep, limestone soils on dry but not too warm hills.

It ripens early.

Fig. 14.15. Pinot noir.

Wine. – Pinot noir produces the most magnificent red Burgundies. Unlike the famous reds of the Médoc, which are a blend of three varieties, the best red Burgundies are made from Pinot noir only.

Burgundian wines stay in contact with the skins for from five to eight days only. Consequently, red Burgundians, not having as much tannin as the wines of the Médoc, are ready to drink sooner.

The wine of Pinot noir is beautifully ruby-red-coloured, not very dark, well balanced, velvety, delicate with an unparalleled fruity flavour.

Geographical distribution. – Pinot noir is extensively grown in France not only in Burgundy, but in Champagne, where its black grapes are very carefully pressed to give white wines without a trace of colour. The first pressing gives the quality wine, the *vin de cuvée.* The grapes must be ripe, but not overripe. Thus Pinot noir, which predominates in the Champagne, gives red grapes for the making of wines of the purest gold, the best sparkling wines of the world.

Outside France, Pinot noir is extensively grown in Germany, Switzerland, Austria, Hungary, Rumania, Russia, California and Australia. The variety grown in California under the name 'Pinot Saint George' has nothing in common with the noble Pinot noir.

After Dr. H. Ambrosi and the author imported four clones of Pinot noir from Wädenswil in January 1964, there was considerable criticism in high places, as Pinot noir was regarded as an example of an imported variety which does not accommodate well to South African climatic conditions. Only Carignan, a variety which the author recommended should replace Cinsaut, Pinotage and Tinta Baroccas, has been more passionately slandered than Pinot noir. After 1969, when the excellent performance of the imported Pinot noir material could no longer be denied, the quality, especially the colour, of locally made experimental wines of Pinot noir was declared disappointing.

In 1976, i.e. during the first pressing-season after his arrival in South Africa, Dr. J. László made an experimental wine from the same grapes at the O.V.R.I. which was highly appreciated by such visiting French authorities as Professors Branas and Boubals, and Director Huglin in February 1977.

Growers now became eager to plant Pinot noir on a large scale, but there is very little propagation material available. There are two reasons for this:

(1) The mother block of Pinot noir, consisting of 410 vines established by the author in 1968 at Nietvoorbij — headquarters of the O.V.R.I. — was uprooted two years ago (luckily, after Dr. László had made his superb experimental wine from this block).

(2) Pinot noir this year (1978) disappeared from the annually published list of varieties obtainable through the official propagation scheme (*Die Wynboer*, April 1978, p.60).

It is understood that the 'discovery' of some 'dangerous virus' in the material is the latest reason for the undesirability of planting Pinot noir in South Africa.

Indexing results of three consecutive years indicated that three clones of the imported material were free from the harmful viruses of the grapevine, and consequently the material was released to the O.V.R.I. for evaluation on 7 July 1967. The author received them personally.

5. Syrah

Synonyms. — Shiraz, Sirah.

Origin. — Syrah has been grown in the Côte de Rhône probably since Roman times.

Description

Leaves medium, cuneiform, 136-2-57 (4), five-lobed, light grass-green, bullate, dull, tough leathery structure; petiolar sinus U-shaped, open but narrow; dentition uneven, convex, fairly blunt.

Bunches medium, long, loose, cylindrical with long peduncles; *berries* small, oval; skin tough and thick; pulp juicy, sweet, no particular varietal flavour.

Shoots very long and fairly thick, light green, brittle and they are very easily broken off by winds; *canes* light brown, ribbed with long internodes; wood soft with a large pith.

No *subvarieties* are known.

Fig. 14.16. Syrah.

Cultural aptitudes. — Syrah is a very vigorous grower and bears well when pruned long. It does not graft easily, and its affinity for 101-14 Mgt is unsatisfactory. It does excellently on 99 and on 110 R.

Not particularly susceptible to the fungoid diseases of the grapevine, even if it rains abundantly, the ripe grapes of Syrah do not rot easily. Syrah seems to adapt itself well to hot climatic conditions but after véraison its ripe grapes shrivel and drop easily if the vines suffer from drought.

It ripens mid-season.

Wine. — At the Cape, Syrah produces very dark-coloured, full-bodied wines with high alcohol content, rich in tannin, somewhat low in acidity. Young Syrah wines taste somewhat bitter and often have an unpleasant smell. They improve with maturity in wood and bottle. The French also consider young Syrah wines to be rough and harsh but with age they develop a rich aroma and aftertaste, forming a heavy sediment (7). In order to make Syrah wines finer, the most famous French Syrah wines, produced near l'Ermitage in the Rhône valley, are blended.

Geographical distribution. — Outside France, where Syrah is grown only on a very limited scale, the variety is practically unknown in the

other great red wine producing countries such as Italy, Spain, Portugal,
Greece and central and south-east Europe. Syrah is quite extensively
planted in Australia, South Africa and the Argentine.

The author is not quite sure whether it was justified to include Syrah
into the 'high aristocracy' of red wine grape varieties.

The 'Petite Syrah' imported to South Africa from California, is not
identical with Syrah proper.

Long life to the grape! For when summer has flown,
The age of our nectar shall gladden our own;
We must die — who shall not? — May our sins be forgiven
And Hebe* shall never be idle in heaven.

— Byron

---

* Hebe, the daughter of Zeus and Hera, was worshipped by the Greeks as the
goddess of youth. Her chief duty was to hand round nectar and ambrosia to the
gods during their feasts.

Appendix

In Chapter 6, some of the problems of the improvement of propagation material were discussed. It is necessary to amplify this by detailing some of the events and decisions which have led to the present impasse in South Africa.

Because of a strong conviction that the expertise and experience of European viticulturists were highly relevant to South African viticulture, Dr. Hans Ambrosi and the author, both then working for the Oenological and Viticultural Research Institute (O.V.R.I.) at Stellenbosch, began in 1963 the country-wide organized mass-selection of propagation material. At the same time, i.e. immediately after their appointment to the O.V.R.I., they started the systematic importation of the best available select-ed clones of all those premium-quality wine-grape varieties, as well as of rootstocks, which are well known all over the world, but which had never been imported to South Africa, or, like Pinot noir, Chardonnay, Merlot, etc., had degenerated here to such an extent that their culture had become uneconomic. As far as could have been ascertained from available documents, no new varieties had been imported to South Africa since World War 1, with the exception of 99 and 110 R (1934) and Salt Creek, Dogridge and 1613 C (1939).

However, the effects of their efforts have not been felt in South Afri-can viticulture, because of the introduction of a revised official policy, designed in December 1964, which promised to supply the local nursery industry with 'virus- and disease-free material' in the shortest possible time.

Dr. H. Ambrosi and the author strongly opposed the imposition of this virus-obsessed policy on their work at the O.V.R.I. Dr. Ambrosi's con-tract expired in November 1965 and was not renewed. Shortly afterwards he returned to Germany, to become managing director of the wine-producing estates of the German government in the Rhineland.

The 1964 decision, which was intended to be the 'salvation' of South African viticulture, was based exclusively on the scheme proposed by Californian virologists working at Davis for the improvement of vine-propagation material, and totally ignored the tremendous success already achieved in Europe by the methods of mass, type and clonal selection.

Further systematic importation of selected material from Europe was also restricted when the material from the Foundation block of Davis was officially declared — against the author's strongest objections — to be 'the best available' from overseas sources.

Because local virologists by means of indexing 'discovered' invisible viruses in nearly all varieties and clones already imported from Europe before December 1964, the material was kept under quarantine for 7 to 12 years. In fact, the best clones of Weisser Riesling (239 G.m.), Olasz-rizling (Pécs 2), and Pinot noir (2/10) — imported in February 1964 — as well as the highly regarded phylloxera-resistant rootstocks of the hot-test and driest grapegrowing regions of the world, such as 1447 P, 44-53 M and 140 Ru — imported in December 1963 — have still not been re-leased to the public. It is a well-known fact that up to this date the caus-ative agents of most of the grapevine 'viral' diseases, with the exception of fanleaf, and perhaps leafroll, on which there has been an initial report, have not been isolated.

The improvement of vine-propagation material by means of selection is extensively discussed in this book. This topic is completely ignored in all textbooks which have appeared in English. However, in all advanced European grapegrowing countries, selection is considered to be the most important work viticulturists and growers have to do, and to go on doing continuously. In November 1964, however, officialdom forbade the per-sonnel of the O.V.R.I. to do mass selection on private farms because 'this could promote the spreading of viruses in our vineyards'. In January 1965 growers and Co-operative cellar-managers demanded the continuation of mass-selection, organized by Dr. Hans Ambrosi with great success during the previous season. Because this was now against official policy, nursery-men were informed that no official recognition would be provided for such mass-selected material unless it had been approved by the field per-sonnel of the Division of Plant Pest Control in Stellenbosch from the 'phytosanitary point of view' ('daar mag nie voortgegaan word met massaseleksie as 'n skema nie'). And so the viticulturists of the O.V.R.I., under the leadership of the internationally known authority Dr. H. Amb-rosi, had to defer to the judgement of local plant-pathologists, outside the O.V.R.I., who were not qualified viticulturists.

At the professional meeting of the German breeders and nurserymen, 12-14 February 1975, Prof. Helmuth Becker of Giesenheim said:

'It is of no practical value to produce extremely vigorous rootstock clones, presumably "cleaned" from all known viruses, without evaluating them in comparative field-trials in the grafted stage under different eco-logical conditions. It will still be a very long time before it can be established whether heat-treated rootstocks can successfully be used in practice. The opinions of viticulturists and virologists differ greatly on this point. We have proved in Germany that visual selection, carried out in three stages, also in the case of rootstocks, is the most efficient method of eliminating harmful viruses from local propagation material. The entire modern German viticulture, based exclusively on visually selected and approved clonal material, the adaptation of which has been tested in all viticultural regions, can be considered as a huge "indexing programme" demonstrating its efficiency. How could the method of indexing, as practised by virologists *in vitro* on a few plants, for a short period, and without even attempting to take the practical value of the examined material into consideration, be compared with it?'

Davis-educated and Davis-oriented South African plant-pathologists prevented the attempts by Dr. H. Ambrosi and the author to begin a systematic visual selection of local rootstocks and to evaluate them in comparative field-trials in the different locations, with the remark, 'The rootstock does not bear grapes, consequently it is only its virus-status which decides its viticultural value.'

During the past fourteen years numerous 'virus-free' clones of 99 R, 101–14 Mgt and Jacquez were released to the industry. While the virus state of this material was supposedly known, its practical performance in the grafted stage still had to be ascertained by the grower himself at his own risk and expense. This is a very unsatisfactory procedure. There have also been some embarrassing cases. The vines in the rootstock mother-plantation from which all 'virus-free' 99 R and 101–14 Mgt were supplied to the nursery industry were purposely killed by herbicides in November 1975. The reason for this 'massacre', given by a high official (*Landbouweekblad,* 9 July 1976), was, that in this way viruses which were also in the roots of the vines could be killed, and thus after the removal of the dead plant residues from the soil, material 'cleaned' from viruses could be immediately planted in the same place.

Two questions remained unanswered: (1) Why was it necessary to kill viruses in the roots of such rootstocks, which for years had been declared, and consequently sold to the public, as 'free' from viruses? (2) Where is the 'cleaned' material that has already shown that it performs better in the field?

'Super grapes out of quarantine' were promised by plant-pathologists to local nurserymen three years ago (*Farmer's Weekly,* 22 October 1975). Thus, material which has been 'cleaned' from viruses by means of heat-treatment has been officially declared to be 'super grade' long before it has proved its presumably superior value in the vineyard.

While promising 'breeding plants completely free from infection', they do not mention the well-known facts that (a) some viruses, for example yellow speckle, could not be removed even after heat-treatment periods up to eleven months, and (b) from a practical point of view, re-infection cannot be prevented under field-conditions. What if the so-called 'super grapes' perform poorly against visually selected clones of the same variety in comparative field-trials?

It is not the author's intention to stir up controversy for its own sake, but rather to present the problems of South African viticulture in its historical perspective. Although the members of the 'triumvirate' who were mainly responsible for the far-reaching decisions of 1964 have since disappeared from the scene, the results of their policies remain. The grape-grower of South Africa is still paying the price. Further, there seems to be neither official recognition of past failures nor any discernible intention to remedy them in the light of the bitter experiences of the years from 1964. The problem presented by a critical shortage of good propagation material shows no signs of solution — in fact, the situation will probably deteriorate unless there is a change of policy.

By way of comment on this unhappy controversy, one might refer to Captain Liddell Hart, the eminent military historian, who wrote: 'We learn from history that men have constantly echoed the remark ascribed to Pontius Pilate: "What is truth? " It may be a justifiable question, in the deepest sense, but it is too often used as a smokescreen. The longer I have watched current events, the more I have come to see how much trouble arises from the habit, on all sides, of suppressing or distorting what we know quite well is the truth, out of loyalty to a cause or institution — at bottom, this loyalty being usually a care for our own interest. Another lesson of history is that the most dangerous folly of all is man's failure to recognize his own aptitude for folly. The pretence of infallibility is instinctive in a hierarchy.'

Felix qui potuit rerum cognoscere causas' — Virgil.

Bibliography

Ahrens, K., 1929, 'Physiologische Untersuchungen an *Plasmopara viticola* unter besonderer Berücksichtigung der Infektionsbedingungen', *Jhb. Wiss. Bot.*, 70: 93-157.

Alleweldt, G., & G.H. Balkema, 1931, 'Über die Anlagen von Infloreszenz-und-Blüteprimordien in den Winterknospen der Rebe', *Zt. Acker-Pfanzenbau*, 123: 57-74.

Alleweldt, G., 1958, 'Eine Frühdiagnose der Bestimmung der Fruchtbarkeit von Reben', *Vitis*, 4: 230-6.

Alley, D., 1973, 'Status of grapevine improvement in California', *Problemen der Rebenverdedlung*, 9: 88-99.

Ampelografia SSSR., 1946-1956. I-VI. Moskwa: Pistshepromizdat.

Bábó, Frhr. von, & E. Mach, 1909, *Handbuch des Weinbaues und der Kellerwirtschaft*, I-II. Berlin: Parey.

Baggiolini, M., 1952, 'Les stages repères dans la dévelopment de la vigne', *Rev. Romande Agr. et Vitic.*, 8: 4-6.

Bailey, J.H., 1934, 'The species of grape peculiar to North America', *Gentes Herbarum*, 3: 151-244.

Baranov, P., 1927, 'Zur Morphologie und Embryologie der Weinrebe', *Ber. d. Dt. Bot. Gaz.*, 45: 97-114.

Basserman-Jordan, F., 1907, *Geschichte des Weinbaues*, I-III. Frankfurt am Main: Keller.

Becker, H., 1971, 'Neue Ergebnisse der Technologie und Lagerung in Rebenveredlung', *Problemen der Rebenveredlung*, 8: 29-48.

Becker, H., 1973, 'Über die Situation der deutschen Rebenpflanzguterzeugung', *Problemen der Rebenveredlung*, 9: 12-23.

Bernon, G., 1932, 'Sur la fertilité des yeux de la vigne', *Progr. Agr. Vitic.*, 97: 156-9.

Bessis, J., 1956, 'Récherches sur la fertilité et les corrélations de croissance entre bourgeons chez la vigne', Université de Dijon: Thèse Doct. Sc.

Bioletti, F.T., 1926, 'Selection of planting stock for vineyards', *Hilgardia*, 2: 10-23.

Boubals, D., 1954, 'Les nématodes parasites de la vigne', *Progr. Agr. Vitic.*, 141-73.

Branas, J., Bernon, G., & L. Levadoux, 1946, *Éléments de viticulture générale*. Bordeaux: Delmas.

Branas, J., 1950, 'Historique sommaire, situation actuelle, objectifs généraux et moyens de la reconstitution des vignobles. Rapport nationale', *VIe Congr.*, de *l'O.I.V., Athènes*.

Branas, J., & A. Vergnes, 1957, 'Morphologie du système radiciculaire', *Prog. Agr. Vitic.*, 174: 29-32.

Branas, J., 1974a, *Viticulture*. Montpellier.

Branas, J., 1974b, 'Sélection phytosanitaire. Resultats obtenus jusqu'à ce jour en viticulture et en enologie par moyen de la sélection visuelle et de la thermothérapie', *Bull. de l'O.I.V.*, *47*: 369–79.

Braun, H., & E. Riem, 1950, *Krankheiten und Schädlinge der Kulturpflanzen.* Berlin: Parey.

Cornu, M., 1876, 'Études sur le *Phylloxera vastatrix*', *Rec. Mém. Sav. Agr. Sc.*, *26*:1.

Dalmasso, G., & I. Cosmo, 1952–1964, *Principali vitigni de vini cultivati in Italia*, I–III. Roma: Longo et Zopelli.

Dowson, W.J., 1956, 'Review of bacterial diseases of plants', *C. Stapp. Ann. Biol.*, *45*: 238.

Du Plessis, S.J., 1940, 'Bacterial blight of vines', *Dept. Agr. Sc.*, *Bull.* No. 213.

Esau, K., 1948, 'Phloem structure in the grapevine, and its seasonal changes', *Hilgardia: 18*: 217–96.

Esau, K., 1964, *Anatomy of Seed Plants.* New York: Wiley.

Fader, W., 1975, 'Überlegungen zur Mengertragsbeschränkung über den Anschnitt', *Die Weinwissenschaft, 111*: 970–5.

Galet, P., 1958–1964. *Cépages et vignobles de France.* Montpellier: Déhan.

Galet, P., 1971, *Précis d'ampélographie.* Montpellier: Déhan.

Galet, P., 1973, *Précis de viticulture.* Montpellier: Déhan.

Galzy, R., 1971, 'Récherches sur la connaissance de la vigne saine et court-nouée cultivée *in vitro*', *Connaissance de la vigne et du vin, 5*: 127–61.

Gibbon, E., 1776, *The Decline and Fall of the Roman Empire*, I–VII. Oxford: University Press.

Guillon, J.M., 1905, *Étude générale de la vigne.* Paris: Masson.

Hayne, A.P., 1897, *Resistant Vines: Their Selection, Adaptation and Grafting.* Sacramento: State Printing.

Hegedüs, A., P. Kozma, & M. Németh, 1966, *A szölö.* Budapest: Akadémia.

Hillebrand, W., 1974, *Rebschutz-Taschenbuch.* Wiesbaden: Bilz & Fraund.

Hillebrand, W., 1976, *Weinbau Taschenbuch.* Wiesbaden: Bilz & Fraund.

Huglin, P., 1958, 'Récherches sur les bourgeons de la vigne: initiation florale et dévelopment végétatif', *Ann. Am. Pl., 12*: 151–6.

Huglin, P., 1960, 'Causes déterminent les altérations de la floraison de la vigne', *Ann. Am. Pl., 10 (3)*: 351–8.

Huff, P., 1975, 'Einfluss des Anschnittes auf die vegetative und generative Leistung verschiedener Rebsorten', *Giessen: Dissertation.*

Istvánffy, Gy. de, & Gy. Pálinkas, 1913, 'Études sur *Plasmopara viticola*', *Amp. Int. Évk., 4*: 1–136.

Johnson, H., 1971, *The World Atlas of Wine.* London: Mitchell Beazley.

Kádár, Gy, 1973, *Borászat.* Budapest: Mezögazdasági.

Kliewer, W.M., 1975, 'Effect of soil temperature on budbreak, shoot growth, and fruit-set of Cabernet Sauvignon grape vines', *Am. J. Enol. Vitic., 2*: 82–9.

Kliewer, W.M., & K.A. Roubelakis, 1976, 'Influence of light intensity and growth regulators on fruit-set and ovule fertilization in grape cultivars under low temperature conditions', *Am. J. Enol. Vitic., 4*: 163–7.

Kövessi, M.F., 1901, *Récherches biologiques sur l'autment des sarments de la vigne.* Lille: Bigot.

Kozma, P., 1958, 'A szölö fajfenntartó nemesitési módszerei és eddigi eredményei Magyarországon', *Nemzetk. Mg. Szle., 2.*

Kozma, P., 1966, *Szölötermesztés.* Budapest: Mezögazdasági.

Kriedmann, P.F., & M.S. Buttrose, 1971, 'Chlorophyll content and photosynthetic activity within woody shoots of *V. vinifera* L.', *Photosynthetica, 51*: 22–7.

Kroemer, R., 1909, 'Organographie, Anatomie und Physiologie der Rebe', in Bábó & Mach, *I:* 6-157.

László, J., 1977, 'Current trends in overseas viticulture', *Die Wynboer, 545:* 40-7.

Levine, R.P., 1962, *Genetics.* New York: Rinehart & Winston.

Lewin, I., 1976, 'How to use nitrogen fertilizers efficiently in agricultural practices', *Inform. Bull.* No. 336, FFTRI.

Lichine, A., 1967, *Encyclopedia of Wines and Spirits.* London: Cassell.

Lüstner, G., 1909, 'Die tierische Feinde und Krankheiten der Rebe', in Bábó & Mach, *I:* 879-1127.

Malherbe, I. de V., 1962, *Soil Fertility.* Cape Town: Oxford University Press.

Manzoni, G., 1952, 'Considerazioni su differenze anatomiche in radici de barbatelli di *Vitis vinifera, Vitis rupestris, Vitis Berlandieri', ·Annal. Sper. Agr.,* 7: 292-337.

Manzoni, G., 1954, 'La foglia della vite', *Rev. Vitic. Enol.,* 7: 171-8.

Matthee, F.N., A.J. Heyns, & H.D. Erasmus, 1970, 'Present position of bacterial blight (vlamsiekte) in South Africa', *The Dec. Fr. Gr.,* 81-5.

Merjanian, A.S., 1926, 'Über die Dorsiventralität der Weinrebe', *Angewandte Botanik, 19:* 470-502.

Meyer, B.S., D.B. Anderson, & R.H. Bohning, 1961, *Introduction to Plant Physiology.* London: Van Nostrand.

Millardet, A., 1901, 'La fausse hybridation chez les Ampélidées', *Rev. Vitic., 16:* 677-80.

Molon, G., 1906, *Ampelografia,* I-II. Milano: Hoepli.

Moser, L., 1966, *Weinbau einmal anders,* Wien: Österreichische Agrarverlag.

Motorina, M.V., 1958, 'Fotosintez i dihanie v uslovijah Moskowskoj oblast', *Izv. TCXA., Moskwa, 1:* 123-40.

Mottard, G., J. Nespoulus, & P. Marcout, 1963, 'Les porte-greffes de la vigne', *Bull. Inf. Ing. Agr.* No. 182, Paris.

Müller-Thurgau, H., 1908, 'Kernlose Traubenbeeren und Obstfrüchte', *Landw. Jb. d. Schweiz.*

Müntz, A., 1895, *Les vignes.* Paris: Berget & Levrault.

Myburgh, N., 1975, 'Selfsmoordbeleid vir wynbou', *Landbouweekblad,* 21 Maart, 8-12.

Negrul, A.M., 1946, 'Proishozsdenie kulturnogo vinograda i ego klassifikacija', in Ampelografia SSSR, *I:* 216.

Németh, M., 1958, 'L'examen comparatif sur la valeur des cépages de cuve et leur sélection clonale', *Szöl. Kut. Int. Évk., XI:* 261-326.

Németh, M., 1966, *Borszölöfajták határozókulcsa.* Budapest: Mezögazdasági.

Németh, M., 1967, *Ampelografiai Album,* I-II. Budapest: Mezögazdasági.

Perold, A.I., 1926, *A Treatise on Viticulture.* London: Macmillan.

Petit Larousse 1966, 26 ed. Paris: Hollier-Larousse.

Peyer, E., 1963, 'Eine 12jährige Leistungsprüfung von 44 Klonenselektionen der Sorte Blauer Spätburgunder, Pinot noir', *Schw. Zt. f. Obst-und Weinbau, 102:* 250-5.

Peynaud, E., 1875, *Connaissance et travail du vin.* Paris: Bordas.

Planchon, J.E., 1883, *Monographie des Ampélidées.* Paris.

Pongrácz, D.P., 1968a, 'Keur u wynstokke', *Boerdery in Suid Afrika, 11:* 36-8.

Pongrácz, D.P., 1968b, 'The identification of dormant grape rootstock cultivars', *S.Afr. J. Agr. Sc., 11:* 655-72.

Pongrácz, D.P., 1969, 'Dit is nou die tyd om aan seleksie te dink', *Die Wynboer, 448:* 23-5.

Pongrácz, D.P., & E.F. Beukman, 1970, 'Comparative anatomy of *Vitis* roots', *Agroplantae,* 2: 83-94.

Pongrácz, D.P., 1970, 'L'amélioration de material de multiplication dans les vignobles d'Afrique de Sud', *La France Viticole, 3:* 77–83.

Pongrácz, D.P., 1972a, 'Wat elke boer en kweker van die massaseleksie van goeie wingerdvoortplantingsmaterial behoort te weet', *Bladskrif* No. 74. L.T.D.

Pongrácz, D.P., 1972b, 'Affiniteitsprobleem by wingerdenting', *Bladskrif* No. 81. L.T.D.

Pongrácz, D.P., 1972c, 'Hoe kan Cabernet Sauvignon van Cabernet franc in die praktyk onderskei word?', *Die Wynboer, 486:* 17–18.

Pongrácz, D.P., 1972d, 'Die huidige posisie met onderstoksoorte', *Die Wynboer, 489:* 16–18.

Pongrácz, D.P., 1973a, 'L'affinité défecteuse des porte-greffes 101-14 Mgt et 143 B avec nombreuses variétés de *V. vinifera*', *La France Viticole, 8:* 205–9.

Pongrácz, D.P., 1973b, 'Oorenting van 'n slapende ogie van 'n winterloot op die groen lote van 'n onderstok in die lente', *Die Wynboer, 502:* 31–3.

Pongrácz, D.P., 1974a, 'État actuel des travaux sur la sélection clonale, génétique et sanitaire. Méthodes et resultats. Diffusion de material sélectionne', *Bull. de l'O.I.V., 520:* 463–7.

Pongrácz, D.P., 1974b, 'Seleksie van kommersiële wyndruifsoorte in Suid Afrika: ondervindings en gevolgtrekkings', *Die Wynboer, 519:* 34–7.

Pongrácz, D.P., & J.J.A. Meissenheimer, *Die wintersnoei en somerbehandeling van die wingerdstok.* Stellenbosch: Distillers Korp.

Pratt, C., 1971, 'Reproductive anatomy of cultivated grapes – a review', *Am. J. Enol. Vitic., 22:* 92–109.

Pratt, C., 1974, 'Vegetative anatomy of cultivated grapes – a review', *Am. J. Enol. Vitic., 28:* 131–50.

Ravaz, L., 1897, 'Contribution à l'étude de la résistance phylloxérique', *Rev. Vitic., 7:* 109–37.

Ravaz, L., 1902, *Les vignes américaines et producteurs directes.* Montpellier-Paris: Coulet et Masson.

Ravaz, L., & G. Verge, 1921, 'Sur germination des spores du mildiou de la vigne', *Cras., 173:* 142–4.

Ravaz, L., 1930, 'Influence de la taille sur la vigueur et la production de la vigne', *P.A-V., II:* 537.

Riberau-Gayon, P., 1958, 'Les anthocyanes des raisins', *Qual. Plant et Mat. Veg. 3/4:* 491–9.

Ritter, F., & E. Hoffman, 1963, 'Erfahrungen in der Klonenselektion und beim Klonenbau', *Weinberg u. Keller, 8/9:* 350–77.

Sartorius, O., 1926, 'Über die wissenschaftlichen Grundlagen der Rebenselektion in reinen Beständen', *Ztschrft. f. Pflanzenzüchtung, 13:* 79–86.

Sayman, D., 1975, 'Fertilizing according to yield and soil type', *Farming in South Africa,* No. E/3.

Schenk, W., 1975, 'Untersuchungen über die Verwachsungsvorgänge bei Pfropfreben', *Weinberg u. Keller, 22:* 53–75.

Schenk, W., 1976, 'Einfluss der Dorsiventralität auf die Kallusbildung und Verwachsung der Pfropfreben insbesonders im Hinblick auf die Maschinenveredlung', *Weinberg u. Keller, 3:* 89–113.

Schleip, H., 1950, 'Über die Korrelation von Blattbucht und Ertrag bei Burgunder und Ruländer', *Der Weinbau, 4:* 38–45.

Schulte-Karing, H., 1970, *Die ameliorative Bodenbewirtschaftung.* Ahrweiler: Warlich.

Sievers, E., 1969, 'Die Geisenheimer Riesling-Klonen und ihre Bedeutung für den deutschen Riesling-Anbau', *Rebe u. Wein, 22:* 295–9.

225

Sievers, E., 1972, 'Zur Organisation der Vermehrung von anerkannten Edelreismaterial', *Problemen der Rebenveredlung, 9:* 119–44.

Simon, J.L., J. Schwarzenbach, M. Mischler, W. Eggenberger, & W. Koblet, 1977, *Viticulture.* Lousanne: Payot.

Snyder, E., 1936, 'Susceptibility of grape rootstocks to rootknot nematode', *U.S. Dept. Agr. Cir., 405:* 1–15.

Steingruber, P., 1933, 'Die Grenzen des Erfolges bei Selektion im Weinbau', *Gartenbauwissenschaft,* 178–96.

Stout, A.B., 1936, 'Seedlessness in grapes', *New York: Agr. Exp. St. Geneva, Techn. Bull.* 238.

Strasburger, E., 1921, *Das Botanische Praktikum.* Jena: Fischer.

Teleki, Z., 1907, *Die Rekonstitution der Weingärten.* Wien u. Leipzig: Hartlebens.

Toynbee, A.J., 1946, *A Study of History.* Oxford: University Press.

Van der Merwe, J.J.H., & F.N. Matthee, 1972, 'Phytophtora root-rot of grapevines in the Western Cape', *The Dec. Fr. Gr., 22:* 268–9.

Van Niekerk, P.E., & G. Schlieman, 1966, 'Compost making', *The Dec. Fr. Fr., 16:* 351–9.

Van Niekerk, P.E., & W.J. Pienaar, 1967, 'Fertilization programme for fruit trees and table grape vines in the Winter Rainfall Area', *The Dec. Fr. Gr., 5:* 1–8.

Viala, P., 1893, *Les maladies de la vigne.* Paris: Masson.

Viala, P., 1889, *Une mission viticole en Amérique.* Paris: Masson.

Viala, P., & L. Ravaz, 1892, *Les vignes américaines.* Paris: Didot.

Viala, P., & L. Ravaz, 1901, *American vines. Adaptation, culture, grafting, and propagation.* Melbourne: Govt. Printer.

Viala, P., & F. Péchoutre, 1910, 'Morphologie du genre *Vitis*', in Viala-Vermorel, *I:* 113–298.

Viala, P., & Vermorel, 1901–1910, *Ampélographie* I–VII. Paris: Masson.

Vogt, E., 1950, *Weinbau.* Stuttgart: Ulmer.

Vogt, E., & B. Götz, 1977, *Weinbau.* Stuttgart: Ulmer.

Volschenk, J.E., 1969, 'Some soil problems in viticulture in the Winter Rainfall Region', *Inf. Bull.*

Vuittinez, A., 170, 'Méthodes de diagnostic des viroses de la vigne', *Le Progr. Agr. et Vitic. 9:* 242–51.

Weaver, R.J., 1976, *Grape growing.* New York: Wiley.

Wells, H.G., 1920, *The Outline of History.* London: Cassell.

Wildman, W.E., R.A. Naja, & A.N. Kasimatis, 1976, 'Improving grape yield and quality with depth-controlled irrigation', *Am. J. Enol. Vitic., 4:* 168–75.

Winkler, A.J., 1962, *General Viticulture.* Berkeley and Los Angeles: Univ. of California.

Winkler, A.J., J.A. Cook, W.M. Kliewer, & L.A. Lider, 1974, *General Viticulture.* Berkeley and Los Angeles: Univ. of California.

Woodham, R.G., & D.M. Alexander, 1966, 'The effect of root temperature on Sultana vines', *Vitis: 5:* 345–50.

Zimmerman, J., 1957, 'Holzreife, Affinität, Adaptation', *Dt. Weinbau-Kal., 8:* 42–5.

Zimmerman, J., 1960, 'Neuzeutliche Methoden der Selektion und Erhaltungzüchtung', *Der dt. Weinbau,* 600–5.

References

CHAPTER 1. HISTORY AND GEOGRAPHICAL DISTRIBUTION
OF GRAPE-GROWING

1. Basserman-Jordan, 1907, vol. I, pp. 11-14, 15-33.
2. Galet, 1973, pp. 21-2, 13-15.
3. Gibbon, 1776, vol. IV, pp. 64, 66, 68.
4. Hegedüs et al., 1966, p. 19.
5. Johnson, 1971, pp. 13, 14, 140, 234.
6. Lichine, 1967, pp. 2-3, 268-76, 78, 498, 107.
7. Simon et al., 1977, p. 22.
8. Toynbee, 1946, p. 225.
9. Wells, 1920, pp. 553-5, 558.
10. Winkler, 1962, pp. 6-7.

CHAPTER 2. CLASSIFICATION OF THE GENUS VITIS

1. Bailey, 1934.
2. Branas, 1974, pp. 14-19, 65, 122.
3. Galet, 1973, pp. 199-203.
4. Hegedüs et al., 1966, pp. 9, 16.
5. Negrul, 1946, vol. I, pp. 216, 63, 159.
6. Németh, 1967, vol. I, pp. 13-16, 26-7.
7. Planchon, 1883, pp. 2, 5.
8. Simon et al., 1977, p. 39.
9. Weaver, 1976, pp. 3-6.
10. Winkler, 1962, pp. 1, 17, 16, 15.

CHAPTER 3. MORPHOLOGY AND ANATOMY

1. Alleweldt et al., 1931.
2. Alleweldt, 1958.
3. *Ampelografia SSSR.*, 1946-1956, vol. I.
4. Baranov, 1927.
5. Branas et al., 1957.
6. Branas, 1974, pp. 371-4, 376, 378, 244-5, 177, 398, 306-9, 326-9.
7. Esau, 1948.
8. Esau, 1964, pp. 2, 143, 81, 22, 282.
9. Galet, 1973, pp. 52-5, 28-9, 32-3, 57-63, 80-1, 82-3.
10. Guillon, 1905, pp. 265-73, 184-91.

11. Hayne, 1897, p. 53.
12. Hegedüs, 1957.
13. Hegedüs et al., 1966, pp. 60-5, 69, 75, 78, 81.
14. Huglin, 1958.
15. Kriedmann et al., 1971.
16. Kroemer, 1909, pp. 43, 6, 7-9, 13, 11, 60, 62-5, 19-21, 24, 66-8, 25, 27-9, 33-7, 81-3, 32, 28-31, 76-80, 37-41, 42-3.
17. Manzoni, 1952.
18. Manzoni, 1954.
19. Merjanian, 1926.
20. Perold, 1926, pp. 26, 62, 27, 29, 40-1, 36, 35, 39, 49-50, 53-5, 59-60.
21. *Petit Larousse*, 1966, p. 674.
22. Pongrácz, 1968.
23. Pongrácz et al., 1970.
24. Pratt, 1971.
25. Pratt, 1974.
26. Strasburger, 1921, pp. 239-56.
27. Viala et al., 1910, pp. 225, 233-4, 113, 238-43, 276, 304, 282, 123-6, 199, 183, 195.
28. Vogt, 1950, p. 237.
29. Weaver, 1976, p. 13.
30. Winkler, 1962, pp. 68-72, 75, 77, 78, 101-4, 107-9.
31. Woodham et al., 1966.

CHAPTER 4. BIOLOGY OF THE VINE

1. Baggiolini, 1952.
2. Bessis, 1965.
3. Branas, 1974, pp. 241, 299, 324-9, 252-4.
4. Esau, 1948.
5. Galet, 1973, pp. 86-7, 122, 127-33, 331-5.
6. Guillon, 1905, pp. 265-74, 77, 285-300.
7. Hegedüs, 1957.
8. Hegedüs et al., 1966, pp. 129, 65, 130, 125-8, 109, 61.
9. Huglin, 1960.
10. Kliewer et al., 1976.
11. Kövessi, 1901, p. 37.
12. Kroemer, 1909, vol. I, pp. 135-68.
13. Malherbe, 1962, pp. 292, 215, 31.
14. Meyer et al., 1961, pp. 494-5, 190, 121, 122, 301-7, 448, 314-15, 313, 193-4, 198, 259, 260, 332-4.
15. Motorina, 1958.
16. Müller-Thurgau, 1908.
17. Perold, 1926, pp. 107, 113-14, 62, 40, 114, 121, 438, 122, 134, 510.
18. Peynaud, 1975, pp. 69, 61.
19. Pratt, 1971.
20. Pratt, 1974.
21. Riberau-Gayon, 1958.
22. Stout, 1936.
23. Vogt et al., 1977, p. 64.
24. Weaver, 1976, pp. 177, 321, 26, 332, 28, 29, 31, 34.
25. Winkler et al., 1974, pp. 118-20, 129-30, 142, 151-7, 170-1, 95-100, 90-3, 410-17, 423-6.

CHAPTER 5. SOILS AND CLIMATE

1. Bábó et al., 1909, vol. I, pp. 456–88, 443–50.
2. Branas, 1974, pp. 370, 376, 395–402.
3. Guillon, 1905, pp. 322–30, 404–8, 409–11.
4. Malherbe, 1962, pp. 36, 37, 151, 72, 73, 76, 74, 83, 86–8, 63, 167–9, 171, 176, 116, 124.
5. Perold, 1926, pp. 13–16.
6. Volschenk, 1969.
7, Weaver, 1976, p. 155.
8. Winkler, 1962, pp. 63–7, 55–6.

CHAPTER 6. MEANS OF IMPROVING PROPAGATION MATERIAL

1. Alley, 1973.
2. Becker, 1973.
3. Bioletti, 1926.
4. Branas, 1950.
5. Branas, 1974a, pp. 197, 143–50, 139–43, 530–5.
6. Branas, 1974b.
7. Galet, 1973, pp. 216–17, 218–20, 503–5.
8. Galzy, 1971.
9. Hayne, 1897, pp. 37, 15, 20.
10. Kozma, 1958.
11. Levine, 1962, pp. 1–4, 122–4.
12. Millardet, 1901.
13. Myburgh, 1975.
14. Németh, 1958.
15. *Petit Larousse*, 1966, pp. 510, 471.
16. Peyer, 1963.
17. Pongrácz, 1968.
18. Pongrácz, 1969.
19. Pongrácz, 1970.
20. Pongrácz, 1972.
21. Pongrácz, 1974a.
22. Pongrácz, 1974b.
23. Ravaz, 1897.
24. Ravaz, 1902.
25. Ritter et al., 1963.
26. Sartorius, 1926.
27. Schleip, 1950.
28. Sievers, 1969.
29. Sievers, 1972.
30. Steingruber, 1933.
31. Teleki, 1907, pp. 11–34, 145–58.
32. Viala et al., 1892, pp. 70–8, 93–102, 111–23, 128, 160, 190, 193, 202–6.
33. Viala et al., 1901, pp. 42, 117, 198–202, 61–75, 82–96, 104–13, 145–53, 162, 170, 177–9, 187–9.
34. Vogt et al., 1977, pp. 376–80.
35. Vuittinez, 1970.
36. Winkler et al., 1974, p. 467.
37. Zimmerman, 1960.

229

CHAPTER 7. PROPAGATION

1. Bábó et al., 1909, vol. I, pp. 330-3, 336-9, 359-76, 378-82, 406, 415, 429-31.
2. Becker, 1971.
3. Branas, 1974, pp. 197-200, 202-4, 208-13, 204.
4. Esau, 1964, pp. 246-7.
5. Galet, 1973, pp. 268-79, 259-61, 255-8, 277-83.
6. Hayne, 1897, pp. 44, 38, 51.
7. Hegedüs et al., 1966, p. 103.
8. Kozma, 1966, pp. 68, 170-3, 177, 198, 200.
9. Perold, 1926, pp. 372, 363, 375, 184-5, 399, 389, 391.
10. Pongrácz, 1972b.
11. Pongrácz, 1973a.
12. Pongrácz, 1973b.
13. Pratt, 1974.
14. Schenk, 1975.
15. Schenk, 1976.
16. Viala et al., 1892, pp. 209-62.
17. Vogt, 1950, pp. 201, 211.
18. Vogt et al., 1977, pp. 328, 342.
19. Weaver, 1976, p. 155.
20. Winkler, 1962, pp. 158-76.
21, Zimmerman, 1957.

CHAPTER 8. ESTABLISHMENT OF A VINEYARD

1. Bábó et al., 1909, vol. I, pp. 496, 503, 510, 602.
2. Branas, 1974, pp. 512-13, 523-6.
3. Galet, 1973, pp. 329-30, 267.
4. Kozma, 1966, pp. 269-73, 234, 228, 521.
5. László, 1977.
6. Malherbe, 1962, pp. 151-4.
7. Perold, 1926, pp. 540-1, 546, 368-72.
8. Simon et al., 1977, p. 176.
9. Van Niekerk et al., 1967.
10. Vogt et al., 1977, pp. 130, 138, 325.
11. Weaver, 1976, pp. 185-7.
12. Winkler, 1962, pp. 195-6.

CHAPTER 9. FERTILIZER ELEMENTS REQUIRED BY THE GRAPEVINE

1. Hillebrand, 1976, pp. 145-51, 152-7.
2. Lewin, 1976.
3. Malherbe, 1962, pp. 182-4, 191-9, 200-11, 214-18, 31, 224-5, 240-1.
4. Müntz, 1895, pp. 447, 449, 450-1, 458, 488.
5. Sayman, 1975.
6. Van Niekerk et al., 1967.
7. Van Niekerk et al., 1966.
8. Vogt et al., 1977, pp. 96, 97.
9. Winkler, 1962, pp. 350-7, 364-5.

230

CHAPTER 10. TILLAGE, CHEMICAL WEED CONTROL, IRRIGATION

1. Branas, 1974, pp. 504–6, 534–6, 398.
2. Galet, 1973, pp. 418–20.
3. Hayne, 1897, pp. 19, 34–5.
4. Malherbe, 1962, pp. 130–8.
5. Perold, 1926, pp. 554–7.
6. Schulte-Karing, 1970, p. 137.
7. Wildman et al., 1976.
8. Winkler et al., 1974, pp. 394–7.

CHAPTER 11. PRUNING AND TRELLISING

1. Bábó et al., 1909, vol. II, pp. 625–6, 633–41, 642–4.
2. Branas et al., 1946.
3. Branas, 1974, pp. 404–5, 437–41, 417–31.
4. Fader, 1975.
5. Galet, 1973, pp. 358–60, 367, 366.
6. Hillebrand, 1975, pp. 54, 124–6.
7. Huff, 1975.
8. Huglin, 1958.
9. Kliewer, 1975.
10. Kozma, 1966, pp. 312–15, 316–20, 375, 304, 355, 306, 369–78.
11. László, 1977.
12. Moser, 1966, pp. 136–42.
13. Németh, 1967, vol. I, pp. 154, 56, 130, 47, 123; vol. II, pp. 39, 25.
14. Perold, 1926, pp. 560–4, 567–8, 131, 573–6.
15. Pongrácz et al., 1976, pp. 5, 13, 18–19, 15–17, 33–4.
16. Ravaz, 1930.
17. Simon et al., 1977, pp. 87–93.
18. Vogt et al., 1977, pp. 175–9, 153, 157, 156.
19. Weaver, 1976, pp. 176–8, 204–7.
20. Winkler, 1962, pp. 234–5, 244–9, 253, 274–5.

CHAPTER 12. PARASITOLOGY OF THE VINE

1. Ahrens, 1929.
2. Boubals, 1954.
3. Branas, 1974, pp. 830–33, 838, 842, 57, 715, 719–24, 743–8, 760–5, 770–5, 784–8, 755–8, 796–9, 568, 699–702.
4. Braun et al., 1950, p. 315.
5. Cornu, 1876, pp.1–357.
6. Dowson, 1956.
7. Du Plessis, 1940.
8. Galet, 1973, pp. 502–4.
9. Hayne, 1897, pp. 9–14.
10. Hegedüs et al., 1966, pp. 86, 152–6.
11. Hillebrand, 1974, pp. 73–5, 21–3, 35–40.
12. Istvánffy et al., 1913.
13. Kádár, 1973, p. 108.
14. Lüstner, 1909, vol. I, pp. 880–93, 895–913, 1067–77, 1047–51, 1058–62, 1123–6, 1099.
15. Matthee et al., 1970.

16. Perold, 1926, pp. 487–90, 465–7, 469–72, 454–9, 462–5, 475–9, 482–3, 444, 494–9.
17. *Petit Larousse,* 1966, p. 786.
18. Pratt, 1974.
19. Ravaz, 1902, pp. 38–43.
20. Ravaz et al., 1921.
21. Snyder, 1936.
22. Van der Merwe et al., 1972.
23. Viala, 1893, pp. 498, 500–5, 508–12, 58, 82–94, 2–8, 19, 352–6, 174–6, 258–60, 286–9.
24. Vogt et al., 1977, pp. 287, 262–4, 274–6, 270–3.
25. Winkler et al., 1974, pp. 539–42, 543–5, 442, 445, 448–9, 455–7, 446, 462–3, 464–5, 450–2, 470–86, 465.

CHAPTER 13. GENERAL AMPELOGRAPHY

1. Bábó et al., 1909, vol. I., pp. 12–14, 39.
2. *Ampelografia SSSR.,* 1946–1956.
3. Dalmasso et al., 1952–1964.
4. Galet, 1958–1964, vol. I, pp. 25, 48–52, 56–7, 29–38, 43–4.
5. Galet, 1971, pp. 21, 171, 189, 45, 13–17, 42, 31, 34.
6. Molon, 1906.
7. Németh, 1966, pp. 10, 12, 16, 28, 55–8, 79–80.
8. Perold, 1926, pp. 140, 146.
9. Viala et al., 1910, vol. I, pp. 3–4.

CHAPTER 14. SPECIAL AMPELOGRAPHY

1. Bábó et al., 1909, vol. I, pp. 184–99, 279.
2. Branas, 1974, pp. 162–64, 530–1, 535, 57.
3. Galet, 1959–1964, vol. I, pp. 63–6, 56–8.
4. Galet, 1971, pp. 41, 52, 59–60, 71–7, 69–70, 207, 197, 171, 169, 209, 173, 195, 165.
5. Galet, 1973, pp. 263, 264, 407–9.
6. Hayne, 1897, pp. 30–1, 29, 19–20.
7. Lichine, 1967, pp. 267, 522, 348–50, 194, 290.
8. Mottard et al., 1963, pp. 12, 13, 11, 14, 29, 34–5.
9. Németh, 1967, vol. I, pp. 130–4, 56–60, 94–8, 140–9, 123–8, 50, 135–8, 154–6, 153, 299–310; vol. II, pp. 39–41.
10. Perold, 1926, pp. 197, 199, 202–3, 213–14, 352, 247, 266, 271.
11. Pongrácz, 1968.
12. Pongrácz, 1972c.
13. Pongrácz, 1972d.
14. Ravaz, 1902, pp. 77–104, 105–9, 152–7.
15. Viala, 1889, pp. 125–31, 77–81, 11–12.
16. Winkler, 1962, 15–17, 604.

INDEX OF VITIS SPECIES AND VARIETIES

(synonyms and subvarieties are not included)

234